Visual Research Methods in Educational Research

Visual Research Methods in Educational Research

Edited by

Julianne Moss
Deakin University, Australia

and

Barbara Pini
Griffith University, Australia

Editorial matter, introduction and selection © Julianne Moss and Barbara Pini 2016
Individual chapters © Respective authors 2016
Softcover reprint of the hardcover 1st edition 2016 978-1-137-44734-0

All rights reserved. No reproduction, copy or transmission of this publication may be made without written permission.

No portion of this publication may be reproduced, copied or transmitted save with written permission or in accordance with the provisions of the Copyright, Designs and Patents Act 1988, or under the terms of any licence permitting limited copying issued by the Copyright Licensing Agency, Saffron House, 6–10 Kirby Street, London EC1N 8TS.

Any person who does any unauthorized act in relation to this publication may be liable to criminal prosecution and civil claims for damages.

The authors have asserted their rights to be identified as the authors of this work in accordance with the Copyright, Designs and Patents Act 1988.

First published 2016 by
PALGRAVE MACMILLAN

Palgrave Macmillan in the UK is an imprint of Macmillan Publishers Limited, registered in England, company number 785998, of Houndmills, Basingstoke, Hampshire RG21 6XS.

Palgrave Macmillan in the US is a division of St Martin's Press LLC, 175 Fifth Avenue, New York, NY 10010.

Palgrave Macmillan is the global academic imprint of the above companies and has companies and representatives throughout the world.

Palgrave® and Macmillan® are registered trademarks in the United States, the United Kingdom, Europe and other countries.

ISBN 978-1-349-68602-5   ISBN 978-1-137-44735-7 (eBook)
DOI 10.1057/9781137447357

This book is printed on paper suitable for recycling and made from fully managed and sustained forest sources. Logging, pulping and manufacturing processes are expected to conform to the environmental regulations of the country of origin.

A catalogue record for this book is available from the British Library.

Library of Congress Cataloging-in-Publication Data

Names: Moss, Julianne.

Title: Visual research methods in educational research / Julianne Moss, Deakin University, Australia, Barbara Pini, Griffith University, Australia [editors].

Description: New York : Palgrave Macmillan, 2016

Identifiers: LCCN 2015033208 |

Subjects: LCSH: Visual learning. | Learning, Psychology of. | Audio-visual education.

Classification: LCC LB1067.5 .V58 2016 | DDC 371.33/5 – dc23

LC record available at http://lccn.loc.gov/2015033208

Contents

List of Figures   vii

List of Tables   ix

Notes on Contributors   x

1 Introduction   1
  Julianne Moss and Barbara Pini

Part I   Images of Schooling: Representations and Historical Accounts

2 Reading Images of School Buildings and Spaces: An Interdisciplinary Dialogue on Visual Research in Histories of Progressive Education   15
  Julie McLeod, Philip Goad, Julie Willis and Kate Darian-Smith

3 On Using Found Object Photographs in School Research   36
  Jeremy Rowe and Eric Margolis

4 Reading the Visual in the Marketing of Elite Schooling   59
  Barbara Pini, Paula McDonald and Jennifer Bartlett

Part II   Performing Pedagogy Visually

5 The Use of the Visual to Interpret School Cultures: Producing Knowledge and Knowing When You Are Learning to Teach   75
  Kim Senior and Julianne Moss

6 Pedascapes: New Cartographies of Pedagogy   100
  Mary Dixon

7 Using Film to Show and Tell: Studying/Changing Pedagogical Practices   116
  Pat Thomson and Christine Hall

8 Visual Language, Visual Literacy: Education à la Modes   133
  Dawnene D. Hassett

Part III Power and Representation in Visual Educational Research

9 Repeat Photography and Educational Research 153
   Amy Scott Metcalfe

10 Children Framing Childhoods and Looking Back 172
   Wendy Luttrell

11 On 'Gods' and 'Kings' in the Tutorial Industry: A 'Media Spectacle' Analysis of the Shadow Education in Hong Kong 189
   Aaron Koh

12 The Abductive Leap: Eliding Visual and Participatory in Research Design 209
   Elaine Hall and Kate Wall

Part IV Ethical Issues in Visual Educational Research

13 Ethical Challenges in Visual Educational Research 231
   Kitty te Riele and Alison Baker

14 The Gaze and the Gift: Ethical Issues When Young Children Are Photographers 251
   Patricia Tarr and Sylvia Kind

15 Conclusion 267
   Barbara Pini and Julianne Moss

Index 277

List of Figures

2.1 Diagram of school, reproduced by kind permission, Tony Delves — 22
2.2 Exterior image of school, reproduced by kind permission, Coula Mellos — 24
2.3 Interior view of classroom — 29
2.4 Grounds of school, reproduced by kind permission, Tony Delves — 30
3.1 Mathematics lesson in English classroom, unidentified photographer, ca 1860 — 37
3.2 Men's gymnastics class, Arizona Territorial Normal School, unidentified photographer, ca 1907 — 39
3.3 Papago Indian School, San Xavier Mission, near Tucson, stereograph by D. P. Flanders photographer, ca 1874 — 42
3.4 Pima Girls School lunch group, near Phoenix, Arizona, unidentified photographer, ca 1898 — 43
3.5 'Typical' kindergarten class, stereograph, unidentified photographer, ca 1885 — 45
3.6 African American school house, Florida, stereograph by R. K. Bonine photographer, ca 1885 — 47
3.7 Very early class of young boys with flags at the Albuquerque Indian School, ca 1985 — 52
5.1 Pre-service teacher during a collaborative session with Year 8 students — 76
5.2 Year 9 student drawing from collaborative workshop with pre-service teachers — 78
5.3 Teacher educator/practitioner researcher conferring with Year 8 co-researcher — 82
5.4 Shawn on the basketball court — 86
5.5 The moment Kim walked onto the court leaving Nathan with the camera — 87
5.6 One of the thirty-six basketball action shots — 88
5.7 Photograph (see Figure 5.5) put through the 'colour in' effect — 88
5.8 Photograph (see Figure 5.6) put through the 'colour in' effect — 89

viii List of Figures

5.9	Scott and Nic working together	91
5.10	Manga strip using photograph in Figure 5.9 and excerpts from Scott's reflective journal	93
6.1	Pedagogical interaction	104
6.2	Pedascape 1: Amy's drawing, Amy's map of learning sites and constructed NAPLAN numerical image format assessment data	110
6.3	Pedascape 2	111
8.1	Traditional heuristic of reading comprehension	141
8.2	Model of reading/writing with visual texts	141
9.1	Methodological framework for repeat photography	159
9.2	Horticulture Barn, 1925; Barn Coffee Shop, 2007; Owl at the Barn daycare, 2012	166
9.3	Horse Barn, 1925; Old Barn Community Centre, 2012	166
10.1	Kendra: 'This is where I am comfortable and where I feel respect'	177
10.2	Kendra's toys	178
10.3	Gabriel's school library	180
11.1	A tutorial billboard advertisement in an MTR station	200
11.2	A tutorial advertisement flyer	202
12.1	Models of mixed methods use from Onwuegbuzie and Leech, 2006	212
13.1	Self-representation in the young graffiti writers project (Project 1)	236
13.2	Collective photographic narrative (Project 2)	246

List of Tables

6.1	Type of data format: Index of Community Socio-Educational Advantage (ICSEA), Australian Curriculum, Assessment and Reporting Authority (ACARA), *My School* website	107
6.2	Example of constructed table of socio-economic data	110
9.1	Reframing visual sociology	155
9.2	Agricultural facilities listed in Buildings and Equipment of the University of British Columbia, UEC, 1925	165
11.1	A multimodal discourse analytical framework	198
11.2	Translation of Chinese texts in Figure 11.1	201
11.3	Translation of Chinese texts in Figure 11.2	204
12.1	Notation for the arguments	216
12.2	Examples of negative reactions	217
12.3	Analytic matrix	223

Notes on Contributors

Alison Baker is a postdoctoral research fellow at the Victoria Institute for Education, Diversity and Lifelong Learning, Victoria University, Melbourne, Australia. Her research explores youth citizenship through community-based arts and sports with young people in Melbourne. She is interested in blending creative, participatory research methodologies with documentary arts techniques to develop young people's sense of social justice and capacity for action.

Jennifer Bartlett is an associate professor in the QUT Business School specialising in Corporate Social Responsibility (CSR), public relations and corporate communication. Much of her research work is focused around the role of communication in building and managing organisational legitimacy. Her work has appeared in national and international journals, such as *Public Relations Review*, *Journal of Communication Management* and the *Asia Pacific Journal of Public Relations*. She is one of the editors of the award-winning Wiley Blackwell *Handbook of Communication and Corporate Social Responsibility*, which is the seminal work on communication and CSR, and a fellow of the Public Relations Institute of Australia and Chair of the Public Relations division of ICA.

Kate Darian-Smith is Professor of Australian Studies and History, Faculty of Arts and Professor of Cultural Heritage, Faculty of Architecture, Building and Planning at the University of Melbourne, Australia. She has published widely on Australian and imperial histories, memory studies, war and society, children's history, cultural heritage and museology. Her recent books include *Conciliation on Colonial Frontiers: Conflict, Performance and Commemoration in Australia and the Pacific Rim* (2015; co-editor) and *Children, Childhood and Cultural Heritage* (2013; co-editor). Her current projects include a book on the history of Australian press photography and school design in its social contexts.

Mary Dixon is Deputy Director of the Centre for Research in Education Futures and Innovation at Deakin University, Australia. She has worked in higher education in Australia, Singapore and Thailand. She is well known locally and internationally for her expertise in curriculum and pedagogy research and in visual research methodology. Her classroom research moves between primary, secondary and tertiary sectors. Her recent theorisation of images draws on the growing educational work informed by Deleuze. Her research work in classrooms has been built around generative applications of visual data generated by students, teachers and researchers.

Philip Goad is Professor and Chair of Architecture at the University of Melbourne, Australia. An expert on 20th-century Australian architecture, he has written widely on design issues relating to education, health, community, commerce and national identity. He is the author of *New Directions in Australian Architecture* (2001), editor and author of *Bates Smart: 150 Years of Australian Architecture* (2004), co-editor of *Modernism and Australia 1917–1967: Documents on Art, Design and Architecture* (2006), *Modern Times: The Untold Story of Australian Modernism* (2008) and the *Encyclopedia of Australian Architecture* (2012). He is a fellow of the Australian Academy of Humanities.

Christine Hall is a professor and former head of the School of Education at the University of Nottingham, UK. She writes, researches and teaches about the arts and literacy in schools and about the policies and practices that affect teachers' work. Her recent research projects have investigated creative teaching, the impact of arts and cultural learning on school change and the Royal Shakespeare Company's professional development work with teachers. She is writing about place-based approaches to analysing and understanding educational development and the impact of philanthropy on local policy making.

Elaine Hall joined Northumbria School of Law as Reader in Legal Education Research in 2013, having been Lecturer in Research Methods at Newcastle University, UK. Her research career has spanned sixteen years and more than thirty funded projects. This research has been directed towards the experience of teaching and learning from the early years to old age, as curriculum-specific, metacognitive and professional practices. The diversity of context has produced a unifying theory of pedagogic enquiry, which focuses on the intent of the researcher, the potential of research and pedagogic tools and critical engagement in research networks.

Dawnene D. Hassett is an associate professor in the Department of Curriculum and Instruction at the University of Wisconsin-Madison, USA. She studies the social and cultural construction of literacy education, including what it means to be visually literate. Drawing on post-structural theories, she analyses the social forms of reasoning that tightly control current literacy programming. Then, using social semiotics and socio-cultural theories, she pokes holes in that reasoning to find relationships between imagination and the image, print literacies and visual literacies, multimodal communication and dialogic comprehension. She teaches undergraduate and graduate classes in curriculum theory and literacy education.

Sylvia Kind is an instructor in the Department of Early Childhood Education at Capilano University, Canada and works closely with the campus Children's Centre as an atelierista. She is an exhibiting artist, working primarily in textile/fibre processes and photography. Her research and teaching interests are in art education, studio research, the role of materials in early childhood education, atelierista studies and teacher inquiry.

Aaron Koh is Associate Professor of Literacy and English Education in the, School of Education and Professional Studies at Griffith University, Australia. Previously he worked at Monash University, the Hong Kong Institute of Education and National Institute of Education, Singapore. His research interests are critical English education, cultural studies in education and global studies of elite schools. He is on the editorial board of four international journals: *Curriculum Inquiry, Journal of Curriculum and Pedagogy, Discourse: Studies in the Cultural Politics of Education* and *Journal of Adolescent & Adult Literacy*. He is also the co-founding Springer Book Series Editor of *Cultural Studies and Transdisciplinarity in Education*.

Wendy Luttrell is Professor of Urban Education, Sociology and Critical Social Psychology at the Graduate Center, City University of New York, USA. Her research explores educational inequality, featuring how gender, race, class and sexuality systems of inequality take root in students' self-evaluations and actions. She is the author of two award-winning books on this topic, *Schoolsmart and Motherwise: Working-Class Women's Identity and Schooling* (1997) and *Pregnant Bodies, Fertile Minds: Gender, Race and the Schooling of Pregnant Teens* (2003), and is also the editor of *Qualitative Educational Research: Readings on Reflexive Methodology and Transformative Practice* (2010).

Eric Margolis is a sociologist, internationally known for his work on visual ethnography. He is an associate professor at Hugh Downs School of Human Communication, University of Arizona, USA. He holds a doctorate from the University of Colorado, Boulder, and has written many articles on visual ethnographic methods. He is past-president of the International Visual Sociology Association and co-editor with Luc Pauwels of the *SAGE Handbook of Visual Research Methods* (2011). The second edition is currently in the works. His current projects include:

'Visual Research' with Renu Zunjerwad in the *SAGE Handbook of Qualitative Research*, edited by Norman K. Denzin and Yvonna S. Lincoln (5th ed., forthcoming 2015).

Paula McDonald is Professor of Work and Organisation, and ARC Future Research Fellow in the QUT Business School in Brisbane, Australia. She takes a multi-disciplinary approach to her research, addressing complex problems in organisational settings which take account of broader social and regulatory policies and structures. The governance and management of high schools is one of a range of thematic areas on which her research focuses. She is the author of three books and over sixty academic journal articles, and her research has had substantial impact in a range of organisational and policy settings.

Julie McLeod is a professor in the Melbourne Graduate School of Education, University of Melbourne, Australia. She holds an ARC Future Fellowship (2012–2016), is Deputy Director of the Melbourne Social Equity Institute and co-editor of *Gender and Education*. Her research is in the history and sociology of education, with a focus on curriculum, youth, gender and inequality. Her books include *Rethinking Youth Wellbeing: Critical Perspectives* (2015); *The Promise of the New and Genealogies of Educational Reform* (2015); *Researching Social Change: Qualitative Approaches* (2009); and *Making Modern Lives: Subjectivity, Schooling and Social Change* (2006).

Amy Scott Metcalfe is Associate Professor of Higher Education in the Department of Educational Studies at the University of British Columbia in Vancouver, Canada. Her current work examines research policy and the social role of the research university, and her research methods include visual analysis and critical policy studies. She has recently published her research in the *International Journal of Qualitative Studies in Education* and is co-editing a special issue on poststructural policy analysis for *Critical Studies in Education*. She is a coordinating editor for *Higher Education*.

Julianne Moss is Professor of Education Studies Pedagogy and Curriculum at Deakin University, Australia and a past President of the Australian Association for Research in Education (2013–2014). Her research interests lie in visual research and the intersection of these methods with student diversity, teacher professional knowledge and social change. She is CI on recent major Australian government research tenders and research projects in teacher education, and led the programme of research with twelve project schools, university associate researchers and school mentors for the ARC Linkage Grant

Doing Diversity: Intercultural Understanding in Primary and Secondary Schools (2013–2015) with C. Halse, F. Mansouri, C. Arrowsmith, R. Arber, N. Denson, N. Priest and J. O'Mara.

Barbara Pini is a professor in the Faculty of Arts, Education and Law at Griffith University, Australia. She has written extensively in the field of rural and gender studies with her more recent work focusing on the field of education. Her recent books include *Disability and Masculinities: Corporeality: Pedagogy and Critique of Otherness* (2015; co-edited with C. Loeser and V. Crowley) and *Feminisms and Ruralities* (2014; co-edited with B. Brandth and J. Little).

Jeremy Rowe has collected, researched and written about 19th- and early-20th-centuries photographs for over twenty-five years. He has written several books, numerous chapters and articles on photographic history and curated exhibitions with regional museums. He serves on several boards, including the Daguerreian Society (as president) and Ephemera Society of America. His current projects include georeferenced analysis of the development of early photographic studios, initially in New York City, and routes travelled by pioneer photographers. Jeremy lives in Mesa, Arizona, and on the Bowery in New York City, and manages a photographic history resource (Vintagephoto.com).

Kim Senior is Senior Lecturer in Pedagogy and Curriculum at Deakin University, Melbourne, Australia. She has over two decades of experience as an educator in Australia, Japan and South East Asia. Her research interests focus upon pedagogical relationships, literacies and visual methodology/methods in social research.

Patricia Tarr is an associate professor in the Werklund School of Education, University of Calgary, Canada. She has been interested in the Reggio Emilia philosophy since 1990. Her research and published works have focused on the possibilities of the Reggio Emilia philosophy for North American contexts, particularly on classroom environments and pedagogical documentation. Her research in pedagogical documentation has led to her current work in ethical issues in research with and about young children.

Kitty te Riele is a professor and principal research fellow in the Victoria Institute for Education, Diversity and Lifelong Learning at Victoria University, Australia. She researches educational policy and practice for marginalised young people, with a particular focus on alternative education initiatives. She has experience as an active member of faculty and university human research ethics committees. Her books include the edited collection *Negotiating Ethical Challenges in Youth Research* (2013; co-edited with Rachel Brooks) and *Ethics and Education Research* (2014; co-authored with Rachel Brooks and Meg Maguire).

Pat Thomson is Professor of Education and convenor of the Centre for Research in Arts Creativity and Literacy (CRACL) in the School of Education, University of Nottingham, UK. A former South Australian head teacher in disadvantaged schools, she now researches primarily in galleries, communities and museums. She blogs as patter on patthomson.net and tweets as @ThomsonPat.

Kate Wall is Reader in Education at Durham University, UK. She is interested in creative methodologies for facilitating voice (particularly with young children), the ethics of this process and its end result, and how the practices that we use support more authentic perspectives and allow for more democratic ways forward in teaching and learning. Her work is characterised by collaboration between research and teaching communities and, as such, she has worked to transfer and codify affective strategies across domains under the belief that in effective pedagogy there are established techniques that researchers can learn from and vice versa.

Julie Willis is Professor of Architecture in the Faculty of Architecture, Building and Planning, University of Melbourne, Australia and the University's Pro Vice Chancellor (Research Capability). With Philip Goad, she is co-editor of the *Encyclopedia of Australian Architecture* (2012). Her current and recent research projects include studies on government, community, healthcare and educational buildings, equity and the role of women in the architecture profession, architecture and wartime, and international architectural networks.

1
Introduction

Julianne Moss and Barbara Pini

One more book on visual research

In recent years there has been a burgeoning uptake of visual research in the social sciences. The interest is also highly visible in the field of education. In 2011, Margolis and Pauwels published the first handbook on visual methods. The handbook articulated both the growth of the field in recent years and also the diversity of disciplines that are engaged in the production of research that loosely falls under the signature of visual research. So the question we ask is why another book on visual research and why a focus on education? Is there anything new? Or is this the same old? How can a critical focus and a new contribution to visual research methods be established in a single volume?

Overall, there is very little academic literature on the subject of visual research methods in education. In particular, there is an absence of theoretically grounded discussions of the possibilities and challenges of the approach for educational researchers. This book addresses the gap in the literature and brings together some of the leading educational researchers writing on the subject. Rather than offering a 'how to' approach to the method, the authors will use their own experience of engaging visual sources to address some of the complex epistemological and methodological questions which may come to the fore in visual research.

One of the key issues for the uptake of visual research methods (VRMs) in educational research is the way that the field of education has both embraced VRMs yet uses multiple and diverse theoretical perspectives. Education by its very nature is interdisciplinary and nests its theoretical orientations largely within the social sciences. For researchers who are new to the field of VRMs in education there is little literature that explains, weaves together and supports critical discussion of the strengths and weaknesses of diverse interdisciplinary practices used in the uptake of VRMs in education. One self-evident but overlooked issue is that VRMs (as the name suggests) requires an understanding of the visual, visual studies and visual culture. Gillian Rose (2013), a seminal contributor to the field of VRMs, has argued that a lack of understanding in this regard by visual researchers is delimiting the field and is a barrier to understanding how our knowledge of the relationships between the production of knowledge and the production of knowledge by other social groups is emerging in the second decade of the 21st century.

Rather than merely fetishise a collection of case studies that use VRMs, the chapters in the book are selected to trace contemporary debates about the visual in educational research. We are therefore arguing that, given the intense interest in the adoption of VRMs in education, it is now timely to closely analyse the contribution made by educational researchers. As editors, we

- organise thematically the collection of research studies according to four key issues for VRM;
- evaluate the interrelationship of these approaches with visual cultural studies more broadly; and
- analyse the representations of the politics and practices of VRMs to provide a well-needed critical perspective on the contribution of VRMs in educational research, asking what we can take from the new and the old.

This approach affords our publication a unique space in the education and social science literature. As Rose (2013) asks us in the conclusion to her recent paper: Are social science researchers in fact doing anything different from what is occurring in visual culture, or is what is going on in VRMs characteristic of a broader convergence happening in the field of social science knowledge production? These meta issues of knowledge production will unfold in our volume as they relate to educational research.

The editors and authors in this book are researchers who, for some time, have been connected to the field of education, but in differing ways. The book does not focus solely on photography, as visual methods are more than that. The contributors were selected for their working knowledge of social theory and action, and for the points of difference we could see visible in the 'look' of their work. A common thread in the fourteen chapters is the deep reflexivity that is engaged by the authors. As Lather (2014) states, the reflexivity does not, however, assume 'a modernist self, transparent methods, and reflexivity as a "too easy" solution to whatever problems might arise' (p. 8). As editors, we have been both equally captured and caught by the field, and although we have differing disciplinary backgrounds, we are tied through shared concerns for the continuing development of the field of VRMs in education.

Despite the burgeoning publications in visual research from any number of perspectives, there is a continuing need to read the field through a critical consciousness that both celebrates what has gone on in education and questions what has been done and what is yet to be done in contemporary social science research and education in particular. Rather than gesturing towards a paradigmatic slice that understands the visual in educational research as limited to photography and participatory approaches, and has little to say about or speak back to educational policy and practice, we aim to illustrate, through the breadth of chapters, the innovative work that has been achieved in the last decade that keeps critical conversations to the fore. The book is intended to have a diverse audience. The chapters will be of benefit to researchers and policy makers, but also those who may be new to the field of research in education.

As Australian editors, we are accustomed to reviewing the field from the landscapes that are above us in the south. The spatial affordances of scholarship and the temporal nature of work, cliqued as it may be, are very much about what it means to become a researcher 'down under'. We are taught through our graduate years to look out and across bodies of scholarship, research and policy. Increasingly, our Australian education faculties are situated as part of larger social science structures, such as colleges and mega faculties. Further, the higher education sector in Australian is like those elsewhere – globalised and engrossed in all things hybrid, technical and less humanised. Yet our work in education remains in communities, in schools and hyper-real systems where impact is less and less measured by the human touch or in the experiences that are educative.

Editing with the 'signature method' in mind

What can be offered in a short anthology of chapters from authors who are currently working in Anglophone contexts such as Australia, Hong Kong, Canada, the USA and the UK could be interpreted as a highly myopic method. To explain our method we have done some borrowing from Agamben (2009), the well-known contemporary Italian philosopher. We take our known limitation of the selection of contexts as read and are suggesting that while handbooks and publications specific to photography, participatory approaches, the use of film, media and the like have proliferated in recent years, the signature that each researcher presents in this book carefully considers the 'look' and mode of visual research. Education in the global world indeed has a 'look'. It is increasingly codified, and practices appear in Anglophone words as 'look – alike', despite the vastly differing geographical and cultural nuances of place and social sites that situate education and schooling.

In his celebrated work, *The Signature of All Things on Method*, Agamben (2009) introduces us to the philosophy of signatures. Academic scholarship, like art, is readily identified by the author or creator. Academics, however, are rarely praised for their artistry or the 'look' that they bring to knowledge. In this book, the authors have taken a distinctive approach to their analysis and framework and reveal something of their 'look' and 'signature' to visual research. As Agamben has illustrated for us in his 'theory of signatures', 'the paradigm of signatures is further complicated' (2009, p. 38). Signatures etymologically can be connected to the act of signing a document. In Latin, *signare* also means 'to coin' (2009, p. 38), and for many centuries the signature was impressed as a seal on a letter. It is only later, as Agamben reveals, that 'the signature decisively changes our relation to the object as well as its function in society' (Agamben 2009, p. 40). In sum, for Agamben,

> a signature does not merely express a semiotic relation between *signans* and a *signatum*; rather it is what – insisting on this relation without coinciding with it – displaces and moves it to another domain, thus positioning it in a new network of pragmatic and hermeneutic relations. (2009, p. 40)

Thus in the context of a small work which is not a handbook, the signature of the authors and their approach to visual research in education are developed to demonstrate an effective resolution for the field of education. Through the author's selection of problem and visual method(s), visual research is re-positioned with an educative signature that critically reviews the approach taken to VRMs. We are proposing that visual research methods likewise are part of a new network of pragmatic and hermeneutic relations in educational research, but as a developing method we have much to learn from the new and the old. What follows is an overview of what each of the chapter authors have signed off for us: thirteen chapters that we have organised into four parts and bookended by an introduction and conclusion.

Overview of the chapters

Part I is titled 'Images of Schooling: Representations and Historical Accounts'. In this section, three groups of authors develop accounts that capture moments in time and engage with disciplinary and interdisciplinary dialogues. **McLeod, Goad, Willis and Darian-Smith**, drawing on an interdisciplinary study of the history of school design and innovations in pedagogy, explore the socio-spatial arrangements of schools and classrooms as a focus for visual analysis. As with a number of chapters in the book, we get access to knowing more about recent large-scale studies. The chapter situates the explanation of the visual research from an Australian Research Council (ARC) study which examines how the architecture and design of schools interacts with educational ideas and practices, shaping understandings of the child; the citizen; learning; the natural, aesthetic and built environments; and the social world. The larger study brings together researchers working across the disciplines of architecture, urban planning, history and education in order to explore the multi-layered histories and interactions between innovations in school design, educational reforms and pedagogies, attending to the socio-spatial, aesthetic, built and natural environments of schools.

Rowe and Margolis examine the use of 'found object' images in educational research. They introduce the key questions of ethics that confront visual researchers. As they note, while privacy rights and rules protecting human subjects make it increasingly difficult to take photographs in schools, there is a wealth of visual data depicting schooling. The chapter provides several search and research strategies for collecting both old and new school images. Details on how to access sites from major online archives and school collections, to eBay and photo shows, tag sales, or swap meets, to online social-networking sites like Facebook, Pinterest, and Reddit, or simple Google image searches are described for the reader. The chapter also has a particular take on issues of representation through the introduction of photoforensics – the history of photography and photographic apparatus, styles used by professional and amateur photographers, and the specific development of genre schools. Acknowledging that typically materials are not 'historic' until they are more than fifty years old, they provoke us to consider what counts as an historical image in these times and argue that it is valid for visual researchers studying education to use broader definitions that fit their topic.

In the final chapter in this section, **Pini, McDonald and Bartlett** take up a key question that is often addressed to researchers in the form of a critique of visual methods. Rather than arguing that there is one approach that defines the field, the authors contend that an openness to varied and multiple paradigms which are guided by research questions and aims is needed. The researchers build on work which has mapped the use of approaches in elite schools through interviews with the producers of these images; that is, marketing and communication managers whose work is to produce and/or oversee the production processes of brochures, video newspaper advertisements and the like. The authors argue that this group of actors has become key in the educational landscape and the mediation of discourses that pertain to the rendering of schooling and education in this century. Moreover the authors illustrate how research on elite schooling and the take up of the visual have a lineage in the field. Pini, McDonald and Bartlett offer not only a concise overview of the corpus of work on elite schooling and marketing materials but also depart from it by talking to those who have the responsibility for creating the visuality of these schools.

Part II is titled 'Performing Pedagogy Visually', where the four chapters focus on pedagogy and the canvassing of issues that relate to the production of research in teacher education, learning spaces and the use of film in understanding teacher professional knowledge. The authors illustrate how new pedagogical relationships can be understood if we keep the visual in mind.

Senior and Moss introduce the well-known and rehearsed problematic issues and struggles of researching and reconstructing teacher education research in the context of global policy panic and teacher quality discourses. The chapter reports on the tracing of Kodak Easy Share™ method for transforming data and interpretation in a study of teacher education, school culture and pedagogy. Issues of method and analysis are addressed in the context of a project that was collaborative, contextually appropriate, feasible and ethically aware and negotiated over the life of the project. The co-production of knowledge is analysed to disrupt notions of how the visual and teacher education simultaneously get taken up in educational research.

Dixon is currently working in Australia and offers, in her chapter, a performative cartography of pedagogical spaces inside schools developed from a large Organisation for Economic Co-operation and Development (OECD) project on learning spaces conducted in Victoria. In these times, international bodies of classroom data are being assembled and rely heavily on large-scale data collection through, for example, videoing classroom action and international comparative studies. In her chapter, we are reminded of the multiple ways that pedagogical data are presented and how visuals are or are not put to work in educational policy. The chapter calls to account the politics of representation in studies of pedagogy and asks what else is needed or can redress globalising portrayals of pedagogy. Finally she concludes by outlining how pedascapes can address the pedagogical silences in the public portrayal of schools.

Thomson and Hall have extensive research backgrounds in collaborative and arts-based partnerships. In their chapter, they focus on the spaces between educational research, children and young people, and what their approach contributes to the remaking of how we might understand teacher professional knowledge. Through their aim of producing pedagogic resources for teachers *through* research, informed initially by visual research literatures, they explain and problematise what websites and film can do to support teachers' learning. As they note, the visual research literature has less methodological discussion about, and empirical reporting of, research using moving images. The chapter takes up the problem of how to communicate different and more creative approaches to pedagogical practice which do not unintentionally duplicate the notion of a deficient teacher incapable of professional knowledge production. But the contribution of the chapter is not all methodological; there is a substantive and compelling argument developed on how films become resources and change practice and possibilities for alternative pedagogical approaches.

Working in the USA and a specialist in early years' literacy, **Hassett** also reports on work that aims to be put in the hands of teachers. Drawing on social semiotics to push the boundaries of a print-based education, she introduces readers to an educational definition of visual literacy that begins with an analysis of highly visual and interactive children's texts as resources in helping to make meaning (their modes). For educational purposes, this exercise is not only about the study of visual signs and how they might be interpreted, but also about the design of curriculum and instruction where visual signs and representational modes can be played with and manipulated for educational purposes. The chapter ends with a discussion of the ways in which a working knowledge of social semiotics can affect the teaching of visual reading and visual design à la modes, thereby rethinking what an educational definition of visual literacy for the early years may look like.

In Part III's 'Power and Representation in Visual Educational Research', the first chapter is by **Metcalfe**, who is working in Canada. She demonstrates how repeat photography as a visual research method is an approach that fits well with conditions of possibility, displacement, and power and representation in image-based work. As she goes on to explain, repeat photography, the longitudinal analysis of visual methods, is the practice of place-based photography over time, often beginning with archival images as the source for further analysis. Repeat photography has its origins in the natural sciences, specifically geology. The potential for repeat photography in educational research is explored as it might be used to inform educational practice and policy. The chapter signs off with a call for researchers to look deeper and theorise with more complexity, a continuing theme that emerges throughout the four parts of the book.

In the next chapter, **Luttrell** provides us with a review of her distinctive contribution to longitudinal research, through the project *Children Framing Childhoods and Looking Back*. This study has put cameras in the hands of thirty-six children growing up in working-poor and immigrant communities, inviting them to document their lives and schooling over time, specifically at ages ten, twelve, sixteen and eighteen. The research, situated in the USA, has generated an extensive audiovisual archive that includes photographs; video-and audio-taped individual and small group interviews of the participants talking about their images; and video diaries produced by a subset of participants at ages sixteen to eighteen. In the chapter, we are given a considered and reflexive account of how specific analytic moves have been made over time and, as Luttrell reminds us, are necessary for understanding the children's meaning making through photography. Further, we learn more of the traditions of the field that, as she states, are too often neglected in discussions about photography as a form of educational research. The chapter presents strategies that allow for a fuller appreciation of what the children 'do' with their cameras, which Luttrell argues counters deficit and stigmatised visions of their childhoods, families and schools.

In the next chapter, **Koh** introduces readers to the visual ecology of tutorial centre advertisements that are circulating in the mediascape of Hong Kong. As he describes for us, it is difficult to miss these attention-grabbing tutorial centre ads. They are everywhere in the public spaces of Hong Kong. Not only do they appear as huge billboards erected on well-trafficked avenues and public transport such as MTR and double-decker buses, they are also circulated in social media platforms like YouTube and more traditional media formats, such as TV commercials and full-page newspaper ads. Introducing the term, the 'media spectacle' – a term borrowed from Douglas Kellner (2003), Koh works up a critical concept that he uses to unfold the educational politics in Hong Kong's education landscape. Dazzling tutorial ads disclose a great deal about education in contemporary Hong Kong, and the chapter well illustrates the ideological work that these media texts do and the specific politics they embody.

Returning to the UK, **Hall and Wall** at the outset divulge that there are some things that just will not be present in their chapter. The chapter seeks to problematise some of our assumptions about visual methods and their role in relation to participatory design and ethics in educational research. The authors make use of abductive reasoning (after Peirce 1878, 1903) to explore the ways in which other researchers over a number of years have attributed causality and connection in this area. The experience in exploring these assumptions to write this chapter suggests that the use of greater precision and transparency in framing the relationship between the researcher's intent and the use of visual methods is a vital first step, which can set the context for a more reflective data collection process as well as a more reflexive discussion of intent, design and process. The chapter challenges, both in public discourse and in the authors' own thinking, the casual and increasingly frequent elision of 'visual' and 'participatory' in discussions of research design.

The final part of the book is titled 'Ethical Issues in Visual Education Research'. **Te Riele and Baker**, researchers from Victoria, Australia, point out the need for continuing discussions that occur in educational research and social research more generally in respect to the specific ethical dilemmas that visual approaches pose for both researchers and institutional ethical committees. Urging for a creative and reflexive disposition to be adopted towards research ethics guidelines and principles, the purpose of this chapter is to highlight how traditional approaches to applying research ethics principles are challenged by visual research approaches. As the authors argue, ethical challenges are inherently 'grey' rather than 'black and white', so this chapter does not supply solutions. Rather, the authors' intent is to make visible ethical challenges that are particularly relevant for visual research. This is achieved by an overview of three widely recognised principles for research ethics: benefit and harm, respect for persons, and justice. The chapter draws on the expertise of Te Riele and on a discussion of the specific challenges for visual research in relation to each principle, based on two research projects by Baker.

Tarr and Kind, researchers who are based in Canada and working in the field of early childhood education, examine the ethical issues in using photos as part of the documentation processes to understand children's thinking with three- and four-year-olds using cameras. In this chapter they explore the questions and issues that have emerged around the use of photography, which have implications for both educators and researchers, incorporating visual methods with children, especially young children. Their research conversations support us in understanding pedagogical documentation as a process of listening to children. The research further involves processes of photographing and recording children's processes and engagements, revisiting and discussing them together, and collectively proposing new directions for inquiry. It takes children's participation in their own learning seriously and situates children and educators as researchers together. Building on research from education and visual sociology, and the ethical issues which are metaphorically explained through the lenses of the gaze and a consideration of the photograph as a gift, this chapter is a thought-provoking reminder of the centrality of ethical responsibilities in educational research.

This book takes a critical lens to the dramatic increase in visual research methods in education with contributions that

- extend and enliven debates about what constitutes 'the visual' by documenting experiences of a broad and diverse range of visual data and/or revealing the constructed, fluid and contingent nature of the categorisation 'the visual';
- explore the ways in which visual methods may further contribute to critical educational research in disrupting norms, ideologies, discourses and institutions, and in redressing educational inequalities based on gender, sexuality, class, race, geographic location and ability;
- investigate how visual methods with their potential to highlight the embodied, affective and the sensory may open up new research trajectories in areas of key concern in contemporary educational sociology (e.g. the globalisation and marketisation of education and increasing educational inequalities) or contribute to new knowledge in areas of educational research where the visual has been seldom invoked (e.g. policy studies, higher education, alternate educational settings);
- consider how researcher positionality shapes ethnographic knowledge arising from visual sources and/or the use, advantages and limitations of reflexivity in analysing and representing the visual;
- problematise some of the orthodoxies of visual methodological research, such as, for example, the conflation between visual methods and more egalitarian research relationships and/or participatory goals, and the notion that visual research is always qualitative; and

- reflect on visual representational strategies including some of the tensions which exist in communicating visual research to academic and practitioner audiences and/or the possibilities new technologies may offer for representing the visual.

In the concluding chapter, we consider how visual research methods in education have been deployed in this volume and in the recent literature. Re-emergence between what is written and what is meant and read as the visual – subtle and obscure as these practices sometimes can be – are, nonetheless, signatories to education and educational research in a rapidly globalising world. Visual research methods can support education and educational research to frame contemporary research problems, but to ensure that the uptake of VRMs in education is not reduced to fashion and fad, there is much to be understood.

References

Agamben, G. (2009). *The Signature of All Things: On Method*. New York: Zone Books.

Kellner, D. (2003). *Media Spectacle*. London: Routledge.

Lather, P. (2014). To Give Good Science: Doing Qualitative Research in the Afterward. *Education Policy Analysis Archives, 22*(10). http://dx.doi.org/10.14507/epaa.v22n10.2014

Margolis, E., & Pauwels, L. (2011). *The SAGE Handbook of Visual Research Methods*. Los Angeles: Sage.

Peirce, C. S. (1878). Illustrations of the Logic of Science VI. *Popular Science Monthly, 13*(August).

Peirce, C. S. (1903). Pragmatism – The Logic of Abduction. *Collected Papers, 5*, 195–205. Cambridge, MA: Harvard University Press.

Rose, G. (2013). On the Relation between 'Visual Research Methods' and Contemporary Visual Culture, *Sociological Review*, online. DOI: 10.1111/1467-954X.12109.

Part I

Images of Schooling: Representations and Historical Accounts

2
Reading Images of School Buildings and Spaces: An Interdisciplinary Dialogue on Visual Research in Histories of Progressive Education

Julie McLeod, Philip Goad, Julie Willis and Kate Darian-Smith

Introduction

School space is not merely a backdrop to the 'proper' work of schooling. The classroom or the school itself is much more than a simple container in which learning and educational experiences happen, as if indifferent to the spatial and material environment (Burke and Grosvenor 2008, p. 8). The design of schools, from classrooms and school buildings, to play areas and outdoor zones, has been integral to the history of educational provision and in conveying ideas about the purposes and ambitions of schooling. In this sense, the architecture of school buildings and the organisation of school space mediate the experience and aspirations of schooling. They shape – both hinder and enable – pedagogies and classroom dynamics as well as interactions and learning, even in the seemingly unstructured space surrounding school buildings. Acknowledging the significance of space, however, calls for more than attention to the instructional efficacy of learning environments (Leander et al. 2010). It also calls for an account of the kind of student subjectivities and dispositions the space of schooling invites and makes possible (Burke and Grosvenor 2008; Gutman and de Coninck-Smith 2008). In addition, the very look and feel of schools feed into the symbolic and reputational meaning they have in their local communities and beyond. A focus on the design of school environments underscores the significance of the visual and representational dimensions of schooling, across public and community settings as well as in the lived experience of being in school spaces – built, natural, inside, outside – for teachers, students and families. As Christmann (2008) observes: 'Buildings are characterized by the fact that they "communicate" themselves spatially, aesthetically, and, in any case, visually' (para 4).

This chapter reflects on visual research in education by taking a look sideways at the representation of school buildings and the intended as well as the ad hoc arrangement of school spaces. It draws from a project on the spatial history of school design, pedagogy and social change in Australia across the 20th century.[1] The larger study brings together researchers working across the disciplines of architecture, urban planning, history and education in order to explore the multi-layered histories and interactions between innovations in school design, educational reforms and pedagogies, attending to the socio-spatial, aesthetic, built and natural environments of schools. The project combines case studies of specific school sites, buildings and designs with intellectual and cultural histories of the educational and architectural ideas animating and responding to these innovations. This includes international debates regarding educational and architectural experiments and the transnational history of their re-contextualisation (McLeod 2014).

Across the 20th century, innovations in Australian school design have reflected new understandings of education as well as changing relations between schools, communities, forms of citizenship and conceptions of the child and adolescent (e.g. Willis 2014). Modern architecture and urban planning have played a critical role in mediating and realising these educational changes and their attendant aspirations. As Kozlovsky (2010) has noted: 'The study of the environments where education takes place intersects two fields of knowledge, architecture and education'; moreover, 'the study of the school, especially that of the modern school building, requires knowledge in both fields to account for the collaborative nature of the process of design of these environments' (p. 695).

Our purposes in this chapter are, first, to illustrate some of the ways in which the fields of education and architecture come together in the history of Australian schooling and, second, to showcase different methodological and interpretive approaches to working with visual sources. This discussion is advanced via an interdisciplinary dialogue, drawing out insights afforded by approaches underpinned by different disciplinary orientations and 'ways of seeing' – showcasing views from architectural, educational and social historians. Rather than advocate for the authority of a single approach or expose the limitations of another, this chapter illustrates different ways of reading and interrogating visual representations, juxtaposing them to indicate productive divergences and convergences in approach and in how we each make meaning from images. To focus reflections, Julie McLeod begins by outlining methodological matters and the context of the alternative school movement in Australia during the 1960s and 1970s, before we then take turns to consider the visual representations and 'look' of one community school during that time.

Methodological questions and contexts: new schools for new times

Julie McLeod

Within the history of education, a substantial body of scholarship exists on the use of visual records, and in particular photographs, as sources for both enriching prevailing historical understandings and opening up new ways of seeing and making sense of that history, of bringing new matters into view (Mietzner et al. 2005; Dussel 2013). Yet, as Peim suggests, the 'turn to the visual' need not represent 'a turn away from other modes, other senses of doing history'; rather, it offers 'a specific (but certainly not separate) form of knowledge that requires its own mode of apprehension. It offers a *complementary* form of historical knowledge' (Peim 2005, p. 11). The following dialogue seeks precisely to elaborate the 'mode of apprehension' prompted by visual sources, and to do so from the vantage point of the different disciplinary practices. In particular, we seek to show how visual records offer invaluable insights into the dreams and materialisation of radical and alternative education.

The rubric 'visual research' encompasses a wide variety of sources and strategies: collecting and interpreting existing visual sources; generating new visual records as research 'data' from participants; treating visual sources ethnographically as forms of 'thick description', as records of emotionally charged events, as registers of institutional surveillance (school photographs, or military line-ups), or as professional tools (e.g. drawings and models of buildings); and they can be accidental mementos serendipitously transformed into visual sources attributed with collective cultural significance.

Do visual sources demand new repertoires of methodological strategies, injunctions, cautions and forms of reflexivity? Do they present distinctive methodological and ethical dilemmas? In the account developed here, we address two dimensions to these questions in relation to researching the history of education. The first concerns distinctiveness in researching visual rather than textual or oral sources, and the second concerns disciplinary differences and purposes. Simply put, how might an architect compared to an educator respond to an image of a school building? What will stand out, what will not be noticed, what will be accorded meaning and significance, and what will remain a kind of clue whose meaning might remain somewhat opaque?

Questions of methodological distinctiveness are of different order from asking about the *value* or use of visual sources in understanding the meaning and life of educational institutions or the subjective, embodied experiences of being in school. And they are also different from asking about the generation of visual data by research participants – for example, drawings, photographs, digital records – or the use of visual records in the conduct of research to help elicit responses from participants. The methodological dilemma becomes clearer when considering how one might interpret visual sources compared to interpreting textual and oral sources. It is plausible to argue that at one level the analysis of images can proceed along similar lines to textual analysis. Both involve identifying, for example, manifest and latent meanings, contextual and embedded references, absences, understated or concealed signs, layers of intertexuality and referentiality as well as relations between different elements. The visual record, however, arguably amplifies the significance of the juxtaposition of elements, bringing into play the semiotics of meaning in immediate and direct ways. Moreover, in the case of school design, some elements can only be or are most effectively represented visually – in drawings or models that project the anticipated structure, or in images of the actually constructed design, whether that be the built or natural environment.

Yet, as Grosvenor and Lawn observe in relation to photographs of schools, 'Photography constitutes a site of production and representation, a photograph is a product of cultural discourses and as such must be read not as an image but as a text, and as with any text, it is open to a diversity of readings' (Grosvenor & Lawn 2005, p. 88–89). Moreover, as Dussel observes, the use of photographic images tends to dominate visual research in historical studies of education, arguing that this is connected to a widespread social view of photographic images as a form of '"witness" or "capture"' (Dussel 2013, p. 33) that promise to represent 'life in accurate and concrete terms' (Dussel 2013 p. 34). There has been, Dussel suggests, a 'methodological vacuum' concerning the use of visual images in the history of education, linked to under-theorising of conceptual issues, including lack of attention to the 'historicity of visual technologies and visual regimes' (Dussel 2013, p. 38). She calls for an opening out of the relationship between 'schooling and regimes of visuality' so that we can attend to not only the 'social construction of the visual' but also to the 'visual construction of the social': 'the modern subject embodies a particular visuality, a specific way of looking and being looked at that is not external to its configuration' (Dussel 2013, p. 41).

Such arguments are not to deny the perspective and value of photographs but to underscore that, like other modes of representation – textual, oral, visual – photographs are not innocent, tell-all records that offer an unmediated view of the past. There are parallels here with methodological debates about the use of oral history testimony and its seeming promise of the first-hand account to offer direct access to the past. Oral testimony is now widely seen as a record of memory and forgetting; not as a register of the facts of the past, but as biographical and collective narratives of the past – with all the partial perspectives, omissions, projections, exaggerations and so forth that such a narrative inevitably represents (e.g. Perks & Thomson 2006; McLeod & Thomson 2009). So, too, with photographic sources, which cannot be understood as 'all-seeing' pictures of an event or a classroom, or as simply capturing things as they really were in a naturalistic record. Rather, photographs can be staged and stylised, some elements foregrounded or backgrounded in the composition, and even with supposedly candid and random photographs, some things are excluded from view. And, of course, the same image evokes different emotional and analytical responses from viewers and takes on new significance with every re-reading.

We consider here both staged and informal photographs of a school environment – including outside and inside spaces, and a diagram of the school layout in its early days. Before developing a series of vignettes in response to these images, we offer some brief contextual remarks to situate these images within the history of educational and social progressivism of the 1960s and 1970s, and more specifically within Australian government schooling in the state of Victoria.

In Australia, as elsewhere, the 1960s was a time when new educational ideas were gaining ground about the child, pedagogy, freedom and the role of schools as places to foster self-discovery. Initiatives included the expansion of child-centred curriculum development, the establishment of 'open' classrooms and an accompanying mood of 'de-institutionalisation' that looked to the socially transformative potential of schools. New expressions of progressivism began to flourish, alongside radical critiques of conventional schooling and optimism in the critical potential of schooling to disrupt entrenched power inequalities and affirm the intrinsic value of participant learning and new modes of curriculum (Potts 2007; Schoenheimer 1973; McLeod 2014). The alternative schooling movement of the 1960s and 1970s comprised an informal network of educational reforms that spanned curriculum innovation, student-centred and participatory pedagogies and radical social critique. School design was integral to these changes, conveying in highly visible ways a spirit of de-institutionalisation and a rupture with tradition.

Huntingdale Technical School was one such school that was deliberately designed to reflect this new ethos. It began in February 1972 with a collection of temporary portables and makeshift buildings on a former golf links site in a southern suburb of Melbourne, and by 1973 it had 320 students (Maslen 1973, p. 14). The school's establishment was underpinned by three principles: 'learning can only take place in the individual; the school is a community and operates as such; and the school is part of a wider community' (*The Educational Magazine* 1975, p. 5; see also Huntingdale Technical School 1978, pp. 1.1–1.3).

In the section below, we juxtapose responses to four photographs of the school, which chart its movement from a collection of temporary buildings (known locally as 'portables') to a deliberately designed school intended to embody the aspirations for a new way of being a school. The circulation and location of these images is important to note here, and the consequences of this are discussed further in the individual vignettes. The first three photographic images were taken from a public access Facebook site addressed to former students and teachers at Huntingdale Technical School. This large collection contains images from the 1970s, photographs of school activities and excursions, many photographs of individuals – students and teachers – as well as photographs of various school reunions. We have selected photographs that highlight the buildings and school space, and deliberately have not included photographs of individuals. This was determined by the overall focus on school design, in addition to ethical cautions in not wanting to use relatively recent images of people without their permission (notwithstanding that these images were circulating in the highly ambiguous 'public domain' of Facebook). Questions, then, of the mobility as well as the context *and* de-contextualisation of images are relevant here. We knew that the images came from the start up phases of the school, yet more precisely dating the images involved close reading of visual clues.

An architectural eye

Philip Goad and Julie Willis

To the architectural historian, the visual – buildings, landscapes, cities, streets, and images or other representations of them – is read as if it were text. Photographs, both professional and amateur, and drawings that include perspective views, conceptual sketches and diagrams, plans, sections and elevations are critical primary sources that are used in parallel with oral and textual sources as well as, where possible, an actual experience of a building or place (Forty 2000; Robbins 1994; Evans 1995).

Such images become critical windows into how spaces are used on a day-to-day basis, how these spaces and the form of the building were conceived (or not) as part of an overall strategy, what aesthetic choices were made to determine a building's external appearance to the community, how the building sits within a system of political economy that relates to circumstantial pressures of production and construction, and also how environmental factors such as circulation (movement through a building), light, air and ventilation might determine the ability of users to function within such spaces. Some images also tell us whether users might find these spaces comfortable places in which to be and interact. The caveat to the use of visual methods as a research tool is that reliance on images alone must come with the admission that a full story needs the complement of 'reading' across a range of multiple sources – visual, textual and oral (Wang & Groat 2013). In this case, four historic images of Huntingdale Technical School tell us a great deal but cannot, of course, divulge the whole history of the school. But what they do provide is more than enough to draw some substantive conclusions about the character, architectural quality and atmosphere of one of Victoria's most interesting 1970s experiments in secondary education.

The plan of any building is a key document. It allows the viewer to understand functional arrangement of spaces and their adjacencies; it also allows us to understand circulation and the practiced eye to determine spatial or volumetric manipulation. Some plans are drawn specifically for the purposes of constructing the building, while others (e.g. sketch plans) are intended as documents for client interaction. In this case, the plan is a simple line diagram of spaces that appears to have been drawn to scale.

It shows a school strictly organised along two major corridors, each flanking a north-south spine of 'public' teaching functions such as

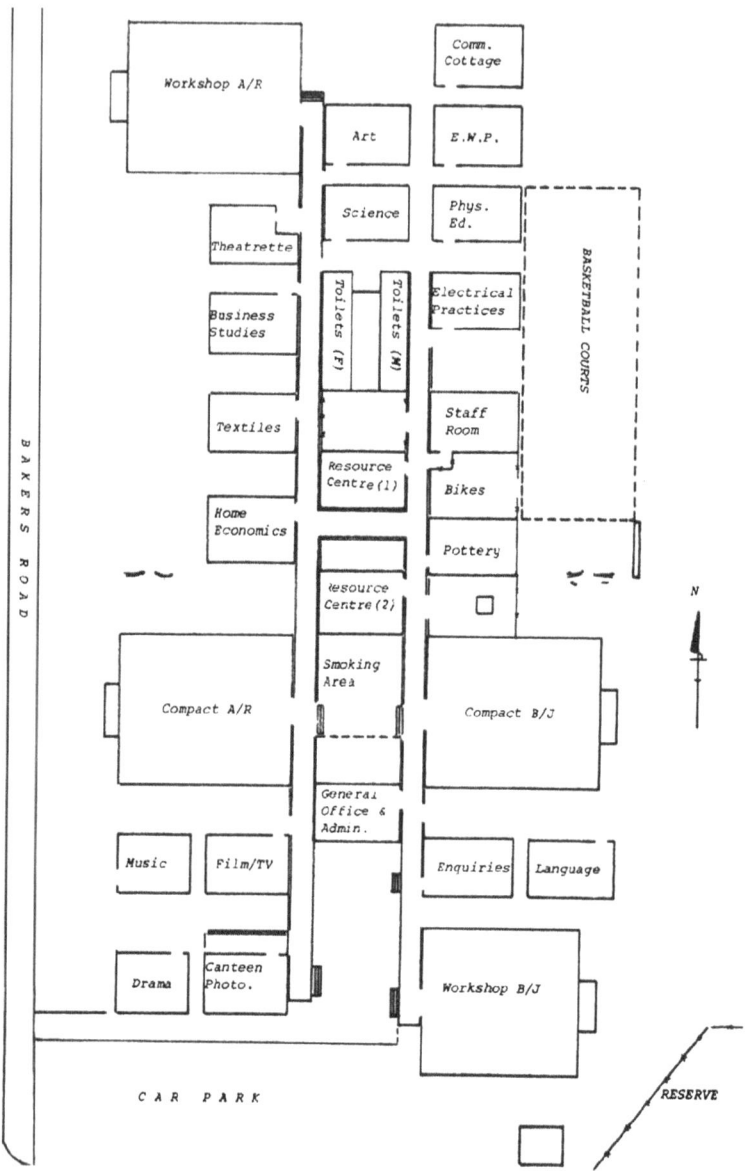

Figure 2.1 Diagram of school, reproduced by kind permission, Tony Delves
Source: Huntingdale Technical School [public group] Facebook site, accessed October 20, 2015.

'Resource Centre 1 and 2', Art and Science rooms and two internal courtyards, with perhaps most interesting of all, one of these designated as a 'Smoking Area' overlooked by the 'General Office & Admin'. While the layout of the buildings may not be intended to signify a hierarchy or institutional control, the formality demonstrated in the diagram and the regular size and repetition of the various study area classrooms appended to the corridors suggests the opposite. It implies, as Hillier and Hanson (1984, pp. 26–51) describe, a particular 'social logic of space'. Further, the panoptic view of the General Office into the 'Smoking Area' offers a mixed message: on the one hand, a relaxed attitude to students and staff smoking together in the courtyard, indicative of a relaxed attitude to conventional mores; but on the other, the presence of supervision and observation. One reading could be of an exercise yard within an institution of control (i.e. a prison or place of detention; for discussion of the panopticon in modern buildings, see Markus 1993). Another reading of the plan, however, is that of external spaces of near equal proportion to the classrooms they separate: in effect, outdoor rooms that break down the scale of the school into more intimate spaces of interaction and engagement for students outside the classroom. What is key, however, to all of these readings is that more information is required to form definitive conclusions. This diagram needs to be complemented by text or other images or another series of more detailed plans to more accurately convey what this school is really about spatial and socially.

The external photograph of Huntingdale Technical School (Figure 2.2) immediately indicates the architectural style of the building at its entry: off-form concrete with chamfered soffits and aluminium-framed windows and doors. This dates the building between the late 1960s and early 1980s, when the Victorian Public Works Department (PWD) reacted against its standard lightweight timber construction (LTC) schools of the post-war years and affected schools that were to appear more 'permanent', attempting to indicate a new, updated form of civic dignity to school architecture. The placement of a work of abstract modern art at the school's entry as well as signage that included an artwork logo based on the letter 'H' indicates an aspiration towards being seen as progressive and creative. A further sign of this progressiveness is the inclusion in the photograph's foreground of a low, treated-pine log-rail fence. Instead of the traditional school fence of cyclone wire, here at Huntingdale the barriers to entry and exit of the school are lowered and made porous. Students could easily sit on the low rails, and come and go between the rails with ease – there appears to be no traditional front school gate.

Figure 2.2 is possible to date and identify through its architectural style. The unlabelled diagram of Figure 2.1 allows no such thing, compounded by the lack of conventional plan drawing techniques; it was not clear if it was the same building or not as depicted in Figure 2.2. Further visual research was required to determine the relationship between the images, and this showed that Figure 2.1 was not the plan of Figure 2.2; furthermore, as Huntingdale Technical School today still stands in the form shown in Figure 2.2, Figure 2.1 was an earlier, demolished incarnation of the school. In order to determine the chronological sequence of the images, we extrapolated the diagram (Figure 2.1) into a three-dimensional form and compared it to the building in Figure 2.2, but such analysis demonstrated that there was no clear architectural connection between both images, including apparently different orientations on the site. We then used a satellite view of the current school site and saw the outline of a building which was closely aligned to that in Figure 2.2, and looked nothing like the plan in Figure 2.1, confirming the different orientation of the site. Inferring from such visual records, it appears that

Figure 2.2 Exterior image of school, reproduced by kind permission, Coula Mellos

Source: Huntingdale Technical School [public group] Facebook site, accessed October 21, 2015.

the new school was built on a section of the site that was not covered by the old, and then the old portables were removed.

If Figure 2.2 was the new school, Figure 2.4 relates to the diagram (Figure 2.1) and explains the school as it was before its 'permanent' replacement. An amateur photograph, it shows a courtyard with a partially covered area formed by two LTC portable classrooms, most likely showing the covered 'Smoking Area' before the addition of one of the 'Compact' LTC blocks. The arrangement in this image appears ad hoc – at odds with the plan diagram – but again it is possible to understand by using the information that is available to determine the connection between the images and not assuming they are de facto representing the same building or period of time. What is interesting here is the apparent mismatch between the formality of the diagram and the relaxed, informal appearance of the school at this time: low key, unpretentious and making do. Even the staff seemed happy to park their cars close and at an angle to the buildings on dusty, apparently unkempt grounds with a backdrop of tall Australian eucalypts in the distance.

The two photographs (Figures 2.2 and 2.4) are of the same school but in different incarnations. Each, however, suggests that a different ethos might be evoked from within, the new school evincing an image of organised or institutionalised 'progress', the other (the old school), a hand-to-mouth government experiment where additions and alterations might be made at will and with standardised elements that do not necessarily mean visual or spatial boredom but instead suggest a 'loose fit' of functions not dependent on specific functionally determined form; in essence, a casual diagram, a messy order. Figure 2.3 is an interior view of a classroom from this period (1972) and is extremely revealing. If the image has been staged, and it appears likely that is has, it gives a vivid account of the creative 'life' and activity of the open-plan classroom experience at Huntingdale. Given the date of the image, the room is almost certain to be one of the double-sized 'Compact' classrooms depicted in Figure 2.1.

For the architectural historian, these images give a composite picture of the same school over time. It is clear that one needs more than one image of the mood, atmosphere and architectural framing of these spaces of education. Images are necessarily partial – they never give the complete picture. The method of the architectural historian is forensic and ultimately just one part of an interdisciplinary task that seeks to elucidate what the spaces of education really mean.

A view from education

Julie McLeod

Alternative schools promised to liberate students from the confines of the classroom and the constraints of institutionalised learning. They variously occupied community buildings, re-created familial and intimate environments in older houses, or embraced innovative open-plan and purpose-built classrooms that reflected flexibility and utility, creating new opportunities for social and educational interactions. Alternative schools were to be different in highly visible ways, not only in philosophy, curriculum or classroom interactions.

The very feel and set-up of alternative and community schools in the 1970s was crucial to their ambitions, not only to enact different modes of curriculum and pedagogy but also to be plainly recognised as different from regular schools. The dual positioning and ambivalent relation to mainstream schools can be understood in Foucauldian terms as *heterotopic* (Foucault 1998, p. 178), in which alternative schools are intelligible as both like school and not like school (McLeod 2014). The images of alternative schools are of heterotopic spaces, counter-sites that stand in 'an ambivalent, though mostly oppositional, relation to a society's mainstream' (Saldanha 2008, p. 2081). The images of Huntingdale suggest how the physical layout of the school buildings and classrooms was integral in conveying and constituting aspirations for difference, and in helping students to become other than passive subjects of conventional schooling.

Figure 2.1 (the diagram of the school layout) shows an orderly arrangement of school portables and includes important details suggesting some of the changed purposes of the school environment and associated shifts in educational mood. For example, a community cottage is incorporated into the layout of the school, reflecting a desire to forge closer relationships between school and community, an overt invitation for the school to be seen as welcoming to the outside world; indeed, encouraging that outside world to come into the once bounded (and protected) space of schools. As a dedicated space, adjacent to other subject area rooms (Science, Art) the community cottage – its very name evoking an atmosphere of closer social ties – points to a breaking down of preconceptions of what activities and social relations should be part of the scope of school life; and in doing so, expands who is included in definitions of the school community.

Looking at the functions of some of the rooms, we see the transformation of the library to a Resource Centre, reflecting the arrival of audiovisual and other non-book resources into schools during this period. The name 'Resource Centre' also implies a creative mode of engagement, accenting the double meaning of resources as materials to be drawn upon and made into something else. This stands in contrast to the more passive consultation of books implied in the idea of the Library, and as such is congruent with a pedagogy driven by student interest, with two resource centres available to support their self-directed learning. A dedicated room for Film/TV, centrally positioned, also shows the spread of new media technologies in schools and, in combination with the number of other rooms dedicated to arts-based learning (i.e. rooms for music, drama, art, pottery, textiles, and a theatrette), suggests a high premium on students' creative pursuits. As a technical school (geared to vocational education), there are rooms dedicated to applied and practical subjects (e.g. electrical practices, business studies) and there are noticeably no classrooms dedicated to the traditional curriculum areas of mathematics and English or the humanities, although science gets its own room, presumably because of the facilities needed for doing experiments.

This simple drawing then tells us something about the type of curriculum favoured and also hints at the pedagogical preferences in the allocation of open-plan and multi-purpose spaces – the Compacts and the Workshops. There are elements of conventional school buildings – rooms named for subject areas, basketball courts, bike sheds, general office, the staff room (although it looks small and is integrated into the arrangement of student spaces, not sequestered in an 'administration wing'). Yet, at the same time, this diagram is also telling us something else about the feel of this school – evident perhaps most strikingly in the designation of a 'smoking area' and the large open-plan spaces. The incorporation of a smoking zone is hard to imagine in the present day, with heightened regulation of public health, widespread knowledge of the dangers of smoking and schools particularly conscious of minimising social risks. But in the drawing of this school layout, we suggest it means much more than a regulated space for smoking. To make sense of this demarcated area, we draw, in part, upon oral histories with former students and teachers from the school, in which the smoking area was a vividly remembered space, often recalled with a wry laugh and a ready supply of funny stories. The significance of the smoking area lies not only in that it meant smoking was seen as an acceptable activity at Huntingdale Technical School – in contrast to it being a punishable offence in most other schools at that time – but also because it was a social space in which teachers and students interacted together;

teachers who wished to smoke did so alongside students. This points to a reworking of hierarchical relations between teachers and students, and a yearning for greater informality and egalitarian social and interpersonal relationships. Teachers are positioned less as remote figures of authority and discipline and, in the community school philosophy, more as people supporting students' education; and students are attributed with the capacity and responsibility to make decisions about their own learning. The smoking area creates a space that displays a sense of shared endeavour in the community school spirit, where teachers and students mix as people on an equal footing.

New understandings of students' subjectivities are also suggested by Figure 2.3, a photograph from *The Educational Magazine*, a publication of the Victorian Department of Education. The direct caption, 'Huntingdale Technical School: About Students as People', declares a philosophy of student participation and the value of student choices, with the classroom image showing a mix of pedagogical activity and student movement across the classroom space. In the background, students are working on their own or in small groups, not directly overlooked by a teacher's gaze; in the foreground, the teacher is like one of the students sitting around the table (even though all eyes are on the teacher); students are sitting, standing, moving around; there are higher desks for arts and craft work, tables for group work and writing, mobiles hanging from the ceiling. There is an air of focus, concentration and purposeful activity on display, and the image gives the look of a deliberate showcasing of the creative possibilities afforded by the open-plan environment and the effectiveness of the student-led curriculum.

Following Herman et al. (2011), it is instructive to think of classroom objects, such as desks or chairs, as 'medial messengers of the variable and dynamic school culture' and as the 'materialisation' of school culture. They propose that the 'turn to things is an extrapolation of the gradual reconceptualisation...of things into active social entities within sociology. Artefacts and objects are, as such, no longer regarded as the socially external world of the environment...but as mediating agencies...Things come to life in their organisational, social and cultural relationships and, as living entities, they also intervene in those relationships' (Herman et al. 2011, p. 98). Photographic images are especially valuable for gaining glimpses of such materialisation, and in the case here, the materialisation of philosophies of radical schooling. The image of students in the open-plan room shows how the desk, a traditional object in schooling, associated with regulating children into the

Reading Images of School Buildings and Spaces 29

Figure 2.3 Interior view of classroom

Source: The Educational Magazine. (1972), 'Huntingdale Technical School: About Students as People', 29(4), p.17, Department of Education, Victoria.

habits of receptive attention – and classrooms structured according to the orderliness of rows of desks – has now become an object for sitting at, for leaning on, for doing art, for writing, for talking; for mediating students becoming people, with desks assembled in clusters, not rows, both casually positioned and artfully arranged in the apparent freedom of the open-plan classroom.

Photographic records can evoke potent memories of both direct and associated experiences of schooling and, as Burke (2001) argues, subjective and, in particular, emotional responses to photographs are important sources for historians of education. These represent a 'universal and complex resource, generally neglected or rejected by scholars but one which...is a key component of understanding the history of education and interpreting the current debate about its future' (Burke 2001 pp. 192–193.) Figure 2.4 a snapshot of the grounds of the school, looking on to the portable classrooms and a sheltered outdoor area, is empty of people but rich in emotional resonance. It tells a lot about the time and place of this experiment in educational innovation, read through biographical and collective memories of alternative schooling and the 1970s feeling of educational possibilities. The portables are

Figure 2.4 Grounds of school, reproduced by kind permission, Tony Delves

Source: Huntingdale Technical School [public group] Facebook site, accessed October 20, 2015.

framed by a jauntily parked car to the side (it looks like a Volkswagen station wagon from the early 1970s, perhaps?), the branches and shadows of gum trees giving it a distinctively Australian feel, a clear blue sky and the empty, flat, sparse grass in front of the school. One can almost feel the dust, the sun, the dirt in one's shoes rubbing between sock and leather. Inevitably perhaps, it calls to mind my own secondary schooling in a more conventional high school, but a new one also put together with portables and make-do arrangements as the rest of the school building program caught up with the expanding population on the outer edge of Melbourne. It evokes for me, the endless waiting of school, the hanging around, the sense of nothing happening, the restless boredom no matter how interesting the classes try to be. Against the flatness, this image of outdoor space also evokes the intensities of friendships and the drama and flow of relationships and hanging out. This image is also buzzing with the voices of former Huntingdale students who talked about the outside areas of the school with such fondness, as the site of formative experiences, in what might be described now as an unmanaged or even neglected 'outdoor environment'. Perhaps it was precisely its unruly ordinariness, its un-designed feel, which made it so appealing for students. It also gives pause to reflect on how young people's education and formation – as students, as people – happens in such outside spaces, the not-school space, and not only or mainly in classrooms, even if they are open-plan, self-directed zones of creativity: the outdoor space is thus integral to the life and community of the school.

A contextual lens

Kate Darian-Smith

For the historian of 20th-century Australia, photographs are essential documents that parallel, confirm and contradict written texts in their evidence about the past. In her useful guide to the use of photographs within historical research, Penny Tinkler (2013) outlines how visual methodology is underpinned by the conceptualisation and contextualisation of an image as the 'everyday' and the extraordinary are traced across time. Despite the 'temptation' to view a photograph as a simple record of an observable historical reality, most contemporary analyses argue that photographs are themselves constructed, and the relationship between any photograph and the moment it 'captures' is highly complex.

Yet, as Price and Wells (1997, p. 34) put it, 'The very ubiquity of the medium has meant that Photographs have always circulated in context for which they were not made'. Reading photos relies on knowledge well beyond the visual and historical clues in the photograph itself. The connections between the photographer and the photographic image, and intention and purpose behind the act of photography, are more opaque when it comes to institutional or official photographs. In such cases, the images may appear depersonalised by a representative mode that is necessarily one of 'objective' recording. For Susan Sontag (1973, p. 156), institutional photographs and the bureaucratic classifications they produced could reduce the world to 'a series of unrelated, free-standing particles; and history, past and present, [to] a set of anecdotes and *faits divers*'. Such institutional pictures may appear unconnected to a broader social and historical context, and as such need to be understood in the broader reference of other archival accounts that might also include non-written forms such as oral histories.

So in interrogating a set of images of Huntingdale Technical School in the 1970s, the materiality of the school, its buildings and grounds, and its students leads to a series of questions that would be asked of other historical documents: How was the image produced and for what purpose? How was it circulated and how was it interpreted both at the time and at later moments?

The external photographs of the school, with their focus on the new buildings and the portable structure (with car), are devoid of staff or students, and in a sense rendered historical and adrift from time and even place by that absence. Architectural styles offer a clue to the dating of the images, but a key question is whether the absence of people is intentional – as in an official image of the school grounds – or merely the fact that this is the empty schoolyard over, perhaps, the summer holiday. And what does the unpeopled environment portray? Are these photographs the documentation of a modern school campus, and thus a testament to the success of a government program in revitalising the physical environment of schools? If, perhaps, the same images were created in 2014, would these be interpreted in a different way – and perhaps, now, as the documentation of older building structures that are now outdated or even obsolete in purpose?

In contrast, the image of students in the classroom provides a more identifiable historical frame, as can be seen in the chronological markers of time – clothing and especially hemlines, hairstyles, even bodily poses and faces. The movement of the students in the classroom points to the later decades of the 20th century and the behavioural conventions of this time that governed the mobility within a classroom setting. In particular, the caption of the photograph does the work of locating the images in place and time and exemplifying the intention of its publication – if not necessarily its production. The image's title 'About Students as People' encapsulates an ideological framing that shaped its historical interpretation within new ideas about learning and teaching. The location of the image in *The Educational Magazine*, a publication aimed at teachers, further shapes the way that it is read as a historical document.

Moreover, a contextual reading of such an image is, for the historian, expansive. This image of the modern student is one that can work at not only a specific but also a representative level. It can thus stand in for the wider social changes that were to be transforming society in the 1970s, a heady period of political reform and turmoil under the federal Labour government of Prime Minister Gough Whitlam between 1972 and 1975, and the reverberations of this around the nation – even in the small and enclosed space of Huntingdale Technical School.

Concluding remarks

Drawing from a larger project examining the history of innovations in school design and pedagogy across 20th-century Australia, this chapter has focused on visual representations of an alternative school setting. Such schools are rich sites for developing an interdisciplinary dialogue across the fields of architecture, education and social history, in large part because their ambitions called for a major rethinking and remaking of the buildings, space and purposes of schooling. The transformations were not confined to a tweaking of the curriculum, or the refurbishment of classroom facilities. Rather, they entailed re-imagining schooling on multiple fronts and, in doing so, sought to make these new forms and practices of schooling highly distinctive, visible and recognisable in the wider community. The look and design of these schools was thus crucial, and photographic representations of them are an important means for conveying these aspirations. However, as each of the above vignettes indicates, the visual record on its own can only ever tell one part of the historical story. This is neither particularly surprising nor methodologically troubling as historians of all ilk typically need to draw on a range of sources to develop their accounts, and the visual record, despite its illusion of capturing things as they really are, is no exception. We have attempted to show here the various types of clues, contexts and interpretive strategies we have drawn upon to read the visual sources as useful records in the history of alternative schooling; and to show how these are linked to disciplinary and professional differences (and commonalities) in the fields of architecture, education and social history.

Note

1. Australian Research Council Discovery Project, 2011–2013, *Designing Australian Schools: A Spatial History of Innovation, Pedagogy and Social Change*, Julie Willis, Kate Darian-Smith, Philip Goad, Hannah Lewi, David Nichols, Elain Harwood, Julie McLeod, with Research Fellows Sianan Healy and Cameron Logan. Research for this chapter was also supported by an Australian Research Council Future Fellowship, 2012–2016, 'Youth identity and educational change since 1950: Digital archiving, re-using qualitative data and histories of the present', Julie McLeod.

References

Burke, C. (2001). Hands-on History: Towards a Critique of the 'Everyday'. *History of Education, 30*(2), 191–201.
Burke, C., & Grosvenor, I. (2008). *School*. London: Reaktion Books.
Christmann, G. B. (2008). The Power of Photographs of Buildings in the Dresden Urban Discourse. Towards a Visual Discourse Analysis. [29 paragraphs]. *Forum: Qualitative Social Research, 9*(3), Art 11, September.
Dussel, I. (2013). The Visual Turn in the History of Education: Four Comments for a Historiographical Discussion. In T. S. Popkewitz (Ed.), *Rethinking the History of Education: Transnational Perspectives on Its Questions, Methods and Knowledge* (pp. 29–49). New York: Palgrave Macmillan.
The Educational Magazine (1972). Huntingdale Technical School: About Students as People. *29*(4), 17–18.
The Educational Magazine (1975). Community and Continuing Education: The Current Explosion. *32*(4), 3–8.
Evans, R. (1995). *The Projective Cast: Architecture and Its Three Geometries*. Cambridge, MA: MIT Press.
Forty, A. (2000). *Words and Buildings: A Vocabulary of Modern Architecture* (pp. 29–41). London: Thames and Hudson.
Foucault, M. (1998). Different Spaces. In P. Rabinow (Ed.), *Michel Foucault, Aesthetics, Method and Epistemology: The Essential Works of Michel Foucault, 1954–1984, Volume 2* (pp. 175–185), Harmondsworth: Penguin.
Grosvenor, I., & Lawn, M. (2005). Portraying the School: Silence in the Photographic Archive. In U. Mietzner, K. Myers, & N. Peim (Eds), *Visual History: Images of Education* (pp. 85–107). Bern, Switzerland: Peter Lang.
Gutman, M., & de Coninck-Smith, N. (Eds) (2008). *Designing Modern Childhoods: History, Space and the Material Culture of Children*. New Brunswick, NJ: Rutgers University Press.
Herman, F., van Gorp, A., Simon, F., & Depaepe, M. (2011). The School Desk: From Concept to Object. *History of Education, 40*(1), 97–117.
Hillier, B., & Hanson, J. (1984). *The Social Logic of Space*. Cambridge: Cambridge University Press.

Huntingdale Technical School (1978). *The Evaluation Book*. Huntingdale, Victoria: Huntingdale Technical School.

Kozlovsky, R. (2010). The Architecture of Educare: Motion and Emotion in Post-war Educational Spaces. *History of Education, 39*(6), 695–712.

Leander, K., Philips, N. C., & Taylor, K. H. (2010). The Changing Social Spaces of Learning: Mapping New Mobilities. *Review of Research in Education, 34*(March), 329–394.

Markus, Y. (1993). *Buildings and Power: Freedom and Control in the Origin of Modern Building Types*. London: Routledge.

Maslen, G. (1973). Huntingdale Technical School. *The Educational Magazine, 30*(4), 14–15.

McLeod, J. (2014). Experimenting with Education: Spaces of Freedom and Alternative Schooling in the 1970s. *History of Education Review, 43*(2), 172–189.

McLeod, J., & Thomson, R. (2009). *Researching Social Change: Qualitative Approaches*. London: Sage.

Mietzner, U., Myers, K., & Peim, N. (Eds) (2005). *Visual History: Images of Education*. Bern, Switzerland: Peter Lang.

Mietzner, U., & Pilarczyk, U. (2005). Methods of Image Analysis on Research in Educational and Social Sciences. In U. Mietzner, K., Myers, & N. Peim (Eds), *Visual History: Images of Education* (pp. 109–127). Bern, Switzerland: Peter Lang.

Peim, N. (2005). Introduction: The Life of Signs in Visual History. U. Mietzner, K., Myers, & N. Peim (Eds), *Visual History: Images of Education* (pp. 7–34). Bern, Switzerland: Peter Lang.

Perks, R., & Thomson, A. (Eds) (2006). *The Oral History Reader* (2nd ed.). Abingdon, Oxon: Routledge.

Potts, A. (2007). New Education, Progressive Education and the Counter Culture. *Journal of Educational Administration and History, 39*(2), 145–159.

Price, D., & Wells, L. (1997). Thinking about Photography: Debates, Historically and Now. In L. Wells (Ed.), *Photography: A Critical Introduction* (pp. 9–54). London: Routledge.

Robbins, E. (1994). *Why Architects Draw*. Cambridge, MA: MIT Press.

Saldanha, A. (2008). Heterotopia and Structuralism. *Environment and Planning A, 40*, 2080–2096.

Schoenheimer, H. (1973). *Good Australian Schools and Their Communities*. Melbourne: Victorian Technical Teachers Association.

Sontag, S. (1973/1979). *On Photography*. London and New York: Penguin Books.

Tinkler, P. (2013). *Using Photographs in Social and Historical Research*. London: Sage.

Wang, D., & Groat, L. N. (2013). *Architectural Research Methods* (2nd edition). New York: John Wiley and Sons.

Willis, J. (2014). From Home to Civic: Designing the Australian School. *History of Education Review, 43*(2), 138–151.

3
On Using Found Object Photographs in School Research

Jeremy Rowe and Eric Margolis

Introduction

Educational research has focused heavily on first-person observation and, more recently, on researcher-produced photographs and videos of schools and educational settings (Costello 2001; Prosser 2007; Prosser & Loxley 2002; Sekula 1980; Tobin, Wu & Davidson 1989). Another approach, 'photovoice', includes the analysis of subject-produced photographs and drawings to investigate children's lives in school. Photovoice is also used to gain subjective insight into student and teacher experiences (Mitchell & Weber 1999a; Burke & Grosvenor 2003; O'Donoghue 2007; Ganesh 2007; Shohel & Howes 2007; Mitchell 2008). However, as privacy and liability issues increasingly influence decisions about research access, particularly in the United States, this type of visual research has become increasingly cumbersome, difficult and, in some cases, virtually impossible. Schools held to high-stakes performance standards are less willing to allow access since they feel that researcher presence might 'take away' from lesson time. Parents and teachers are less willing to sign informed consent forms – much less modelling-performing-narration releases – due to concerns of distraction and privacy. In addition, even when access is possible, oversight by 'institutional review boards' (IRBs), administrators, or ethics panels often place restrictions on photographs that may infringe on the anonymity or confidentiality of informants, especially protected populations like children. These restrictions make visual research in educational settings challenging, if not impossible.

In reaction to these pressures, and to increasing interest in the evolution of education over time, historians of education and other

On Using Found Object Photographs 37

Figure 3.1 Mathematics lesson in English classroom, unidentified photographer, ca 1860
Source: Collection of Jeremy Rowe Vintage photography – Vintagephoto.com.

educational researchers have begun to employ photographs as data in compelling investigations (Vinao 2005; Lawn & Grosvenor 2005; Burke & Grosvenor 2008; Burke, Howard & Cunningham 2013) Interestingly, researchers that turn to photographs as research tools find they have access to more images of schooling and educational settings than ever before. In the past, researchers seeking photographs had to physically visit historical collections and archives. More driven researchers also explored antique shops, collectors and shows seeking new material relevant to their research. Today, millions of images are available online. Some are self-produced and populate personal, school, Web, and social media sites. Millions more are pre-digital images scanned and posted for their aesthetic, social or historic context. The combination of digital and digitized images, the availability of sophisticated cataloguing and search and retrieval mechanisms, and online access have brought a wealth of images to the researcher's desktop. With little effort, researchers can find images that depict educational settings and activities from many sources, such as historical archives, online social-networking sites like Facebook, Pinterest, and Reddit, or simple Google image searches. Many other images are available for sale on sites, like eBay or Etsy, which offer an ever-changing array of photographs for sale and have become another valuable resource for educators and researchers. Other sources include yearbooks and, increasingly, advertising images designed to 'sell' or 'brand' a school. Our discussion will centre on the use of 'found' photographs, including commercially produced and distributed images, as well as vernacular, amateur images as research data.

Although historians traditionally do not consider materials 'historic' until they are more than fifty years old, it is valid for visual researchers studying education to use broader definitions that fit their topic. By identifying and analysing a photograph in a historic and indexical sense, the researcher can make inferences about the subject, setting and intent to inform their analysis. Hypotheses can be generated and tested using photographs as research data. Within this context, like tracks on a beach, photographic images can be understood and accepted as 'causal evidence' related to and reflecting the objects they depict. We take for granted that images, and the objects represented, disappear into the mists of history as soon as the shutter is released. Annette Kuhn noted the central issue of photographic images:

> The truth/authenticity potential of photography is tied in with the idea that seeing is believing. Photography draws on an ideology of the visible as evidence. The eye of the camera is neutral, it sees the world as it is: we look at a photograph and see a slice of the world. (Kuhn 1985, pp. 27–28)... [However] A photograph, however much it may pretend to authenticity, must always in the final instance admit that it is not real, in the sense that what is in the picture is not here, but elsewhere. (pp. 30–31)

We do not adopt the naïve, realist view that photographs are merely 'pencils of nature' passively documenting the scene before the lens, still less as 'peepholes into history' as Errol Morris put it (2007b, np). In this discussion, we see photographs as a multi-layered resource of embedded information and a visual vocabulary. Photographs can provide researchers with socially constructed texts for detailed analysis whose

Figure 3.2 Men's gymnastics class, Arizona Territorial Normal School, unidentified photographer, ca 1907
Source: Collection of Jeremy Rowe Vintage photography – Vintagephoto.com.

meanings require a visual literacy to be explored and understood. In this regard, images become exceptionally valuable research tools, particularly in study of the history of education. We can accept photographs as providing important data about the forms and practices of schooling to inform research. It is important to note that although inferences can be made, it is not possible to take photographs or make drawings of 'education' per se. Determining whether teaching or learning is actually taking place is an important issue, but it requires different methods. This is another compelling argument for the importance of explicitly stating and documenting researcher assumptions.

Photography and education have a long and intertwined relationship. One of the first photographs made in the United States, a daguerreotype in 1839, was of Central High School in Philadelphia. This was the first of millions of 'school photographs' taken by everyone from professional photographers to teachers, parents and even school children today. Our discussion of post-positivist, ethnographic and interpretivist paradigms is divided into three overlapping historical periods:

1. The 'early history' period, where photographs were only made by professionals and existed as direct positive images (e.g. daguerreotype,

ambrotype, and tintype) or paper or collodion negatives produced primarily by commercial photographers and publishers;
2. The 'snapshot' period, where professionals and amateurs alike could create photographs, and amateurs produced negatives, prints and direct positives like colour slides; and
3. The 'digital' period, where the number of photographic images exploded, but there has been a dichotomy between ease of online access and ephemeral nature of digital files.

We will similarly address three periods of time in terms of ownership and copyright permissions:

1. The historic period before January 21, 1923, where published photographs are in the public domain and are free for research unless copyright has been asserted and renewed;
2. The 'grey area' period between January 21, 1923, and the Digital Millennium Copyright Act (DMCA) protection, where marking with © (copyright) and requiring periodic renewals have made the granting of researching permissions challenging; and
3. The modern period, where photographs are copyrighted upon creation but can be 'donated' for several types of use via creative commons licenses.

This chapter also briefly examines three methodological approaches and practical methods for studying found images of school: post-positivism, ethnography and interpretivism. The discussion is necessarily 'methodological' because what constitutes evidence, standards of proof and a trustworthy conclusion differs for each approach. However, used together, the three paradigms provide powerful ways to examine the representation of schooling. In order to remain firmly grounded in imagery, we will present and analyse representative examples of the various approaches.

- Photoforensics – gathering concrete information based on film and negative type, photographic style, archival notes and chains of provenance, clocks, calendars and other sorts of evidence embedded in images (Morris 2007a; Rowe 2002).
- Ethnographic approaches may make use of grounded theory in examining images (Charmaz & Mitchell 2001). Methods include:
  - Constant comparison,
  - Simple coding,

- Axial coding,
- Theoretical coding, and
- Construction of mid-level theories.
- Interpretivism deals primarily with the symbolic meanings embedded in images but may also employ a number of methods, including:
  - Iconography,
  - Semiotics,
  - Marxist,
  - Critical pedagogy,
  - Feminist, and
  - Critical race theory.

In addition to the serendipity of which images were made, saved or preserved, passed down, and still retain identification or documentation to add meaning beyond the image, 'happenstance' also impacts what the researcher has been able to identify and acquire. Despite the power of search engines, results rely on the scope and quality of unreliable user-supplied descriptions and metadata. Moreover, while progress is being made in searching by image alone, keywords are still essential. Keywords are typically user assigned by photographers or archivists, usually with little regard to control vocabulary or standards. To find school photographs, one may need to do a series of searches using words like 'school', 'teacher', 'classroom', and so on and then sort out tangential results such as schools of fish or piano teachers, for example. One's research questions will determine which images are available, identified by the researcher, and recognised as meaningful. This holds true for physical images sought in archives, collections, and shops, those that are found or acquired first-hand as well as those that have been posted and made available online. Abigail Solomon-Godeau (1991, pp. 182) highlights the well-defined qualities of visual research:

> individual documentary projects, themselves the product of distinct historical circumstances and milieus, 'speak' of agendas both open and covert, personal and institutional, that inform their contents and, to a greater or lesser extent, mediate our reading of them. It is properly the work of historians and critics to attempt to excavate these coded and buried meanings, to bring to light these rhetorical and formal strategies that determined the work's production, meaning, reception, and use.

Photoforensics

Early history

The early history of photography included many formats which produced unique images, including daguerreotypes and collodion positive photographs like ambrotypes and tintypes. The physical object that holds your gaze is the original that was made in the camera by the photographer. Copies could initially only be made by re-photographing the original, or later by using a multiple-lens camera to create several identical images on a single plate. Interior views, such as classrooms, were very rare in the first decades of photography, providing few examples of educational settings other than exterior views of schoolhouses, class portraits made in the studio, or posed teachers with books from the era before 1860. Due to the cost and complexity of photography at this time, most images were printed on albumen paper from collodion wet plate negatives by professional photographers or commercial publishers in formats including cartes de visite, cabinet cards, and stereographs. Cartes de visite are roughly the size of business cards and were primarily used to produce portraits from the mid- to late 19th century. A later slightly larger version, the roughly 4½" × 6½" cabinet card was similarly used from ca 1860 into the early 20th century, again primarily

Figure 3.3 Papago Indian School, San Xavier Mission, near Tuscon, stereograph by D. P. Flanders photographer, ca 1874

Source: Collection of Jeremy Rowe Vintage photography – Vintagephoto.com.

for portraits but occasionally for interior views such as classrooms and school interiors.

Stereographs required a camera with two lenses that produced images from perspectives matching the separation between human eyes. When placed in a viewer, the brain fused the two images into an immersive three-dimensional view. Stereographs were incredibly popular as both documentary resources and (after the 1890s) teaching tools in their own regard (Rowe 2014). Early stereographs provide one of the best sources of information about educational settings, initially from posed genre scenes that became popular in England and Europe and were marketed and copied in the United States. Some are clearly parodies of educational settings, others more allegorically accurate, eventually documenting actual classrooms and educational settings. Though primarily photographic, stereographs also occasionally depicted cartoons, printed illustrations and drawings. Many classrooms had stereoviewers for each student; boxes of stereocards were marketed expressly for schools, often

Figure 3.4 Pima Girls School lunch group, near Phoenix, Arizona, unidentified photographer, ca 1898

Source: Collection of Jeremy Rowe Vintage photography – Vintagephoto.com.

including associated scripts and texts. The sets were often tailored to specific academic disciplines: three-dimensional views of palaces and pyramids accompanied geography, images of solids and graphs accompanied math, and views of dissections supplemented medical school curricula. Several thousand titles in areas such as history, social sciences, botany and biology were offered by companies like the Keystone View Company. Stereographs continued to be a valuable resource for educational documentation into the mid-20th century. To date, we have seen little evidence of the use of stereographs for analysis from the perspective of curriculum studies.

Snapshot

After about 1890, we see the era of amateur photography supplanting professionals. As availability of roll film and inexpensive, handheld cameras made photography simpler and less expensive, the volume of photographs increased exponentially. As the technology evolved and film became more sensitive, views of interiors such as classrooms became more frequent. Amateur photographs, such as snapshots – and after about 1905, photographic postcards – provide a fertile source of visual data for researchers interested in real educational settings. This snapshot era continued as cameras became smaller and simpler and as simple flash and then colour improved the ability to photograph indoors. The ability to easily document educational settings, and to empower teachers and students to make images, led to an ever-greater volume of photographic documentation, from school photos to classroom interiors, auditoriums, gymnasiums and other educational settings. While collectors prize historical images, including daguerreotypes, tintypes, and 19th-century images, the very desirability can make them prohibitively expensive to acquire. However, peers and private and public collections can still provide potential sources for researchers.

Though the vernacular school photographs from the 'snapshot' era are also collected and increasing in value, many images potentially valuable for research can be reasonably purchased from collectors, shops or shows, or from online auction sites. Examples include a recent search on eBay that revealed 26,910 results for 'photographs school' under 'Collectibles'. Another popular source, Etsy, returned almost 1000 items related to school photographs. Overall, simple, quick keyword searches can turn up an ever-changing array of tens of thousands of images related to schools and education.

Digital

The most recent quantum change has been the digital era, which has facilitated massive numbers of 'modern' images and increased access to historic photographs through search engines, huge digital archives and other online sources.

It is important to note the corresponding decrease in physical evidence produced by photographers as more photographs are posted online to be viewed on computers, pads, and phones. Silver-based photographs of the past have an inherent physicality that allows them to be placed in scrapbooks or collected in boxes and passed on to researchers, collectors, libraries and archives. It is also the case that 'prints' require no additional software or hardware to view. Though digital files can be and are printed, it appears that fewer and fewer physical prints are being produced as more material is 'born' and lives only in digital form.

Digital files have the benefit of simplicity regarding copy and transfer, as well as the ability to be easily 'improved' and 'corrected', using tools like digital-imaging software, in ways that required difficult and costly lab work in the past.

A primary weakness of digital files is their ephemeral nature. Without tangible, physical form the image files are at the mercy of accidental deletions, over-recording, hard-drive crashes, or other storage issues. Over time the additional issues of file format compatibility and the ability to access files raise additional concerns; that is, in twenty-five years, who

Figure 3.5 'Typical' kindergarten class, stereograph, unidentified photographer, ca 1885

Source: Collection of Jeremy Rowe Vintage photography – Vintagephoto.com.

will know what a JPEG or TIF file is or how to open it? Finally, there is an issue of resolution. Though many digital files are now fairly large, big files are rarely posted online. Without access to full-sized files, it is often difficult to enlarge the image to see detail important to researchers, or to reproduce in print.

Over the past two decades, online access to photographs has dramatically changed photo research. No longer must researchers travel to collections to view catalogues of holdings in person. Many collections, like the Library of Congress American Memory project and online collections being released by institutions such as the J. Paul Getty Museum, Reuters, and The Metropolitan Museum of Art, are relatively and accurately well catalogued, and as a result can be extremely valuable research tools. Over time these resources become heavily used, as researchers seek material and individual images are repeatedly published and referenced. Many archives of important images from WWII to the present are useful to researchers and important for viewing and studying; however, access, reproduction and use fees are often large. Fees for publication vary from libraries, museums and historical societies on the low end, to commercial 'stock' houses like Getty Images and Corbis, which typically charge higher commercial rates. Though fees are frequently lower for academic research, most institutions have a separate fee structure for publication. Issues related to fees and agreements for online use are complex and beyond the scope of this chapter.[1]

Online collections, though readily available, may be riddled with misinformation or offered without provenance (collateral information about the history and source of the item) or other identification. It is incumbent upon the researcher to validate and verify the associated captions and citations and to use whatever techniques possible to correctly and accurately identify images regardless of source (see our unpacking of the Albuquerque Indian School photograph below). Sadly even when knowledgeable researchers provide corrections or valid new information about images held in institutional collections, correcting errors and disseminating accurate information is very difficult. Unfortunately, there is often a 'chain of command' required to make changes, and this information is often delayed or lost before metadata can be corrected.

Images from sources other than institutions, such as sales and private collections, are extremely valuable but under-appreciated resources for photo researchers. Browsing antique shops, flea markets or other sources often provides access to new images. Online sources such as eBay provide access to thousands of images each week. Though many are searchable,

On Using Found Object Photographs 47

Figure 3.6 African American school house, Florida, stereograph by R. K. Bonine photographer, ca 1885
Source: Collection of Jeremy Rowe Vintage photography – Vintagephoto.com.

most collectors and many researchers find that mislabelled material is often most interesting – though great amounts of time and effort are needed to explore and find relevant images.

Social media sites such as Facebook and Pinterest have grown to be fora where collectors and researchers exchange information. The accuracy of the information is variable but can provide a starting point for researcher verification. An additional complication is the cavalier nature of many posters in failing to cite original sources for the images. The lack of credit and citation adds additional researcher time and effort to track sources, verify information and obtain permissions for reproduction and use.

While the original photographic intent can sometimes be gleaned from captions or context, unfortunately provenance information is frequently limited or missing. Photo albums made by parents, students or teachers are all too often destroyed when purchased at auction or tag sale – broken into component parts and offered for resale with key words like 'school', 'sports', 'Christmas', and so on. Thus any chain of provenance is sundered. Nevertheless, these sources can still provide a treasure trove of images depicting the materiality of schools, educational settings and processes.

It is important for the researcher to understand and analyse within the historic, technical and aesthetic context in which the image was created (Rowe 1997, 2007). Researcher assumptions made about the validity of the documentation and intent of the creator are critical to the analysis and should be explicitly documented as part of the process. Creating an audit trail of the research question, process of selecting, acquiring and accessing the images, and assumption in terms of using the photographs as evidence or catalysts for the research are critically important; audit trails permit others to question, refute or validate the research.

Photoforensics was coined by the first author as a term for understanding the physical and technical evidence associated with and embedded within the photograph. Provenance refers to the collateral information about the history and source of the photograph. Included is data that may be associated with the image or available in terms of who made the photograph, where was it made, where has it been since its creation, what manuscript or collateral information is or has been associated with it, and if and where it has been reproduced.

Good researchers examine and explore the provenance to verify its potential accuracy (Rowe 2011; Margolis 2004; Margolis 2004). For example, if notes on a 19th- or early-20th-century photograph were made in ballpoint pen (after its invention during WWII), then they were likely made by descendants, and thus may include second-hand recollections as opposed to primary source, first-hand evidence. Even where there is no associated provenance, the photograph itself often includes embedded information that can prove valuable to researchers. The type and style of the photographic mount can provide clues as to date of production or distribution based on size and style. The style of dress, classroom size, equipment being used, messages on the walls and blackboards, lighting and so on or other clues in the photograph can help identify or better validate other information about the possible age of a school photograph.

Often the photographic mount includes a photographer's imprint on recto or verso, providing potential clues to geographic source. With a little research into city directories or other sources, photographer address can often be identified to provide additional potential dates for creation of the image. Knowledge and experience with photographic processes permits researchers to evaluate whether the image is an original print from the negative, or possibly a copy or 'pirate' photograph (see the 'Popular Series' example illustration) that may have been produced at a later date.

For later images from the 'snapshot' era, there is often caption information, and on still later photos, processing lab or dating information printed on the edge or back of the print. Photographic postcards are a valuable source of information both for the image and collateral information they can provide (Rowe 2007). Messages written on the card often provide contextual information about the image and occasionally dating. Postmarks are helpful as indicators of the latest date that the image could have been produced. Sometimes photographers identified themselves by writing in the negative or on the card itself. Interestingly, it was common practice to copy earlier images onto postcards, so additional scrutiny is required to confirm dates. Under magnification or scanning, many images are sharp enough that it is possible to read calendars at the back of the classroom or to find other clues as to date or location embedded within the image.

A good metaphor when analysing photographs is the story. Photographs, and perhaps more importantly photographic archives, tell stories that gain complexity as the context and embedded information they contain is explored and understood by the researcher. Each layer of information – aesthetic, historic provenance, embedded physical and technical – provides additional depth and validity to the story for knowledgeable researchers. There is a growing cadre of collectors and researchers knowledgeable in photographic history that can be invaluable to educational researchers. Resources such as collectors' organisations, like the Daguerreian Society and Ephemera Society of America, as well as expanding research interactions to include researchers in history, social and material culture, in addition to photographic history, can provide valuable assets to assist in analysing and interpreting photographs. Good researchers present good stories; the best researchers tell the best and most compelling stories, grounded in empirical, 'validateable' evidence.

Using interpretivist tools

Interpretivism has a long history in the social sciences, going back at least to Wilhelm Dilthey and Max Weber. Dilthey especially drew on biblical hermeneutics, the interpretations of sacred texts and an alternative/companion to exegetics. Interpretivism is a critical appraisal of a text – in our case, an image – adding historical comprehension, social meanings, symbolism and iconic understanding to the photoforensics discussed above. Weber, for instance, in his critical study on the *Protestant Ethic and Spirit of Capitalism* (1904–1905) provided an *interpretation* of two major social movements. His discussion does not look for causes as much as various understandings of how Protestants and Catholics interpret how to live a good and just life, and how these interpretations affect economic behaviour. Perhaps the most important interpretivist of the later 20th century was Clifford Geertz, an anthropologist, who wrote:

> (My) concept of culture... is essentially a semiotic one. Believing, with Max Weber, that man is an animal suspended in webs of significance he himself has spun, I take culture to be those webs, and the analysis of it to be not an experimental science in search of law but an interpretative one in search of meaning. (Geertz 1973, p. 5)

Maybe a decade or two ago there were what were termed 'paradigm wars' between post-positivist and interpretivist positions in most of the social sciences. This has been generally resolved so that, for example, the two authors of this chapter work together and make substantial contributions to understanding images of school, drawing on both paradigms.

Like currency and other commodities, photographs of educational settings circulate; today, as Alan Sekula (1981) noted, there is an unprecedented 'traffic in photographs'. A simple look at the volume of material available online clearly validates this statement. Moreover, as the exchange value of photographs has begun to triumph over their initial meaning (or use value), they become semantically available:

> the subordination of use to the logic of exchange thus not only are the pictures in archives often *literally* for sale, but their meanings are up for grabs.... This semantic availability of pictures in archives exhibits the same abstract logic as that which characterizes goods on the marketplace. (Sekula 1983, p. 444, emphasis added)

This semantic availability is precisely what makes 'found photographs' useful in educational research. Photographs transition from emic to etic as they are trafficked. A graduation photograph taken to commemorate a beloved daughter's success becomes one of thousands of images of 'coming of age ceremonies'.

The goals of the photographic documentary efforts of the U.S. Farm Security Administration (FSA) were:

> to tell people, through pictures, about the great human problem with which the Farm Security Administration is struggling: the problem of giving a decent break to the lowest third of our farm population. The other basic aim is equally sweeping – to make a photographic record of rural America. (Howe 1940)

A search of some 3000 images of schools in the FSA archives revealed 'Black schools' and 'White schools' but included no images of racially integrated schools. It was probably not the intent of either Roy Striker or the Roosevelt administration to support Jim Crow schools, but a systematic investigation revealed that the evidence depicted by the number of segregated and lack of integrated schools in the archive mirrored the practices of boards of education in the areas documented by the FSA (Margolis 2005). As in the famous Sherlock Holmes story, 'Silver Blaze', of the dog that didn't bark in the night (Doyle 1894). Detailed interpretative studies of photographic archives can also reveal what is not included.

As noted earlier, images of school can provide information for researchers from nearly every time period since the 1850s and were produced in virtually every nation. Photos show classrooms settings with students both sitting in rows and columns, and engaging in more active educational pursuits. They depict change through the ages: in interior and exterior architecture, playgrounds, educational technology, student and teacher dress, posture and deportment, and the arrangement of bodies in space (Fram & Margolis 2011); important occasions for photography range from ceremonial occasions, like rites of passage, to degradation rituals (Chappell, Chappell & Margolis 2011). One can easily find evidence of race, social class, and gender as well as segregated and integrated schools or classes (Margolis 1999). There are also ongoing historical studies of the visual culture of schools (Howard, Burke & Cunningham 2013).

Ethnography may make use of grounded theory in examining images (Strauss & Corbin 1998; Charmaz & Mitchell 2001).[2] The researcher systematically collects photographs and sorts them into categories (folders). This process can be aided by software such as ThumbsPlus.[3] First using simple codes perhaps 'date', 'photographer'.... As images are compared with one another the codes become more complex; for example, students seated in rows and columns, or actively involved in a project. The process of axial coding involves examining the categories for 'mother-daughter' subcategories (e.g. 'seated and lecture', 'seated and watching media').

Persistence and constant comparison will produce theoretical categories; for example, 'coming of age ceremonies' (Chappell, Chappell & Margolis 2011) or a null category of 'integrated classrooms' in the enormous archive of the Farm Security Administration (Margolis 2005). If one has a very large collection or archive to work with, simple statistical measures can help identify and define categories. In the end, the researcher works to develop theoretical categories like the function of schools as sites of ceremony and ritual, or race and social class hierarchies. Visual images of schools can also inform feminist (Mitchell & Weber 1999a, 1999b) and Marxist analyses (Sekula 1980) using a priori categories like social class, sex and gender.

One can use the tools of semiotics/iconography to formulate hypotheses about what story the photograph is telling. For example, Margolis (2004) published an article using the image in Figure 3.7 of students holding flags at the Albuquerque Indian School. Following Foucault, he noted many of the images constituted 'visual evidence of how teacher, school and photographer collaborated to force children's bodies to "emit signs" of assimilation, Americanization, rank, discipline, symmetry and order.' (p. 57)... Examining the closed faces of the Indian children and their teachers, Margolis wrote... 'Like mug shots and rogues' galleries they suggest the facial expressions of those who have no ability to

Figure 3.7 Very early class of young boys with flags at the Albuquerque Indian School, ca 1985
Source: National Archives https://research.archives.gov/id/292873.

resist the gaze of the lens or the power of the photographer to take a picture.')...(and) demonstrated to administrators of the BIA, not only the students' state of socialization, but the teachers' ability to establish discipline and order' (p. 62).

A simple photoforensics analysis suggested that this image could not have been produced in 1895. The caption in the National Archives:

> Very early class of young boys with flags at the Albuquerque with the following caption: Indian School. Production Date ca.1895 [sic.]. National Archives and Record Center (BIA)NRG-75-AISP-10 (Margolis 2004, p. 77)
>
> Note: Based on information in the photograph, this photograph was actually made after 1912 – at some point after New Mexico (January 6) and Arizona (February 14) were admitted to statehood and President Taft established the 48-star flag with six horizontal rows of eight (June 24).

One hypothesis was that the photograph was made to celebrate New Mexico becoming a state. The 'statehood' hypothesis is likely also wrong, as may be some of the conclusions about demeanour based on facial expressions. In a great example of the value of the benefit of cross-disciplinary input, during a spring 2014 seminar taught by Margolis, a student named Ian Punnett noticed the stars in the window and identified them as probably indicating participation in WWI. In addition, Ian noted there is also a Red Cross banner in the window. The photo is, of course, black and white, so it is not possible to tell colour of the stars. A blue star indicates a family member serving in the armed forces and a gold star indicates one who died. Ian also discovered that 'The U.S. government took over the banner specs for "service flags" and mandated their consistency for WWII. Before that, there were as many as 40 competing designs'.

Thus the original reading of the enormous number of symbols embedded in the image may be wrong; the patriotism indicated by flags, the dark uniforms and unhappy faces may honour a student from the Albuquerque Indian School who died during the war which the United States entered on April 6, 1917; the war ended in November 1918. That would date the image as likely being created within that twenty-month period.

Symbolic readings of what an image denotes and connotes, like all scientific findings, are iterative and subject to revisions based on additional evidence.

Copyright and limitations to use

There are a number of practical considerations for anyone planning to use pre-existing photographs in educational research. Identifying ownership and obtaining rights are significant challenges for researchers using photographs, particularly for publication. In the past, there was a seventy-five-year window of copyright protection for photographs protected by U.S. copyright. Each year, on January 1, millions of images and documents 'timed out' of their protection and became public domain. The copyright holder could no longer restrict access or the ability to use, reproduce or publish public domain material, making the usage of this material simpler and less complex for research and publication. As a result of the limit of copyright protection and rolling deadline for transition to public domain, each year a wealth of historic books and photographs became available for re-publication and use.

Largely as a result of years of pressure by copyright holders with valuable assets closing in on seventy-five years of age, such as Disney and the estate of George Gershwin, U.S. Congress passed the DMCA in 1998.[4] The DMCA froze the transition to public domain at January 1, 1923, retaining copyright protection for materials created after that date. The act also strengthened protections, removed the required copyright © symbol, and made copyright protection automatic upon creation of a work in tangible form.

One result of the DMCA has been additional requirements for researchers to acquire and prove permission to use images. Scrutiny by publishers increased, and their contracts focused even further on author liability. Virtually all publication contracts place the burden, and often the expense, of obtaining permissions for publication of images on authors. Contracts usually also require authors to assume liability for any claims of infringement against publishers (Rowe 2011). As a result of these limitations many researchers have focused their research and use of historic images to those made before 1923 in order to simplify rights and permissions issues.

One example of an accessible online resource is the American Memory archive at the Library of Congress (LOC), which had grown to over forty separate photograph archives, including millions of public domain photographs, by March 2014. American Memory image searches are currently limited to 5000 returns. Interestingly a search for the keyword 'education' exceeded the 5000 item limit, and 'school' returned over 4500 results. A search for photographs of 'students' returned 2295 results. Though many of the images in the American Memory collections are public domain and available for research use, the LOC does not charge permission fees and, in general, does not grant or deny permission to publish or otherwise distribute material in its collections. Like most institutions, this places the burden of researching and obtaining copyright permissions, and any associated fees, on the researcher/author.

Most modern images, such as those of education from the post-WWII era, including the American civil rights movement and 'duck-and-cover' drills, are owned and controlled by stock photo agencies or news agencies like Time Life or Reuters, which charge for use. While they may be available for study, obtaining permissions for publication is often prohibitively expensive for academic researchers. Similarly, most private and public collections, such as museums and archives, also limit access and charge for reproductions and use in publication. Recently several major collections, such as the J. Paul Getty Museum and the Metropolitan Museum of Art in New York, under the **Open Access for Scholarly Content (OASC)** have granted permission for non-commercial use without cost as long as the source is credited. Some institutions make only low-resolution images available online, and may be charge fees for obtaining high-resolution files needed for reproduction.

Conclusion

Historical photos are a potentially valuable but little appreciated resource for educational researchers. Text alone has a limited ability to convey complex information about what is going on in schools; the authors argue that using images and combining images and text provide a rich environment for research and powerful tools for dissemination.

Extracting the information contained in photographs requires its own tools and forms of literacy; the broader the knowledge of the researcher, the more effectively these resources can be mined and the information they contain extracted. Understanding of photographic techniques, aesthetic trends, clothing and material culture, and historical context can each add to the information extracted from an image. Identifying and assembling groups of images around themes, such as classroom practice, educational technology, or ethnographic background, can provide further fertile ground for researchers.

Grounded theory, interpretive techniques, and symbolism have their own vocabulary. Different disciplines see the images through different lenses and interdisciplinary integration of information and techniques can expand the scope and quality of research analysis.

The importance of audit trails – standpoint assumptions, analytic processes, selection criteria, coding, interpretations in context, and other subjective research elements – cannot be overemphasised. The ability to understand, re-analyse and assess is critical in the context of the original research and helps other researchers understand the thought processes behind the interpretations and results.

The authors have found that an analytic approach that incorporates and blends a post-positivist, photoforensics and technical analysis with interpretivist, hermeneutic perspectives adds depth and value to photographic analysis and image-based research. Hopefully this discussion will provide a foundation for education researchers to recognise the potential value of historic photographs as research tools and encourage them to become literate in techniques to identify, analyse and interpret these valuable resources.

Notes

1. For additional information about licenses and permissions see Rowe (2011).
2. There are other ethnographic possibilities, like 'photo-elicitation', where the meaning of images is derived by showing them to people in interviews and recording responses. Subject-produced drawings like Florence Goodenough's 'Draw-a-man Test' (Goodenough 1926) may be another way to use visual research in education; regrettably, there is not space here to discuss them.
3. Thumbs Plus software: www.cerious.com; for a full discussion of software useful in visual research, see Bassett (2011).
4. DMCA: www.copyright.gov/legislation/dmca.pdf

References

Bassett, R. (2011). Visual Conceptualization Opportunities with Qualitative Data Analysis Software. In E. Margolis & L. Pauwels (Eds), *The SAGE Handbook of Visual Research Methods* (pp. 530–547). London: Sage.

Burke, C., & Grosvenor, I. (2003). *The School I'd Like: Children and Young People's Reflections on an Education for the 21st Century*. London: Routledge.

Burke, C., & Grosvenor, I. (2008). *School*. London: Reaktion Books.

Burke C., Howard, J. Cunningham P. (2013). *The Decorated School: Essays on Visual Culture of Schooling*. London: Black Dog Publishing.

Chappell, A., Chappell, S., & Margolis, E. (2011). School as Ceremony and Ritual: Photography Illuminates Moments of Ideological Transfer. *Qualitative Inquiry*, 17(1), 56–73.

Charmaz, K., & Mitchell, R. (2001). Grounded Theory in Ethnography. In P. Atkinson, A. Coffey, S. Delamont, J. Lofland, & L. Lofland (Eds), *Handbook of Ethnography* (pp. 160–174). London: Sage.

Costello, C. Y. (2001). Schooled by the Classroom: The Reproduction of Social Stratification in Professional School Settings. In E. Margolis (Ed.), *The*

Hidden Curriculum in Higher Education (pp. 43–60). New York and London: Routledge.
Doyle, S. A. C. (1894). Silver Blaze. In S. A. C. Doyle (Ed.), *The Memoirs of Sherlock Holmes*. London: George Newnes.
Fram, S., & Margolis, E. (2011). Architectural and Built Environment Discourses in an Educational Context: The Gottscho and Schleisner Collection. *Visual Studies, 26*(3), 229–243.
Ganesh, T. G. (2007). Commentary through Visual Data: A Critique of the United States School Accountability Movement. *Visual Studies, 22*(1), 41–47.
Geertz, C. (1973). Thick Description: Toward an Interpretative Theory of Culture. In C. Geertz (Ed.), *The Interpretation of Cultures; Selected Essays* (pp. 3–30). New York: Basic Books.
Goodenough, F. L. (1926). *Measurement of Intelligence by Drawings*. New York: Harcourt Brace.
Howe, H. E. (1940, April 1). You Have Seen Their Pictures. *Survey Graphic, 29*, 236.
Kuhn, A. (1985). *Power of the Image*. Routledge.
Lawn, M., & Grosvenor, I. (Eds) (2005). *Materialities of Schooling: Design, Technology, Objects, Routines*. United Kingdom: Symposium Books.
Margolis, E. (1999). Class Pictures: Representations of Race, Gender and Ability in a Century of School Photography. *Visual Sociology, 14*(1–2), 7–38.
Margolis, E. (2004). Looking at Discipline, Looking at Labour: Photographic Representations of Indian Boarding Schools. *Visual Studies, 19*(1), 54–78.
Margolis, E. (2005). Liberal Documentary Goes to School: Farm Security Administration Photographs of Students, Teachers and Schools. In D. Holloway & J. Beck (Eds), *American Visual Cultures*. London and New York: Continuum.
Mitchell, C. (2008). Taking the Picture, Changing the Picture. Visual Methodologies in Educational Research in South Africa. *South African Journal of Educational Research, 28*(3), 365–383.
Mitchell, C., & Weber, S. (1999a). Picture This: Using School Photographs to Study Ourselves. In *Reinventing Ourselves as Teachers: Beyond Nostalgia* (pp. 74–123). London: Taylor & Francis.
Mitchell, C., & Weber, S. (1999b). Undressing and Redressing the Teacher's Body. In *Reinventing Ourselves as Teachers: Beyond Nostalgia* (pp. 124–163). London: Taylor & Francis.
Morris, E. (2007a). Which Came First, the Chicken or the Egg? (Part One). *New York Times*, September 25. Retrieved from http://morris.blogs.nytimes.com/2007/09/25/which-came-first-the-chicken-or-the-egg-part-one/?scp=1&sq=errol%20morris%20cannonballs&st=cse
Morris, E. (2007b). Which Came First? (Part Two). *New York Times*, October 4. Retrieved from http://morris.blogs.nytimes.com/2007/10/04/which-came-first-part-two/
O'Donoghue, D. (2007). 'James Always Hangs Out Here': Making Space for Place in Studying Masculinities at School. *Visual Studies, 22*(1), 62–73.
Prosser, J. (2007). Visual Methods and the Visual Culture of Schools. *Visual Studies, 22*(1), 13–30.
Prosser, J., & Loxley, A. (2002). *Playgrounds of Inclusion? Rituals, Rhetoric and Rubbish Bins: The Micro-Processes of Playground Life in England and Ireland*. Paper presented at British Sociological Association Annual Conference.

Rowe, J. (1997). *Photographers in Arizona 1850–1920: A History and Directory.* Nevada City, CA: Carl Mauts Publishing.
Rowe, J. (2002). Evidence, Interpretation, and Speculation: Thoughts on Kaloma, the Purported Photograph of Josie Earp. Retrieved March 2, 2003. http://www.vintagephoto.com/reference/kaloma/1-02JosieKaloma%20article.htm
Rowe, J. (2007). *Arizona Real Photographic Postcards: A History and Portfolio.* Nevada City, CA: Carl Mautz Publishing.
Rowe, J. (2011). Legal Issues of Using Images in Research. In E. Margolis & L. Pauwels (Eds), *Sage Handbook of Visual Research* (pp. 707–722). Los Angeles, London: Sage.
Rowe, J. (2014). *Arizona Stereographs 1865–1930.* Nevada City, CA: Carl Mautz Publishing.
Sekula, A. (1980). School Is a Factory. *Exposure, 18*(3/4), 77–91.
Sekula, A. (1981). The Traffic in Photographs. *Art Journal, 41*(1), 15–25.
Sekula, A. (1983). Photography Between Labor and Capital. In B. H. D. Buchloh & R. Wilkie (Eds), *Mining Photographs and Other Pictures, 1848–1968.* Halifax: Nova Scotia Press.
Shohel, M. M. C., & Howes, A. J. (2007). Transition from Nonformal Schools: Learning through Photoelicitation in Educational Fieldwork in Bangladesh. *Visual Studies, 22*(1), 53–61.
Solomon-Godeau, A. (1991). Who Is Speaking Thus? Some Questions about Documentary Photography. In A. Solomon-Godeau (Ed.), *Photography at the Dock: Essays on Photographic History, Institutions, and Practices.* Minneapolis: University of Minnesota Press.
Strauss, A., & Corbin, J. (1998). *Basics of Qualitative Research Techniques and Procedures for Developing Grounded Theory (2nd edition).* London: Sage.
Tobin, J. J., Wu, D. Y. H., & Davidson, D. H. (1989). *Preschool in Three Cultures: Japan, China, and the United States.* New Haven: Yale University Press.
Vinao, A. (2005). The School Head's Office as Territory and Place: Location and Physical Layout in the First Spanish Graded Schools. In M. Lawn & I. Grosvenor (Eds), *Materialities of Schooling: Design, Technology, Objects, Routines* (pp. 47–70). United Kingdom: Symposium Books.

4
Reading the Visual in the Marketing of Elite Schooling

Barbara Pini, Paula McDonald and Jennifer Bartlett

In a provocative and engaging paper, Prosser (2008, p. 6) has argued that there is a 'darker side of visual research' which resists epistemic and methodological pluralism and favours prescriptive orthodoxies and boundary setting over flexibility, creativity and reflexivity. Illustrative of the more negative rendering of visual methods is, he argues, the prescriptions outlined by Emmison and Smith's (2000, p. 110) *Researching the Visual,* including their claim that it is possible to 'get by without' talking to the people within and behind images. In this chapter, our aim is not to engage directly with Emmison and Smith's (2000) thesis, given it has been elaborated upon and responded to by a range of visual studies scholars (e.g. Pink 2006; Henry 2012). Indeed, we wish to avoid the type of challenge/attack discourse that Prosser (2008) suggests sometimes characterises the field of visual research and rightly argues is unproductive. Rather than arguing that one approach needs to supplant another, we contend that what is needed is an openness to varied and multiple paradigms which are guided by our research questions and aims. Thus, in this chapter we build on work which has very usefully mapped the visual in elite schools, through interviews with the producers of these images; that is, marketing and communication managers. We argue that this is a group which represents an increasingly important set of actors in the educational landscape creating and shaping the images associated with schools, and thus mediating the discourses which they communicate.

Visual research and elite schools – background

In introducing visual research in the field of education it is customary for writers to begin by noting the paucity of work in the area (e.g.

Fischman 2001; Matthews & Singh 2009; Woolner et al. 2010). In this respect, the study of elite schooling is somewhat different. Unlike many other areas of educational inquiry, the power of the visual and its inflection into all facets of schooling life has been recognised by scholars of elite educational institutions. Even when iconography has not been the sole or even a significant data source, it has still often imbued studies. Rizvi (2014) reports, for example, on how selected artefacts and pictures and the new building in which they were placed, were part of a broader strategy by which an elite Indian school strategically positioned itself as both celebrating tradition and embracing global modernity. Similarly, Koh (2014, p. 208) uses the visual in a study of an elite school in Singapore to provide insights into his positionality as a researcher, while also emphasising the affective and embodied power of images, writing that 'I was in awe the moment I stepped into the school grounds'. In other work, Allan and Charles (2014) examine a poster and collage at one of the two elite schools they investigated in Australia and the United Kingdom to identify the discourses which constitute contemporary configurations of class and femininity in these settings. They explain how the images convey intertwined discourses of globalism, mobilities, responsibilities and whiteness which collectively constitute a subject position they label 'cosmo girl' (Allan & Charles 2014, p. 333).

In contrast to the above studies is another sub-set of scholarship on elite schooling which has given more concentrated attention to the visual, most typically, through studies of prospectuses. Illustrative are two companion papers in which Wardman, Hutchesson, Gottschall, Drew and Saltmarsh (2010) and Gottschall, Wardman, Edgeworth, Hutchesson and Saltmarsh (2010) take a gender lens to the images and layout of the prospectuses of elite Australian schools to compare and contrast hegemonic representations of masculinity and femininity. McDonald, Pini and Mayes (2012) also draw on the prospectuses of elite Australian schools to identify the key rhetorical strategies engaged to enhance reputation and to leverage advantage in the context of marketisation. Importantly, they demonstrate that it is not just language but the visual which is deployed to bolster and promote, whether it be the formatting and fonts or the type and range of photographs. In recognition that elite schools increasingly utilise multiple marketing materials Forbes and Weiner (2008) and Drew (2013) rely not only on prospectuses but also websites in their analysis of elite schools. In this work they attend to the ways in which marketing materials of elite schools mobilise physical, economic, cultural and social capital. Further to this Meadmore and Meadmore

(2004) and Symes (1998) include brochures, advertisements and billboards in their data sets on the subject of marketing and elite schools. Across these data sources the visual is central, particularly as there are now typically images embedded within brochures linked to websites, and in turn, videos and animations embedded in websites. As Meadmore and Meadmore (2004, pp. 375–376) note, the marketing materials are a means by which elite schools march 'to the tune of performativity' which demand to be read as 'cultural texts'.

While the corpus of work on elite schooling and marketing materials described above informs our own study, we depart from it in talking to those who have the responsibility for creating the images. We ask who is producing the enormous range of visual materials associated with elite schools in the contemporary educational sector, probe the practices and cultures of the work of these image producers, and explore their understandings of the role of the visual for schools.

Methodology

This chapter emerges from a larger study of marketisation in Australian secondary school education. One component of this larger project comprised semi-structured interviews with marketers/communication managers at nineteen independent high schools located in south-east Queensland, Australia. All schools enrolled students from Years 8 to 12, but some also enrolled students from preparatory level through to Year 7. Four schools were co-educational (offered education to both boys and girls), while fifteen schools were single-sex (ten boys-only; five girls-only).

Interview questions addressed how the school differentiated itself from other schools (on the basis of, for example, secular/religious underpinnings, sector and status); details of student recruitment practices; relationship management practices with key stakeholders; the extent and nature of marketisation and commercialisation strategies engaged in by the school; how the school was governed; and staff engagement activities with families, students and the community. In responding, visual data was frequently invoked. That is, during the interviews, respondents referred us to or gave us copies of school documentation, including newsletters, prospectuses, annual reports, websites, CDs and DVDs, photographs displayed in their offices, and school signage. This provided an opportunity to ask more specific questions about the production of particular images, including the choices surrounding the selection of images.

Producers of the visual in elite schools

Interviewees had a range of occupational titles such as Communications and Enrolments Manager, Director of Communications, Marketing Manager and Director of Development. There was also some variation in terms of their positioning within the organisational structure of the schools whereby some reported directly to the principal and others to roles such as Business Manager or General Manager. Only a few had representation on the senior leadership team, but this was changing and under challenge. A number had occupied high-level executive marketing positions in the private or public sphere prior to taking up the position at the school.

Despite differences in school characteristics and the precise roles and responsibilities of marketing/communications managers, a dominant and common theme across the data was the way in which schools represent themselves internally and externally through the visual, which is increasingly viewed as important and professionalised. This was reflected in interviewees' own biographies in that the majority were inaugural appointments. One who had commenced employment in the school in 2005 following a career as a marketer for a large tourism corporation recalled a story (that was repeated across the sample) in that her appointment occurred as marketing tasks previously undertaken by teachers expanded and increased in significance.

> Up until that time the school had enabled some of the functions of marketing to be undertaken by teaching staff as part of, you know, part load scenario. For example, our yearbook was done by an English teacher, and she was still doing English teaching, but part of her load would be dedicated to producing the yearbook. Similarly, other teaching staff had responsibility for photography. They used to outsource public relations and advertising activities. So the Council decided to bring it all in under the one umbrella, and so I started here in 2005. (Girls-Only, Independent School)

Further evidence of the formalisation and expansion of the place of the visual in elite schools was provided by interviewees as they outlined the types of managerial documents guiding their working days. One interviewee, for example, prefaced a discussion of her typical week by stating that this was informed by the school's 'five-year strategic marketing plan' and, in turn, annual 'operational plan', which were developed with the assistance of external business consultants and approved by the school board (Girls-Only, Independent School). Another had used a 2012 study tour to the United States for four school administrators (including the marketer) as a means of 'badging and marketing' (Boys-Only, Catholic School). He provided exemplars of the types of visual materials he had collected on the visit and outlined how he intended to replicate what he had seen done at his own school. This illustrates that the ways in which the visual are being engaged in elite schooling has been extended to the globalisation of education.

To different degrees, all those interviewed whose roles are encompassed under the rubric of 'marketing specialist' continue to take responsibility for producing some of the more conventional visual materials associated with elite schools such as the photographs found in prospectuses or the formatting of a parental newsletter. This is with two caveats. First, the scope of this work has been significantly extended so that today there is a huge volume of official visual material produced by schools on a daily basis. It is now common, for example, for schools to have sanctioned 'Facebook' pages to which the marketing/communication manager as well as select staff provide daily updates (including over weekends). At another school, an online 'parent lounge' is attached to an 'email blast' sent home after the final lesson which includes video and photographs documenting what has occurred over the course of the school day (Girls-Only, Independent School). A second key difference between the visual images of the recent past and present is that while there is still evidence of more traditional texts these have been radically transformed in light of the marketers' input and the broader corporatisation of education. Interviewees were eager to highlight, for example, their previous and sometimes extensive experience in other industry sectors and organisational environments where the creation and use of the visual has been professionalised to a greater extent and over longer periods of time. They also highlighted their unique contribution to the school in attempting to push the boundaries of the various means through which visual materials could be utilised by schools – which are relative newcomers to utilising the visual on social media platforms, for example – to promote the organisation and appeal to stakeholders.

Corporatisation of the visual in elite schools

Summing up the nature of the changes they had instigated in producing visual materials for the school, a number of interviewees referred to visual materials as 'more corporate' or, as the following argued, have a 'corporate feel'.

> You have to keep that corporate feel, I think, as well, because that gives you a higher level of what you do here. Whereas you see a lot of schools go for those kiddie feel, you know what I mean? Getting kids' artwork, involved in their promotional stuff and that sort of thing. That's fine, I understand that student touch there. But you are also losing some of that stature, because you need a corporate feel as well. Does that make sense? (Boys-Only, Catholic School)

Asked to explain what this meant, one interviewee used the schools' new prospectus as an example:

> It sounds silly, choice of colours, choice of language, and actually we have used the three themes of the strategic intent document as the themes that will guide the prospectus. So it really does stem from the strategic intent document. It's not just a pretty, glossy brochure anymore, in terms of a warm fuzzy to bring your daughter here. (Girls-Only, Independent School)

In another interview a participant used the following anecdote to illustrate the 'professionalising' of the visual associated with her school. She reflected, 'It's almost like you don't know how bad your house was until you renovate and then you're in this new beautiful renovated house and you'd never go back' (Girls-Only, Independent School).

In other instances interviewees illustrated their 'more corporate' approach by referencing the way more mundane communication was now handled by the school, including classroom or sports newsletters. They recalled that an early task they had accomplished was developing compulsory style guides to direct teachers in their visual and textual communication with parents and students.

> Everything that goes out of the school must go on the school letterhead. I mean they were sending things out all differently. Someone had a house letterhead, someone had a sports letterhead. No, no, no. It goes out on school letterhead. That hadn't been co-ordinated before. If you use that crest, you use the proper crest; you don't use one that has oars sticking out of it because you are doing a rowing thing or you know a basketball. (Boys-Only, Catholic School)

Consistency was repeatedly highlighted as critical not only to a 'professional' or 'corporate' image, but also key to 'branding'. Further, branding through image was described as an ongoing process and as necessary to an internal audience as much as to external audiences. This was evident, as one marketing manager explained, in what she believed the purpose of the visual to be:

> I am thinking about their [parental] needs and expectations in that there's some reassurance going back to them. That they've made the right decision for their daughter...A lot of our parents come in at primary and go through to secondary. So they might have thirteen years at the college. So a publication like that [pointing to document] also helps them to envisage the type of girl their daughter is going to grow up to be or the types of things that she's going to do when she gets to secondary. So it kind of keeps them on that journey with you a bit. (Girls-Only, Independent School)

What is conveyed in the above quotation is that the visual plays multiple roles in elite schools. It certainly positions the schools, as interviewees contended, in very particular ways. At the same time, photographs operate to discipline students (as well as teachers and parents), circulating gendered and classed scripts about ways of being in the world that are valued and legitimated. Such an observation points to the need for future research on visual and elite schooling to ask students to reflect upon and respond to the images associated with their institution. That is, to explore the visual, not as static or singular, but as shifting and multiple, able to be read in different ways and potentially reworked and resisted.

Managing the visual in elite schools

The repeated message from interviews is that any official image associated with elite schools is not circulated without being subject to extensive scrutiny. As we learned, font size and type are afforded considerable inspection before being decided upon so that, for example, they do not look 'too' masculine/feminine, hard/soft, quirky/old-fashioned. Media consultants and/or market research specialists are often engaged to inform these choices. Importantly, it is not only that different layers of management must sign off on images, but consideration is also given to the concerns of varying stakeholder groups and the complexity of the messages that images are asked to convey. This concern was illustrated in an interview with a marketing manager and her assistant graphic designer when asked about the process of choosing visuals. They referred us to what they both described as one of their favourite images they had used to market the school. The image was of a Year 9 student (fourteen years of age) completing an obstacle course at a school camp. As one of the interviewees observed in the photograph, 'she has mud all over her face but she looks like she's having the absolute time of her life'. In prefacing why she wanted to use the image, the marketing manager referred to its role in helping to shift perceptions of the school as producing future university graduates by stating, 'It's not a finishing school – the school and the education means more than that'. What she was seeking to counter, through this particular image, was a dominant discourse of classed femininity associated with the school. However, the marketing manager also needed to ensure the image would not jeopardise relationships with those she thought might disapprove of the photograph, such as the old girls' association who may have objected to this counter discourse of femininity. In this instance, she said she was fortunate that she had some leeway, as the student was not wearing a school uniform and was hence engaged in a recreational activity that would be perceived as somewhat adjacent to the more serious business of learning. Most importantly, however, in achieving approval for the photograph to be published, was that the Principal 'got it'. She explained:

> We weren't quite sure whether it [the image] would run the gauntlet of getting a tick off from the Principal, but she absolutely loved it and she understood. So there was a story in there about our camp program and what it was actually there for. She understood the real authenticity and the soul behind it. It was all about building resilience, and it doesn't matter what you look like. It's even though you're covered in mud but you've achieved something. (Girls-Only, Independent School)

Interestingly, the claim to 'authenticity' in the use of images was one that was made across interviews, and images were clearly inspected for such a quality. The need to convey authenticity is no doubt related to challenging classed assumptions about such schools as out of touch and privileged. It may also, however, be evidence that these schools are seeking to distance themselves from the professionalising and homogenising of the visuals that are today connected to these institutions. Across the interviews there were laughing references to the often seen images of the picture-perfect child in the school hat that prevail across marketing materials in elite schools.

As well as producing and selecting photographic images for school-based publications and outlets (e.g. school websites), communication/

marketing managers are responsible for at least initiating those produced for other media outlets which communicate stories or messages about the school. As one explained, 'We are in a one newspaper town' and therefore there was an ongoing role in 'avoiding negative publicity as well as promoting the positive' (Girls-Only, Independent School). Thus, they would produce stories and photographs and send them as press releases, and/or contact particular journalists/outlets with ideas for a story and have them write and photograph the piece. Those marketers with backgrounds in journalism talked of leveraging former collegiate relationships to their advantage to facilitate the publication of positive visuals about their schools. However, they also acknowledged there was fierce competition for free self-promotion in the press. Indeed, one marketing manager lamented that in the past six months he had sent eighteen press releases with images to the major paper 'on a wide range of things that reflect our strategic message', but none had been taken up (Boys-Only, Independent School). The degree of seriousness associated with the visual, and moreover, producing positive visual images, by elite schools, was no more evident than in the following anecdote by one marketing manager which illustrated how the process was allowed to shape the learning day of students:

> We got a great story in [name of daily newspaper] a couple of months ago about our kindergarten kids with their iPads and the work they are doing in the classroom. The kindergarten teacher was more than happy to work with me and the photographer for literally an hour and a half while we were trying to get the photo because it meant a page 3 story [name of daily newspaper]. It literally took up half the page. They understand that our parents and old girls and prospective parents they read [name of daily newspaper] and they watch the channel ten news. We know what they watch. We know what they are reading because they see it and they repeat it back to us when they come in for the open day or they come in for their interview in the following year. (Girls-Only, Independent School)

The brief of monitoring and managing the visual in elite schools covers not only photographic and graphic images but also student and staff dress. While it is teachers and administrators who police the wearing of the uniform, it is the new marketing-focused entrants in the educational arena who manage any changes to the uniform as part of the school 'brand'. This was evident in a quotation from one marketing manager of an all-girls' Catholic school who described addressing the issue of two distinct school uniforms:

> So let's talk about what we've done with brands – we have two brands as far as uniforms. We have our blue uniform which is blue striped, and that's our day uniform; but our co-curricular uniform is red and gold which is so bizarre for a marketer. And that's probably caused us a few challenges as a school because you have one brand, one crest, one logo, that's it. But we have four colours in our brand so what I've tried to do with people is ask them who are you trying to speak to.
> (Girls-Only, Catholic School)

In a similar respect, school marketing managers also had input into the visual culture of the school in relation to teachers' dress. At an all boys' Catholic school, one had instigated what he described as a 'professional look' with the largely male staff, who were encouraged to wear collared, button-down shirts with the school motto on the pocket. Like so many others we interviewed, he rationalised the need for attention to visuals through reference to the annual revenue of the school and it being a 'big business' which required 'a professional image'.

As interviewees monitor the use of the visual within their own schools to ensure it meets their expectations they also survey the use of the visual across the sector. When asked about other schools, for example, one responded, 'We look very much at what they are advertising, where they are advertising, what they are not doing' (Girls-Only, Catholic School). Certainly, many were able to provide extensive commentary on the visuals of other schools including assessments of the efficacy of images used and the effectiveness of the placement of different images. A final role a number of participants fulfilled concerned new infrastructure developments in the school. They played a role on committees overseeing the establishment of new buildings and/or campuses or directing refurbishments, which were all seen as critical aspects of the visual representation of the school.

Conclusion

Over a period of two decades studies of the prospectuses of elite private schools have noted change in terms of the types of documents being produced and the broader discursive field in which they are produced. Looking at a series of these marketing documents over the latter decades of the 20th century, Hesketh and Knight (1998, p. 33) noted that they had become 'longer and more informative'. More recently in their work, Gottschall et al. (2010) have observed that 'glossy prospectuses' are just one feature of 'the school marketing landscape'. In this chapter we have added to this literature by turning to those who produce the images so central to the promotional material of elite schools; that is, marketing and communication managers. We have documented the way in which the role performed by these managers has gained prominence and expanded so that, for many, their brief covers almost all aspects of the official 'visual culture of schools' (Prosser 2007). As such we have demonstrated that the 'consciousness of appearance' (Marginson 1993, p. 43) in education that has been evident in recent years is now embodied in the work and rhetoric of the marketing and communication manager.

Across interviews participants drew upon a corporatised vocabulary of choice, improvement, quality, effectiveness and efficiency to describe the contemporary educational sector (Ball & Youdell 2009). They stressed their business credentials to highlight their suitability for the role of producing and selecting images to represent the school, differentiating themselves from teachers (and sometimes administrators) who are seen to lack business knowledge and skills. Ensuring that the visual image of the schools at which they worked was 'corporate' was seen as inherently positive. Images produced in the (recent) past were described negatively – often in infantilised or feminised terms. The message was that there has been a significant shift in the visual in elite schools, which, as we were told so often, to one marked by professionalism. Such a message would be an important one for parents to receive given that as elite schools become another commodity that aspirational families seek to acquire, school fees are a significant family investment. The fact that there are now 'professionals' employed who can point to their business credentials in producing and circulating visuals of the school thus legitimates the 'choices' parents have made in selecting elite schooling for their children.

In their constant deployment of the rhetoric of marketisation and privatisation and their privileging of the corporate world, interviewees brought to the fore discourses which are largely obscured in the official visual and textual material they produce on behalf of their schools. As McDonald et al. (2012, p. 15) observe it is typical for 'business-like concepts' to be shrouded behind more 'palatable' terminology and for elite schools to actively distance themselves from 'profit-driven corporations'.

As marketing and communication managers have taken up their roles in the elite schools of Australia they have engaged with a global community of staff at other equivalently prestigious schools soliciting strategies and advice on visual materials. They also describe employing the services of global consultancy companies in media, advertising and new technologies to assist in the same enterprise. The way in which decisions about the visual in elite schools are made is thus another manifestation of these entities operating not simply as national but 'global' actors (Kenway & Fahey 2014, p. 192). Speaking to such actors directly and uncovering the scope and nature of their roles and functions in producing the visual yields important new insights that can, at best, only be inferred from visuals themselves. Indeed, our analysis revealed some of the organisational structures and processes within high schools that influenced how visuals are produced, selected, manipulated and communicated in the education context. Such an approach informs notions of the types of images which are *not* chosen or utilised in visual materials, the stakeholder groups targeted for different types of images and the authority of those who have the final say on what and how visuals are deployed. As we have argued, this is not to dismiss the importance of examining visuals themselves, as has been the primary focus on previous work in the field, but our approach and subsequent findings challenges Emmison and Smith's (2000, p. 110) claim that insights from those who produce the visuals are not also relevant.

References

Allan, A., & Charles, C. (2014). Cosmo Girls: Configurations of Class and Femininity in Elite Educational Settings. *British Journal of Sociology of Education, 35*(3), 333–352.

Ball, S., & Youdell, D. (2009). Hidden Privatisation in Public Education. *Education Review, 21*(1), 73–83.

Drew, C. (2013). Elitism for Sale: Promoting the Elite School Online in the Competitive Educational Marketplace. *Australian Journal of Education, 57*(2), 174–184.

Emmison, M., & Smith, P. (2000). *Researching the Visual*. Thousand Oaks, CA: Sage.

Fischman, G. E. (2001). Reflections about Images, Visual Culture and Educational Research. *Educational Researcher, 30*(8), 28–33.

Forbes, J., & Weiner, G. (2008). Under-stated Powerhouses: Scottish Independent Schools, Their Characteristics and Their Capitals. *Discourse, 29*(4), 509–525.

Gottschall, K., Wardman, N., Edgeworth, K., Hutchesson, R., & Saltmarsh, S. (2010). Hard Lines and Soft Scenes: Constituting Masculinities in the Prospectuses of All-Boys Elite Private Schools. *Australian Journal of Education, 54*(1), 18–30.

Henry, L. M. (2012). Trend Report: Theory and Practice of Visual Sociology. In J. Hughes (Ed.) *Visual Methods: Volume One Principles, Issues, Debates and Controversies in Visual Research.* (pp. 1–64). London: Sage.

Hesketh, A. J., & Knight, P. T. (1998). Secondary School Prospectuses and Educational Markets. *Cambridge Journal of Education*, *28*(1), 21–35.
Kenway, J., & Fahey, J. (2014). Staying Ahead of the Game: The Globalising Practices of Elite Schools. *Globalisation, Societies and Education*, *12*(2), 177–195.
Koh, A. (2014). Doing Class Analysis in Singapore's Elite Education: Unravelling the Smokescreen of Meritocratic Talk. *Globalisation, Societies and Education*, *12*(2), 196–210.
Marginson, S. (1993). From Cloister to Market: The New Era in Higher Education. *Journal of Tertiary Education Administration*, *15*(1), 43–63.
Matthews, J., & Singh, P. (2009). Visual Methods in the Social Sciences: Refugee Background Young People. *International Journal of Interdisciplinary Social Sciences*, *4*(10), 61–70.
McDonald, P., Pini, B., & Mayes, R. (2012). Organizational Rhetoric in the Prospectuses of Elite Private Schools: Unpacking Strategies of Persuasion. *British Journal of Sociology of Education*, *33*(1), 1–20.
Meadmore, D., & Meadmore, P. (2004). The Boundlessness of Performativity in Elite Australian Schools. *Discourse*, *25*(3), 375–387.
Pink, S. (2006). *Doing Visual Ethnography*. London: Sage.
Prosser, J. (2008). The Darker Side of Visual Research. ESRC National Centre for Research Methods. Working Paper #09. www.manchester.au.uk/realities.
Rizvi, F. (2014). Old Elite Schools, History and the Construction of a New Imaginary. *Globalisation, Societies and Education*, *12*(2), 290–308.
Symes, C. (1998). Education for Sale: A Semiotic Analysis of School Prospectuses and Other Forms of Educational Marketing. *Australian Journal of Education*, *42*(2), 133–152.
Wardman, N., Hutchesson, R., Gottschall, K., Drew, C., & Saltmarsh, S. (2010). Starry Eyes and Subservient Selves: Portraits of 'Well-Rounded' Girlhood in the Prospectuses of All-Girl Elite Private Schools. *Australian Journal of Education*, *54*(3), 249–261.
Woolner, P., Clark, J., Hall, E., Tiplady, L., Thomas, U., & Wall, K. (2010). Pictures Are Necessary but Not Sufficient: Using a Range of Visual Methods to Engage Users and School Design. *Learning Environment Research*, *13*(1), 1–22.

Part II
Performing Pedagogy Visually

5
The Use of the Visual to Interpret School Cultures: Producing Knowledge and Knowing When You Are Learning to Teach

Kim Senior and Julianne Moss

Researching teaching and learning in education presents with its own problematic issues and struggles. In this century, persistent neoliberal attacks on teachers, teacher education and schools has led to fragmented realities in the doing of educational research. In the knowledge-based and knowledge-driven global economy, the healthy cacophony of educational debate and research is reduced to metred discussion upon those things that are tangible, measurable and scientific. Teaching and learning is reduced to a representational practice (Ellsworth 1997) that can be ascribed to, and accounted for, by specific agents.

Within the teacher education research canon, Cochran-Smith and Lytle (2009) report that 'the considerable range and variation of practitioner research have contributed to its richness and vitality but at the same time, perhaps undermined its coherence as an intellectual and social movement with a palpable impact on emerging policies' (p. 35). There are issues, but, as Cochran-Smith and Donnell (2006) pointed out earlier, 'Either explicitly or implicitly, practitioner inquiry raises questions and interrupts expectations about the relations of inquiry, knowledge, and practice...practitioner research raises many questions about whether it is possible or desirable to do research that privileges the role of neither practitioner nor researcher, but instead forges a new role out of their intersections' (p. 514). This chapter reports on the tracing of Kodak EasyShare™ software for transforming data and interpretation in a study of teacher education, school culture and pedagogy. Issues of method and analysis are addressed in the context of a project that was collaborative, contextually appropriate, feasible and ethically aware and negotiated over the life of the project. The co-production of knowledge is analysed to disrupt notions of how the visual and teacher education gets taken up in educational research.

Introduction

Learning, and learning to teach, is greater than the sum of its individual parts; it is greater than a clinical and technicist practice. Learning to teach is a tense and precarious undertaking in which we learn to (re) learn and learn to (un) teach while simultaneously defining ourselves in the classroom as well as in this new professional world. We struggle both consciously and unconsciously with 'us' and 'them'. It is a struggle that sometimes leaves all of those intimately involved speechless: 'For is it not true that face to face with the primal mystery of Being, we are brought to an awareness that language which has

Figure 5.1 Pre-service teacher during a collaborative session with Year 8 students

served us well to describe the phenomena of the world begins to falter; at best, it merely points and then passes into silence' (Pinar & Irwin 2005, p. 400). In terms of social science research in education, it leaves a rest, a pause that is easily dismissed as an empty silence – a void to be filled by the tangibility of measureable scientific research. Elliot Eisner (1997) has also long reminded us that 'research [does] not belong to science alone' (p. 5), and in *The Enlightened Eye* (Eisner 1991) he argues comprehensively that there are many ways in which our world can and should be known. He argues that expanding the ways in which the socio-cultural nature of schools and schooling is described and interpreted enhances educational research. Indeed, instruments and tools, questionnaires and standard deviations will not satisfactorily explore the relational in teaching and learning. Living pedagogy is embodied in both the autonomy and continuity of relationships including dreams, failings and the ordinary. It may be alluded to and, just sometimes, glimpsed.

In 2006, a group of twenty-five pre-service (primary and secondary) teachers volunteered to participate in an initiative instigated by Dr Mary Dixon, a teacher educator and colleague of the authors. Drawing upon a professional relationship she had developed with a recently opened secondary school on the urban fringes of Melbourne, Dr Dixon negotiated that twenty-five volunteer Year 8 and Year 9 students would collaborate with the pre-service teacher cohort as they learnt to teach. Over one academic year, once a week, the pre-service teachers would participate in combined workshops with the secondary students led by two teacher educators at the school. The workshops and after-school debriefing sessions counted towards four units of study towards the pre-service teacher's bachelor or diploma certification, working across issues of teaching, learning, curriculum and assessment. The study outlined in this chapter was situated within this initiative and *began* with the participation of eight of the twenty-five pre-service teachers and three of the twenty-five secondary students.

Working from an unabashedly post-post positioning, the study did not seek to *find*, or tell, *the* truth of learning to teach. It did seek to learn and give some account of the process of teaching how to speak of/to/with 'others' whilst recognising 'that every word is also a hiding place, an apparent nakedness is but a mask that conceals a will to power' (Lather 2007, p. 17). Initially, drawn to the literary genres (Barone 1997; Cahnmann 2003; Clandinin & Connelly 2000; Gough 2001, 2004; Richardson 2003a; Stronach 2006; Vallack 2005) of Arts Based Educational Research (ABER) to 'deepen the conversation' and enhance perspectives on some of the 'taken-for-granted' (Barone & Eisner 2006, p. 96) issues in teacher education, the study asked: How can the indirect and entangled relationships of living pedagogy be explored and represented? Early stages of the study relied upon letters and emails as a means of data generation (see Senior 2008). In order to document the processes of coming to learn to teach within the situated context of this school-based cohort, data collection included photographing: planning sessions between the pre-service teachers and teacher educators; planning and workshop notes; and products from sessions with the pre-service teachers such as mind-maps, drawings, sketches and session posters. Six months into the study, glimpses of living pedagogy and an organic exploration of what it means to learn to teach led to a re-imagination of visual ethnographic data with ten more of the secondary students joining in the research and five more of the pre-service teachers (twenty six participants in total).

Framing the story

Figure 5.2 Year 9 student drawing from collaborative workshop with pre-service teachers

There has been a keen interest taken by successive Australian federal governments in teacher preparation. During the 1980s in Australia, there were fifteen Commonwealth inquiries into teacher education and again fifteen in the 1990s; between 2000 and 2007, there have been twenty-two reports, inquiries and reviews (House of Representatives Standing Committee on Education and Vocational Training 2007, pp. 169–179). Recently the Teacher Education Ministerial Advisory Group (TEMAG) has called for Australian teacher educators to 'lift the quality of initial teacher education programs' (Craven et al. 2014, p. xvi). Concurrent and consequential to the increasing federal invigilation, there have been state-level pushes for systemic curriculum reform emphasising deeper and transdisciplinary learning while creating stronger links to community (Department of Education, Tasmania 2000; Department of Education, Tasmania 2006; Education Queensland 2002; Victorian Curriculum and Assessment Authority 2004). As well as recognition that the 'quality of pedagogy most directly affects the quality of learning' (Department of Education and Training, NSW 2003; Department of Education and Training, Victoria 2004; Gore, Ladwig & King 2004). Pedagogical approaches underpinned by innovation, flexibility and responsiveness are not only imperative to the knowledge-based economy (Victorian Curriculum and Assesment Authority 2004) but to a truly democratic plural society. Such approaches affirm inclusion over exclusion and connection over disconnection if they are truly concerned with student responsiveness. However, these developments are being played out within a contemporary rhetorical discourse increasingly restrained by literalism, over-simplification and mercantilism. It would appear that the balance between students' 'intellectual, physical, social, moral, spiritual and aesthetic development' and recognition for 'supportive and nurturing' learning environments (Ministerial Council on Education, Employment, Training and Youth Affairs 1999) runs contrary to the unfolding neoliberal agenda seeking infallible, direct causal relationships between specific individuals, groups or institutions.

Investigations by the federal government (Department of Education, Science and Training 2003; House of Representatives Standing Committee on Education and Vocational Training 2007) and Victorian state government (Victorian Parliament, Education and Training Committee 2005) into teacher education and a national inquiry into the teaching of literacy (Department of Education, Science and Training 2005) recommend a number of changes to the way in which teachers are prepared for teaching in the classroom. In each review there was reportedly an overemphasis on 'theory' at the expense of 'practice' in initial teacher education courses (Department of Education, Science and Training 2005, p. 105; Department of Education, Science and Training 2003, p. 177). In the current neoliberal climate and at a time when federal and state governments are coming to terms with an aging teaching population, an under-supply of teachers in specific learning areas and the difficulty of recruiting and retaining teachers in specific regions (Department of Education, Science and Training 2003, pp. 15–16), some groups are pushing a deregulation agenda. Such an approach, it is argued, would provide aspiring teachers with the practical teaching skills that would better prepare them for 'the realities of the classroom' than 'too much educational theory' (Buckingham 2005, p. 3).

Marilyn Cochran-Smith urges 'the education research community to make it clearer to the public and to policymakers that there are significant complexities in what happens' (2005b, p. 14) from the creation of policy through to the classroom. Researchers such as Sonia Nieto (2002), Jacqueline Irvine (2003), Deborah Britzman (2003), Linda Darling-Hammond (2000, 2006), Geneva Gay (2000, 2003), Ana Maria Villegas and Tamara Lucas (2002), and Susan Davis Lenski et al. (2005) have all done so. Their respective works confirm the province of pedagogy as the responsibility of teachers:

> Enacted in every pedagogy are the tensions between knowing and being, thought and action, theory and practice, knowledge and experience, the technical and the existential, the objective and the subjective. Traditionally expressed as dichotomies, these relationships are not nearly so neat or binary. Rather, such relationships are better expressed as dialogic in that they are shaped as they shape each other in the process of coming to know. (Britzman 2003, p. 26)

Pedagogy, that is dialogic, ongoing and attentive to presence or 'indwelling of teachers and students' (Pinar & Irwin 2005, p. 191) is complicated, chaotic and contingent.

In 2005, the American Educational Research Association (AERA) published their comprehensive report (Cochran-Smith & Zeichner 2005) on teacher education. The report provides a critical analysis of research into pre-service teacher education in the United States as it presently stands and recommends a future research agenda by 'outlining topics that need further study...describing promising lines of research, and pointing to research genres and processes most likely to define new directions and yield useful findings for policy and practice' (p. viii). In summarising the findings for each of the nine topics covered by the report, the AERA panel repeatedly identified a need for qualitative research that 'probes relationships' of teacher knowledge, attitudes and practice (p. 11); 'examines interactions' between teaching techniques and teachers' thinking (p. 16); investigates 'interactions between...pedagogical approaches and programmatic contexts' (p. 20); 'rich descriptive studies' (p. 23); and 'ethnographic analyses' (p. 33). Indeed, in their final recommendations they explicitly call for research that, while they concede will be 'exceedingly complex and difficult to do', will 'examine the complex links among teacher preparation programs and contexts, teacher candidates' knowledge growth, teachers' professional practices, and pupils learning within the contexts of schools and classrooms' (p. 35).

Such calls are consistent with Wideen, Mayer-Smith & Moon's (1998) earlier critical review of teacher education. The authors expressed concern about the 'isolated nature of research programs' which led them to suggest that educational researchers need to refocus attention on the interconnected nature of being – an ecological approach – 'we become aware of different levels of complexity, new properties and insights emerge' (p. 168). They argued the need for research that interrogates and challenges 'the structures, approaches and mythology of teacher education'; involves in-depth studies of 'how other players affect the landscape and process of learning to teach'; resists the tendency 'to treat the participants as objects of research'; and provides 'a clearer understanding of the perceptions of...teacher educators, their background and their images of power' (pp. 168–169). Both these international reviews into teacher education indicate that there is a gap in the research literature regarding in-depth descriptive ethnographic research on learning to teach that may illuminate the interdependent teaching/learning nexus.

In 2005, Marilyn Cochran-Smith referred to an earlier presidential address made nearly a decade and a half before by another AERA President Larry Cuban (1992, cited in Cochran-Smith 2005a) in which he asked whether it was the responsibility of the research community to speak up against public policies believed to be 'flawed in both logic and evidence, and ultimately, hostile to [our] vision for students'. He continued by asking if, in the face of almost inevitable/certain implementation of such policies, the research community should 'accommodate', or collude, to mitigate any damage or use their voice 'in order to influence the policy debate'. Cuban raised these ethical questions in the face of high-stakes testing and the neoliberal educational reform shift evident from the beginning of the 1980s. For the teacher/teacher educator/researcher, the heart of the matter lies within Cuban's original concern – *our vision for students*. How does the teacher education research literature address the preparation of teachers guided by a vision for, or *by*, students?

In Australia, a federal inquiry into teacher education (House of Representatives Standing Committee on Education and Vocational Training 2007) found that 'there is simply not a sufficiently rich body of research evidence to enable it to come to any firm conclusions about the overall quality of teacher education in Australia' (p. 5). This inquiry spanned two years and received 195 submissions from 170 individuals and organisations across all states and territories. Public hearings and forums heard a total of 446 witnesses from teacher professional bodies, faculties of education, parent advocacy groups, public administrators and private and public schooling bodies. The committee noted that 'there is not even agreement on what quality in teacher education means' (p. 5). As mentioned earlier, discourses of teacher and initial teacher education program quality continue to circulate in the Australian political arena. Findings from a recent large-scale teacher education study commissioned by the federal government has identified, almost contrary to these discourses, that those most intimately involved in teacher education report high levels of satisfaction. Indeed, principals had 'more positive perceptions of the effectiveness of graduates than the graduates themselves' to plan and implement teaching and learning (Mayer et al. 2013, p. 15). The 'quality' conundrum is not just confined to the Australian context; consistency and clarity of definitions in teacher education research has been highlighted as a concern internationally (Cochran-Smith & Zeichner 2005; Noffke & Zeichner 2006). Reflecting upon three decades in teacher education, Zeichner (2006) notes that some advocates of the deregulation agenda strenuously support taking teacher preparation out of universities and placing responsibility back to schools where the school and classroom environments are the best preparations for the realities of teaching.

Practitioner inquiry: ~~native/observer~~ as framer

From the radical deregulation position, theory and practice are seen as binaries: theory the province of academics and practice the work of teachers. The deregulation agenda mirrors the general pedagogical knowledge and pedagogical content knowledge (Shulman 1986, 1987) split that continues to frame the pedagogical discourse in teacher education. What constitutes effective or quality pedagogy continues to be contested and debated by policy makers, practitioners and researchers within the dichotomous position set up between general pedagogical knowledge and pedagogical content knowledge. One of the attractions of pedagogical content knowledge is its focus on topic specificity, which lends itself to boundedness and stability. Therefore, in the neoliberal market

Figure 5.3 Teacher educator/practitioner researcher conferring with Year 8 co-researcher

climate it is little wonder that pedagogical content knowledge and the 'what' of teaching have found ascendancy. However, binaries serve as much to exclude as they include. Pedagogy and the pedagogue are excluded in this polarising debate: 'pedagogical content knowledge is the category most likely to distinguish the understanding of the content specialist from that of the pedagogue' (Shulman 1987, p. 8). Cochran-Smith (2005a) suggests that the apparent rejection of pedagogical knowledge is a reflection in teacher education of the 'popular myth that there is little to know about teaching and schools, and what little there is can be easily picked up on the job' (p. 12).

Mythology surrounding teacher education is not surprising given that it is a relatively new field of inquiry (Noffke & Zeichner 2006; Borko, Liston & Whitcom 2007). Furthermore, the nature of research conducted in the field of teacher education has, in part, contributed to its perceived unknowablility, especially in the highly contextualised and relational aspects of pedagogy. Broeckmans (2003) points out that most research in the field is behaviourist in nature, concentrating on overt behaviours that can be measured and do not look into the process over an extended period. Submissions made by education faculties, individual senior academics, and the Australian Association for Research in Education (AARE) to the 2007 federal inquiry into teacher education *Top of the Class* (House of Representatives Standing Committee on Education and Vocational Training 2007) resonated the above observation by expressing concern that it was difficult to gain competitive grant funding for research that was 'applied rather than experimental in nature' (p. 12). Kincheloe (2003) clearly observed that 'rarely do the most significant questions of human affairs lend themselves to quantification and the pseudo-certainty which accompanies them' (p. 142). This is further borne out in the 2007 *Top of the Class* report when the committee observed that most data available was based on surveys of graduates, teachers and principals and that is 'not sufficient to fully inform policy and practice in teacher education' (House of Representatives Standing Committee on Education and Vocational Training 2007, p. xxii).

Noffke and Zeichner (2006) acknowledge that radical research frameworks such as critical and feminist theory have made important methodological contributions in teacher education, but research is often conducted by researchers in 'social foundations areas' and not 'in the teacher preparation programs deeply connected to practical work in schools' (p. 830). This will remain the case until teaching and its poorer cousin teacher education are taken more seriously by the academy. As Zeichner (2006) notes, teacher education is largely seen as a 'cash cow' that feeds the more prestigious research agenda of the faculty (p. 335). Practitioner research (Cochran-Smith & Lytle 2004; Cochran-Smith & Donnell 2006; Borko, Liston & Whitcom 2007), on the other hand, has for decades faced criticism by those within the academy that research by teachers into their practice lacks legitimacy or creditability (Zeichner & Noffke 2001; Yates 2004). In some ways, research in teacher education finds itself in a catch-22 situation. Practitioners, to varying degrees, accept that 'the relations of knowledge and practice are complex and distinctly nonlinear' (Cochran-Smith & Donnell 2006, p. 508) and therefore may produce 'risky' research

> where researchers look at their own or other people's crises as pedagogues, their disorientations, and their incompetence. It may also produce research where what is pointed to is silence rather than words, and stillness rather than action. (Rhedding-Jones 2003, p. 11)

There is a need for in-depth, descriptive and situated research that calls for researchers 'to get their hands dirty' (Groundwather-Smith & Mockler 2006, p. 111) and yet the methodological and theoretical promise of radical research frameworks remain largely unexplored.

Myths such as 'good schools', 'quality teachers' and 'successful students' abound in current educational discourse, and not always originating from those with 'hostile' intent. As Elizabeth Ellsworth (1992) has pointed out 'repressive myths' are also generated by the very emancipatory or critical discourses used by those seeking to address a social justice agenda. Perhaps as a consequence some in educational research call for researchers to re-envision generative 'conceptions of meaning' (Hostetler, Macintrye Latta & Sarroub 2007, p. 242) in teacher education 'to make their lives and the lives of their students more complex, complicated, and connected' (p. 237). A vision for students, or a vision for improving the quality of teacher education, 'must relate both to existing conditions and to something we are trying to bring into being, something that goes beyond a present situation' (Greene 1995, p. 51). Dewey's (1938, 1997) position that meaning is derived from 'conflict and entanglement' between teachers and learners and not diminished by it, would suggest that this is a rich site to begin exploring existing conditions in pedagogical research.

There is a body of research in teacher education literature emerging from the multicultural or cultural diversity tradition that seeks to examine the entanglement between teachers and learners. It is possible to trace such examination in the research of Sonia Nieto (1999, 2000, 2002), Geneva Gay (1978, 2000, 2003), Antonia Darder (1991, 1997, 2002) and Marilyn Cochran-Smith (2000, 2004). However, because of its origins there is a tendency to focus on 'characteristics' or 'background' of teachers and students (the 'what' becomes the 'who' of I am/they are). This lends itself to stable notions of identity and processes that deal with, manage, or even attempt to resolve relationships between teacher and learner.

In 2000, Brady and Kanpol criticised modernist paradigms in teacher education as 'hegemonizing its agents and its vision of the present and the future' (2000, p. 40). Both authors resonated the earlier arguments of Greene (1995) and Ellsworth (1992) by consigning concepts such as 'empowerment' and 'effective teaching' as merely talk 'because many of these concepts are devoid of the social, political and philosophical pursuits within them' (Brady & Kanpol 2000, p. 40). Their article lamented that many teacher educators fell into reproducing the content and skills methodology to preparing teachers. Alison Cook-Sather (2002) challenged the theory and practice divide even further by bringing together those learning to teach and school students. Formerly a teacher, and now a teacher educator, Cook-Sather described how she felt the loss of the irrepressible insights of her school-aged students. She endeavours to close the theory/practice divide by breaking the accepted and reproducing hegemonising relations between theorists or researchers and practitioners and teachers and learners. Through Cook-Sather's research (2002, 2006a, 2006b), and her research with Youens (2007), it has been found that there are significant benefits to both pre-service teachers and their mentors by providing an opportunity for direct and unprivileged dialogue.

The research project outlined in this chapter, like those above, is embedded in the intuitive, contexualised and contingent understandings of teacher/researchers. It is interested in the generative possibilities that teacher/researchers may bring to research, particularly if they take up the challenge to resist the irresistible (Eisner 2006) and reflexively consider the construction of Other (Trinh 1989, 1991). It is interested in further problematising the entangled relationships of teaching and learning to illuminate what may appear beyond the representational in learning to teach. Where are the voices, or faces, of those deeply embedded in the pedagogic relations at the heart of school culture? 'How can the extinguished light be lit again so that teachers and learners can appear before one another and show, in speech and action, who they are and what they can do?' (Greene 1995, p. 44, our emphasis).

Transformative data – one thing leading to another

Figure 5.4 Shawn on the basketball court

At the end of the first six months at the secondary school with the preservice teacher cohort, two incidents marked a significant shift in the role that photographs played in the research project. One event was a basketball match and the other was an accident whilst playing around with photographs taken of the basketball match. Shawn, one of the Year 9 students, did not let us forget a promise made on the first day at the school concerning a basketball challenge against 'you uni people'. A few minutes shooting baskets with some of the more athletic pre-service teachers would not suffice; it had to be everyone down on the courts for a full-on match. The last day of school before midterm holidays was set aside, cutting short one of the scheduled joint workshop sessions. The Year 8 and Year 9 students almost exploded out of the classroom as they headed for the courts; there was a mixture of excitement, exhilaration and nervous energy in us all.

For most of the first six months of the project, Kim, the first-named author, had comfortably snapped around 150 photographs of the preservice teachers group work activities. Every evening she downloaded the images into the Kodak EasyShare™ software that came with the camera. It would automatically place all the images into dated albums.

She would click through the pictures, delighted that there was no need to ration shots with digital technology or to worry about blurred or over/under-exposed shots. While this digital camera was a cheap, non-chargeable camera that ran on batteries, a 1 GB memory card could hold up to 500 images if needed. During this first six-month period, Kim had been reticent about using the camera when the Year 8 and 9 students were around. She was unsure how they would feel about being photographed and was unsure about what she *should* photograph. There was also the issue of what *could* be photographed within the parameters of this rather amorphous 'classroom'. This all changed on the afternoon of the basketball challenge. Nathan, one of the Year 8 students, bounded up to Kim and asked if he could have the camera, urging Kim to join in the basketball game.

It was an interesting afternoon on and off the basketball court. Some pre-service teachers played enthusiastically, some chatted and cheered alongside the small crowd of secondary students on the sidelines, and others chose to sit apart from any action. Shawn conversed directly with Kim for the first (and only) time. At the end of the match, a student other than Nathan returned the camera. Nathan had passed it onto someone else when he decided to join the game too. What images would appear when the memory card was downloaded that evening? What had Nathan and the other student chosen to photograph? The result was a series of thirty-six photographs.

Figure 5.5 The moment Kim walked onto the court leaving Nathan with the camera

88 *Kim Senior and Julianne Moss*

Figure 5.6 One of the thirty-six basketball action shots

Kim clicked through them, over and over. Who could be seen? What had others 'seen' or captured of the afternoon? How did they get those action shots without blurring? Did cropping the photos bring a focus on particular individuals? While learning how to use the cropping feature on images, Kim noticed a 'fun effects' tool in the editing function. Intrigued she gave all of the effects a try, finally deciding upon the 'colour in' effect.

Figure 5.7 Photograph (see Figure 5.5) put through the 'colour in' effect

The Use of the Visual to Interpret School Cultures 89

Figure 5.8 Photograph (see Figure 5.6) put through the 'colour in' effect

The photographs became something more when emptied. The environment, background and shadows bespoke of something different; bodies and objects denuded of colour spoke more emphatically, producing images which invite the viewer to be touched by their 'rays' (Barthes 2001, p. 61). The rays and lines of movement merge autonomy and continuity to appear in what may otherwise be overlooked or hidden in the distinct and coloured photographs. They invite the reader to engage with them in a less discernible but equally compelling way. Artist and author Shaun Tan describes this kind of engagement with the visual image as a 'gap of recognition' (Dunford 2007, p. 35) between writer/drawer and reader/viewer. It is a space in which the usual hegemonic relationships do not apply; a space in which the writer as creator lets go of ownership and tempts the reader's imagination forth.

Mitchell (2005) reveals our response to images as a 'double consciousness' in which we may suspend ourselves in and amongst visual representations. We are capable of maintaining a 'magical attitude' (p. 7), or imaginative state of awareness with images, while at the same time a capacity to question their veracity, motives and value. Even if we suspend our imaginative awareness by recognising that 'every image is manipulated', the content of images is based upon the producer's intent and the response of the reader 'will be based on content, perception of intent and context' (Goldstein 2007, p. 79), the generative possibilities for educational research are significant. Mitchell (2005) offers another way in which we can critique and interrogate images; a sensitive approach that sounds the 'images with just enough force to make them resonate' (p. 9). Rather than getting caught up with what they *mean*, he suggests we ask what images *want*.

Framed? Disrupting visual method and representation

The research project into the pedagogy of learning to teach began by inviting the pre-service teachers and Year 8 and 9 secondary students to write to the researcher: emails, postcards, handwritten letters, text messages and notes from three of the Year 9 students (Annalise, Ashley and Stevie-Lee) and eight of the pre-service teachers continued regularly. But the more Kim tried to grasp what may have been happening with words, the more that letters alone seemed to fall short in some way. After the basketball match and at the beginning of the new school term, the secondary students were invited to the university for a reciprocal 'excursion' – the students wanted to see where 'you uni people hang out'. Nathan and his friend Alexander were eager to see Kim's office and were surprised that photographs from the school were up on the walls. They sought themselves out, they talked about the others in the photographs and they talked in general. They asked why the photos were there, and she reminded them about the research project on learning to teach and how everyone had initially been invited to write or email. 'Yeah, but I don't like writing', Nathan said, as he began to pick up the boxes of goodies to take to the tutorial room that had been booked for lunch.

Who else had been excluded from participating in the research because of an attachment to text? Who was silenced or made absent by writing? *What* else was being excluded? Kim went back to the purpose of and the premise upon which the research was initiated.

> As researchers, we often read about what teachers, parents, principals and politicians have to say about the process of learning to teach, but we don't get to hear what young people have to say. I would like to make sure that my research includes your views and opinions. (Senior 2008, p. 195)

Hadn't Nathan shared his views and opinions when he had commandeered the digital camera? Hadn't the photographs communicated something compelling, surprising and unexpected: another perspective? An amendment to ethics allowed the use of cameras for the final nine months of the project, and a further five pre-service teachers and ten secondary students (including Nathan, Alexander and Shawn) joined the research. In these remaining months, three Kodak cameras were left on the table where all resources were kept and where anyone could use them whenever they wanted. Every week the photographs were downloaded as before, but this time Kim printed A4 copies to take to the school the following week. Prior to setting up the workshop rooms for our afternoon sessions, she would routinely post the previous week's photographs up on the whiteboard for everyone present to look at and comment upon. At the end of the day, the photographs were taken down and brought into the office to put up on the wall in Kim's study. She immersed herself in the photographs and played with the 'colour in' effect.

No effort was made to track, or record, who took what photograph or when, so that the photographs could not be grouped according to photographer and therefore meaning could not be extrapolated. Kim did not want to set up an alternative hierarchical structure within the analysis whereby Nathan's or Keith's or Annalise's photographs were interpreted for the reader. Instead, a way was sought in which the photographs or images could be transliterated for a far more tentative process of correspondence or approximation (Senior 2011). She sought to erase the possibility of 'fixed meaning', as Hélène Cixous (Shiach 1991, p. 36) suggests, by looking at the data from different perspectives or angles of repose (Richardson 2003a). She looked at the data as 'pictures' on walls or laid out – sometimes making trails of photographs down the corridor so that they could be reordered or regrouped together. She looked at the photographs as a whole, as smaller groups and one against another. What could be seen? Who could be seen? What was unexpected? What did the images *want*?

Different ordering, different readings and different conversations lent themselves to complex and 'thick'

Figure 5.9 Scott and Nic working together

(Geertz 1973) interpretations of the photographs and images. Kim kept a visual diary, scrapbooks (with copies of emails, letters and newspaper articles regarding teaching and teacher education) and produced, both individually and collaboratively, art pieces for a public exhibition at the university and the secondary college. She revisited earlier conversations about the photographs and 'colour in' images, and it became clear that while some interpretations reoccurred or resurfaced in dialogue with others involved in the project, they were never closed or finished (Sjöholm 2005, p. 12). Where did all this analysis leave the research? As an ethnographic inquiry into learning to teach, what did this data have to say? What did the images want? How could an ethnographic text be produced that responded to the multiple, complex and incomplete 'voices' at the heart of pedagogical relationships?

Co-production of knowledge in visual research

Resisting the urge to step from the non-knowing space of data analysis, the research data was presented as a transliterative text – an ethnography through intertextual assemblage in manga form. The photographs had played an important part in analysis for the project, but the 'colour in' images offered something more to work with in terms of what this particular project sought to do. From day one at the school, Kim noticed that some of the Year 9 students were interested in manga, and one of the original student co-researchers, Stevie-Lee, wrote and posted her own drawings on fan sites. Discussion about manga writers, writing and drawing played an extensive role in the email exchanges between Kim and Stevie-Lee. As an intertextual narrative form, manga provided a generative way to work with all the data (letters, emails, photographs and field notes) as well as the scraps of paper or snippets of overheard conversations that are common in the classroom. The photographs were left aside and Kim worked only with the 'colour in' images along with textual fragments. The 'colour in' images allowed greater freedom in using data that included non-participants to the research as they were 'de-identified' and yet at the same time remained 'present' in the data. The result was a collection of thirty-two individually titled and interrelated visual strips in the form of a manga about learning to teach.

Even though each strip is a standalone piece (like the one shown above), the underlying currents, associations and 'sub plots' between the strips meant that it was important that the manga was collated in

The Use of the Visual to Interpret School Cultures 93

Stained hands

Figure 5.10 Manga strip using photograph in Figure 5.9 and excerpts from Scott's reflective journal

a particular way. A spreadsheet was created in order to manage this ordering process with columns such as:

- working number for each strip;
- working title;
- those involved in the strip;
- those who appear in the images (checking for identifiable non-participants to the research to either crop image, erase lines or replace the image);
- working number of related manga strip(s);
- comments (e.g. key words or questions/problems that remained);
- JPEG number of images to be used; and
- repetitions (if images are used in other strips).

The strips were then printed up in both A4 and A3 format so that the stories could read through to check for continuity (not in the linear sense but for readability) and clarity in the visual and textual formatting. As mentioned earlier, one of the unexpected features of the images in the manga format was the de-identification of people in the images. On a couple of occasions where images contained students not expressly part of the research, lines or identifying marks could be erased to ensure anonymity (e.g. parts of the school logo could be erased from the students jumpers or name tags or lines on faces that would disclose someone's identity).

Seeing quality in teacher education research

In this chapter the focus has been on teacher education research and the development of an innovative, qualitative, visually informed approach. The theoretical grounding of the project, as Margolis and Pauwels (2011) point out, 'not only involves the visual analytical side (how to deal with the form and content of the visual products) but also includes the main subject matter or the thematic focus of the projects' (p. 13). In the recent TEMAG report recommendation, thirty-four of the report suggests that a national focus into teacher education 'including into the effectiveness of teacher preparation and the promotion of innovative practice' (Craven et al. 2014, p. xvii) be commissioned as part of the quality teacher education agenda. There is a well-understood critique of teacher/researcher inquiry and an accepted practice of silencing of learners. In teacher education where the contingent understandings of relationships are critical to pedagogy, visually informed research designs would support the production of knowledge and knowing when you are 'learning to teach'.

References

Barone, T. E. (1997). Among the Chosen: A Collaborative Educational (Auto)Biography. *Qualitative Inquiry, 3*(2), 222–237.
Barone, T. E., & Eisner, E. (2006). Arts-Based Educational Research. In J. L. Green, G. Camilli, & P. B. Elmore (Eds), *Handbook of Complementary Methods in Education Research* (pp. 95–109). Mahwah, NJ: Lawrence Erlbaum.
Barthes, R. (2001). Camera Lucida: Reflections on Photography. In J. Thomas (Ed.), *Reading Images* (pp. 54–61). New York: Palgrave.
Borko, H., Liston, D., & Whitcom, J. A. (2007). Genres of Empirical Research in Teacher Education. *Journal of Teacher Education, 58*(1), 3–11.
Brady, J. F., & Kanpol, B. (2000). The Role of Critical Multicultural Education and Feminist Critical Thought in Teacher Education: Putting Theory into Practice. *Educational Foundations, 14*(3), 39–50.
Britzman, D. P. (2003). *Practice Makes Practice: A Critical Study of Learning to Teach* (Revised ed.). Albany: State University of New York Press.
Broeckmans, J. (2003). An Attempt to Study the Process of Learning to Teach from an Integrative Viewpoint. In M. Kompf & P. Denicolo (Eds), *Teacher Thinking Twenty Years on: Revisiting Persisting Problems and Advances in Education* (pp. 111–118). Netherlands: Swets & Zeitlinger.
Buckingham, J. (2005). Good Teachers Where They Are Needed. *Issue Analysis* (64), 1–18.
Cahnmann, M. (2003). The Craft, Practice, and Possibility of Poetry in Educational Research. *Educational Researcher*, 29–36.
Clandinin, D. J., & Connelly, F. M. (2000). *Narrative Inquiry*. San Francisco: Jossey-Bass.
Cochran-Smith, M. (2000). The Questions That Drive Reform. *Journal of Teacher Education, 51*(5), 331–333.
Cochran-Smith, M. (2004). *Walking the Road – Race, Diversity, and Social Justice in Teacher Education*. New York: Teachers College Press.
Cochran-Smith, M. (2005a). The New Teacher Education: For Better or for Worse? *Educational Researcher, 34*(7), 3–17.
Cochran-Smith, M. (2005b). Teacher Education and the Outcomes Trap. *Journal of Teacher Education, 56*(5), 411–417.
Cochran-Smith, M., & Donnell, K. (2006). Practitioner Inquiry: Blurring the Boundaries of Research and Practice. In J. Green, G. Camilli, & P. Elmore (Eds), *Handbook of Complementary Methods in Education Research* (pp. 503–518). Mahwah, NJ: Lawrence Erlbaum Associates.
Cochran-Smith, M., & Lytle, S. (2004). Practitioner Inquiry, Knowledge, and University Culture. In J. Loughran, M. Hamilton, V. LaBoskey, & T. Russell (Eds), *International Handbook of Research of Self-study of Teaching and Teacher Education Practices* (pp. 601–650). Amsterdam: Kluwer.
Cochran-Smith, M., & Lytle, S. (2009). *Inquiry as Stance: Practitioner Research for the Next Generation*. New York: Teachers College Press.
Cochran-Smith, M., & Seichner, K. M. (Eds) (2005). *Studying Teacher Education – The Report of the AERA Panel on Research and Teacher Education*. Mahwah: American Educational Research Association.
Cook-Sather, A. (2002). Re(in)forming the Conversations: Student Position, Power, and Voice in Teacher Education. *Radical Teacher* (64), pp. 21–28.

Cook-Sather, A. (2006a). Change Based on What Students Say: Preparing Teachers for a Paradoxical Model of Leadership. *International Journal of Leadership in Education, 9*(4), 345–358.

Cook-Sather, A. (2006b). *Education in Translation – A Metaphor for Change in Learning and Teaching.* Philadelphia: University of Pennsylvania.

Cook-Sather, A., & Youens, B. (2007). Repositioning Students in Initial Teacher Preparation – A Comparative Descriptive Analysis of Learning to Teach for Social Justice in the United States and in England. *Journal of Teacher Education, 58*(1), 62–75.

Craven, G., Beswick, K., Fleming, J., Fletcher, T., Green M., Jensen, B., Leinonen, E., & Rickards, F. (2014). *Action Now: Classroom Ready Teachers – Teacher Education Ministerial Advisory Group.* Canberra: Commonwealth of Australia.

Darder, A. (1991). *Culture and Power in the Classroom.* Westport: Bergin & Garvey.

Darder, A. (Ed.) (1997). *Latinos and Education.* New York: Routledge.

Darder, A. (2002). *Reinventing Paulo Freire – A Pedagogy of Love.* Cambridge: Westview.

Darling-Hammond, L. (2000). How Teacher Education Matters. *Journal of Teacher Education, 51*(3), 166–173.

Darling-Hammond, L. (2006). Constructing 21st-Century Teacher Education. *Journal of Teacher Education, 57*(3), 300–314.

Department of Education and Training. (2004). *Blueprint for Government Schools.* Retrieved March 25, 2006, from sofweb: http://www.sofweb.vic.edu.au/blueprint/

Department of Education and Training, NSW. (2003). *Department of Education and Training.* Retrieved December 10, 2005, from Quality teaching in NSW public schools: Discussion paper: http://www.det.nsw.edu.au/prflearn/docs.pdf/qt_EPSColor.pdf

Department of Education and Training, Victoria. (2004). *Department of Education and Training.* Retrieved January 17, 2005, from Principles of Learning and Teaching P-12 (PoLT): Blueprint for Government Schools: http://www.sofweb.vic.edu.au/blueprint/fs1/polt/default.htm

Department of Education and Training, Victoria. (2006). *Closing the Loop: Curriculum, Pedagogy, Assessment and Reporting.* Melbourne: Department of Education and Training Victoria.

Department of Education, Science and Training. (2003). Retrieved February 18, 2005, from the Report of the Review of Teaching and Teacher Education: http://www.dest.gov.au/schools/teachingreview/

Department of Education, Science and Training. (2005). *Teaching Reading, National Inquiry into the Teaching of Literacy.* Canberra: Commonwealth of Australia.

Department of Education, Tasmania. (2000). Retrieved October 4, 2005, from http://www.education.tas.gov.au/ocll/publications/valuespurposs.pdf

Department of Education, Tasmania. (2006, October 10). Refining Our Curriculum – Curriculum Statement.

Dewey, J. (1938). *Experience and Education.* New York: Touchstone.

Dewey, J. (1997). The School and Social Progress (originally published in 1899). In J. H. Stouse (Ed.), *Exploring Themes of Social Justice in Education – Readings in Social Foundations* (pp. 81–89). New Jersey: Prentice-Hall.

Dunford, G. (2007, Nov/Dec). Drawing Breadth. In A. Attwood (Ed.), *The Big Issue* (292), 34–35.

Education Queensland. (2002). Retrieved October 2, 2005, from Destination 2010 – The Action Plan to Implement State Education, 2002–2010: http://education.qld.gov.au/publication/production/reports/pdfs/2002/dest-2010-actionplan.pdf
Eisner, E. (1991). *The Enlightened Eye – Qualitative Inquiry and the Enhancement of Educational Practice*. New York: Macmillan Publishing.
Eisner, E. (1997). The New Frontier in Qualitative Research Methodology. *Qualitative Inquiry*, 3(3), 259–267.
Eisner, E. (2006). Signature Ideas Sailing on a Skeptical Sea. Unpublished speech notes for the invited presidential session's Grawemeyer Award in Education at the American Educational Research Association conference. San Francisco.
Ellsworth, E. (1992). Why Doesn't This Feel Empowering? Working Through the Repressive Myths of Critical Pedagogy. In C. Luke & G. Jennifer (Eds), *Feminisms and Critcal Pedagogy* (pp. 90–119). New York: Routledge.
Ellsworth, E. (1997). *Teaching Positions – Difference, Pedagogy, and the Power of Address*. New York: Teachers College Press.
Gay, G. (1978). Viewing the Pluralistic Classroom as a Microcosm. *Educational Research Quarterly*, 2(4), 45–59.
Gay, G. (2000). *Culturally Responsive Teaching: Theory, Research, Practice*. New York: Teachers College Press.
Gay, G. (2003). Introduction: Planting Seeds to Harvest Fruits. In G. Gay (Ed.), *Becoming Multicultural Educators – Personal Journey toward Professional Agency* (pp. 1–16). San Francisco: Jossey-Bass.
Geertz, C. (Ed.) (1973). *The Interpretation of Cultures*. New York: Basic Books.
Goldstein, B. (2007). All Photos Lie – Images as Data. In G. Stanczak (Ed.), *Visual Research Methods – Image, Society, and Representation* (pp. 61–81). Thousand Oaks: Sage Publications.
Gore, J. M., Ladwig, J. G., & King, B. M. (2004). Professional Learning, Pedagogical Improvement, and the Circulation of Power. Australian Association for Educational Research conference. Melbourne.
Gough, N. (2001). Learning from Disgrace: A Troubling Narrative for South African Curriculum Work. *Perspectives in Education*, 19(1), 107–126.
Gough, N. (2004). Read Intertextually, Write an Essay, Make a Rhizome: Performing Narrative Experiments in Educational Inquiry. In H. Piper & I. Stronach (Eds), *Educational Research: Difference and Diversity* (pp. 155–176). Ashgate: Aldershot.
Greene, M. (1995). *Releasing the Imagination*. San Francisco: Jossey-Bass Publishers.
Groundwather-Smith, S., & Mockler, N. (2006). Research that Counts: Practitioner Research and the Academy. *Review of Australian Research in Education*, 105–117.
Hostetler, K., Macintrye Latta, M. A., & Sarroub, L. (2007). Retrieving Meaning in Teacher Education. *Journal of Teacher Education*, 58(3), 231–244.
House of Representatives Standing Committee on Education and Vocational Training. (2007). *Top of the Class – Report on the inquiry into teacher education*. Canberra: Commonwealth of Australia.
Irvine, J. (2003). *Educating Teachers for Diversity*. New York: Teachers College Press.
Kincheloe, J. L. (2003). *Teachers as Researchers – Qualitative Inquiry as a Path to Empowerment*. New York: Routledge.

Lather, P. (2007). *Getting Lost – Feminist Efforts toward a Double(d) Science*. Albany: State University of New York Press.
Lenski, S., Crawford, K., Crumpler, T., & Stallworth, C. (2005). Preparing Preservice Teachers in a Diverse World. *Action in Teacher Education, 27*(3), 3–12.
Margolis, E. & Pauwels L. (Eds) (2011). *The SAGE Handbook of Visual Research Methods*. Thousand Oaks: Sage Publications.
Mayer, D., Doecke, B., Ho, P., Kline, J., Kostogriz, A., Moss, J., North, S., & Walker-Gibbs, B. (2013). *Longitudinal Teacher Education and Workforce Study (LTWES) Final Report*. Canberra: Commonwealth of Australia.
Ministerial Council on Education, Employment, Training and Youth Affairs. (1999). *The Adelaide Declaration on National Goals for Schooling in the Twenty-first Century – Preamble and Goals*. Retrieved March 7, 2005, from Australian Government, Department of Education, Science and Training: http://www.dest.gov.au/sectors/school_Education/policy_initiatives_reviews/national_goals_for_schooling_in_the_twenty_first_century.htm
Mitchell, W. J. (2005). *What Do Pictures Want? The Lives and Loves of Images*. Chicago: University of Chicago Press.
Nieto, S. (1999). *The Light in Their Eyes – Creating Multicultural Learning Communities*. New York: Teachers College Press.
Nieto, S. (2000). *Affirming Diversity* (3rd ed.). New York: Longman.
Nieto, S. (2002). *Language, Culture, and Teaching*. Mahwah, NJ: Lawrence Erlbaum.
Noffke, S., & Zeichner, K. M. (2006). Programs of Research in Teacher Education. In J. L. Green, G. Camilli, & P. B. Elmore (Eds), *Handbook of Complementary Methods in Education Research* (pp. 823–832). Mahwah, NJ: Lawrence Erlbaum.
Pinar, W. F., & Irwin, R. (Eds) (2005). *Curriculum in a New Key – The Collected Work of Ted T. Aoki*. Mahwah, NJ: Lawrence Erlbaum.
Rhedding-Jones, J. (2003). Complexity in Research: The Risky Business of Including It. New Zealand and Australian Associations for Research in Education conference. Auckland, New Zealand.
Richardson, L. (2003a). Writing: A Method of Inquiry. In N. Denzin & Y. Lincoln (Eds), *Collecting and Interpreting Qualitative Materials* (pp. 499–541). Thousand Oaks: Sage Publications.
Richardson, L. (2003b). Writing: A Method of Inquiry. In Y. S. Lincoln & N. K. Denzin (Eds), *Turning Points in Qualitative Research* (pp. 379–396). Walnut Creek: AltaMira.
Senior, K. (2008). Letters as an Imaged-Based Methodology in Educational Research. In *Researching Education Visually – Digitally – Spatially* (pp. 183–208). Rotterdam: Sense Publishers.
Senior, K. (2011). Incorrigible and Undisciplined Lines in Visual Social Research: Ways of 'Writing' and 'Drawing' at the Interstices. *ACCESS Critical Perspectives on Communication, Cultural & Policy Studies, 30*(1), 57–70.
Shiach, M. (1991). *Helene Cixous – A Politics of Writing*. London: Routledge.
Shulman, L. (1986). Those Who Understand: A Conception of Teacher Knowledge. *American Educator*, 9–15.
Shulman, L. (1987). Knowledge and Teaching: Foundations of a New Reform. *Harvard Educational Review*, 1–22.
Sjöholm, C. (2005). *Kristeva and the Political*. London: Routledge.

Stronach, I. (2006). Enlightenment and the 'Heart of Darkness': (Neo)imperialism in the Congo, and Elsewhere. *International Journal of Qualitative Studies in Education, 19*(6), 757–768.
Trinh, M. (1989). *Woman Native Other*. Bloomington: Indiana University Press.
Trinh, M. (1991). *When the Moon Waxes Red – Representation, Gender and Cultural Politics*. New York: Routledge.
Vallack, J. (2005). 'I Know What I Like!' *Qualitative Research Journal, 5*(2), 99–111.
Victorian Curriculum and Assesment Authority. (2004). *Victorian Curriculum Reform Consultation Paper*. Retrieved Spetember 29, 2005, from http://vels.vcaa.vic.edu.au/VELSoverview.html
Victorian Parliament, Education and Training Committee. (2005). *Step Up, Step In, Step Out: Report on the Inquiry into the Suitability of Pre-service Teacher Training in Victoria*. Melbourne: Victorian Government Printer.
Villegas, A. M., & Lucas, T. (2002). Preparing Culturally Responsive Teachers – Rethinking the Curriculum. *Journal of Teacher Education, 53*(1), 20–32.
Wideen, M. F., Mayer-Smith, J., & Moon, B. (1998). A Critical Analysis of the Research on Learning to Teach: Making the Case for an Ecological Perspective on Inquiry. *Review of Educational Research, 98*(2), 130–178.
Yates, L. (2004) *What Does Good Education Research Look Like? Situating a Field and Its Practices*. Maidenhead: Open University Press.
Zeichner, K. (2006). Reflections of a University-based Teacher Educator on the Future of College- and University-based Teacher Education. *Journal of Teacher Education, 57*(3), 326–340.
Zeichner, K., & Noffke, S. (2001). Practitioner Research. In V. Richardson (Ed.), *Hanbook of Research on Teaching* (pp. 298–330). Washington: American Educational Research Association.

6
Pedascapes: New Cartographies of Pedagogy

Mary Dixon

Introduction

In recent decades distinctive forms of visual representations of classrooms have received significant attention. Large international bodies of classroom data are being assembled and rely heavily on videoing classroom action, particularly teacher pedagogy (Stigler et al. 1999; Luke et al. 2005; Clarke 2009). These images are being used to inform educational research. In the public sphere 'numerical images' are receiving greater attention. In the globalised phenomenon of education, pedagogical data is largely rendered through numerical representations (Bloom 2006) and usually these are not read as being images or image based. These public portrayals of pedagogy typically employ hard data of student learning outcomes produced in and about schools (OECD 2014; *My School*® 2015). These demographic statistics and national testing results can be read as 'numerical pedagogical' images.

The work in this chapter draws upon an OECD Innovative Learning Environments Study project for the Victorian Department of Education and Early Childhood (Blackmore et al. 2011). Through an innovative and unexpected turn, still photographic classroom images are juxtaposed with 'numerical pedagogical images' to create a performative cartography of spaces inside Australian schools. This turn is unexpected as, in the original research design of the project, the classroom images were not intended to be used alongside the public data. The project sought to identify the pedagogical affordances of newly modified and/or newly built classrooms and schools. The project brief directed attention to the links between spaces and student learning. In the analysis, the research team considered, amongst other data, the pedagogical images they generated in the classrooms and the school learning outcomes data available on public sites. It is usual to utilise these as distinct readings and the two data sets do provide differing pedagogical readings. It is well established that images are generative sites of pedagogical readings (Dixon 2008), but they have limited uptake in the public sphere. However, by reading the public data as 'numerical pedagogical images' and by placing the two 'image' data sets side by side, what has emerged are new cartographies of classroom pedagogy.

Initially in this chapter I give account of the learning spaces project and the visual work employed there. I use images from two cases in the project to provide pedagogical readings of classroom spaces. I then turn attention to the publicly available numerical pedagogical images about the schools. Finally, I use the learning spaces data from the project and place it alongside the public representations of pedagogy. This results in the creation of new pedagogical cartographies, a juxtaposition of soft and hard terrains, which I name 'pedascapes'. These pedascapes go some way to address the pedagogical silences evident in the public portrayal of statistical imagery of our schools. In a doubling effect, the pedascapes increase the visibility of the pedagogical encounter in both the photographic images and in the numerical images.

Pedagogy and space

In the Innovative Learning Environments Study project for the Victorian Department of Education and Early Childhood (Blackmore et al. 2011), researchers from Deakin University undertook twelve case studies in primary and secondary schools over a three-month period. Data were gathered in each case study and included publicly available school data, curriculum and policy documents, interviews with teachers and students, direct observation of teaching, learning and resources, principal-led tours and, of particular interest for this chapter, a range of visual data. The project's innovative use of visual data included the generation and analysis of student maps, cartographic annotations, student and researcher photographs, Google images and design blueprints. A publicly available research showcase of the project is readily accessible (see CREFI 2011a). The website is detailed and contains a vast amount of material which is evocative and emotes notions of innovations for learning environments. The visual work from these case studies is, as stated above, publicly available and is employed in this chapter to show the possibilities of visual data in pedagogical research.

The pedagogical encounter

The literature on the pedagogical encounter has often reverted in unsatisfactory ways to body language and to metaphorical abstractions. As Aoki eloquently states he was brought 'to an awareness that language which has served us well to describe the phenomena of the world begins to falter; at best, it merely points and then passes into silence' (Pinar & Irwin 2005, p. 400). In one sense it is true to say that words from interviews, field notes, policy documents and outcome reports fail to capture, elaborate or communicate the complexity and depth of pedagogical encounters. The everyday words and metaphors from teachers and researchers have gestured towards bodily extensions of pedagogical engagements: for example, it is colloquially said that the teacher can 'hold the class in their hands'. These metaphorical turns are often employed to illustrate rather than to evidence. When faced with the complexity of the teaching and learning relationship, where we must include bodies, spaces, objects and the entangled relationship between all of these, Roy (2003) argues that 'sensation in the smallest interval must be watched' (p. 174). To make pedagogical sense of what is occurring we need to focus on the very space around/between bodies and objects as well as the bodies and objects themselves. The pedagogical relationship involves bodies of teachers and of students, object and spaces and the matter-energies between these bodies, objects and spaces (Zembylas 2007). Attention must be given to all of these constituents. Images from inside the classroom are considered here not for what they show of action but for what they portray of pedagogical relationships. The soft work of images offers an opportunity for the researcher to see what occurs in the pedagogical relationships between bodies, objects and spaces. The focus is on the quality and the occurrence of that relationship. This visual pedagogical reading has a recently established history in the work of such methodologists as Mazzei (2013) and MacLure (2013).

The use of visual data calls on a pedagogical seeing which is understood through the use of an epistemic eye (Eisner 1991). An epistemic eye, which can discern the quality of learning and teaching encounters, draws on a tradition of connoisseurship in which our ability to see and to read these physical connections is a learned one. The pedagogical affordances of images are more readily available to those pedagogues, to those teachers and researchers, who have strong backgrounds in pedagogy and in reading the classroom. Just as for Deleuze and Guattari (1987) there is considerable and intentional slippage between concept and metaphor so the soft approach of the pedagogical reading will not only recognise but also see, for example, the teacher holding the class in her hand.

Classroom images

I have chosen to include only one classroom image in this section to elaborate the generative work of photographs in giving access to the pedagogical encounter. This decision was made as the main focus of this chapter is the placement of photographic images alongside numerical image work.

Mitchell asserts that images require the reader to maintain a 'magical attitude' (2005, p. 7), or an imaginative state of awareness to which we bring to bear a double consciousness. In this state we may suspend ourselves in and amongst visual representations while at the same time maintaining a capacity to question their veracity, motives and value. One such image from a young student in the project called on this capacity for a magical attitude. The image is a schoolyard space and was identified by a student as a learning site.[1] The young student and the concrete lizard on which he lies mirror each other's bodies. They are bodies merging in this pedagogical event. Inside the classrooms, teachers and students connect in formal learning spaces. In the same document, figure 3, entitled 'Openness within', one evocative image, the interplay of carpet, books, bodies, teacher and students, is evidenced as the teacher and students come together on the floor in a 'learning street' inside the school.

In the project case studies, teachers, students and researchers photographed and mapped the newly developed learning environments and classroom engagements. Attention to the spatial construction of learning was afforded when students were given an A3 sheet of paper and pencils (water colour and lead) and asked to draw a map of their school. Upon completion, students were then asked to overlay their map with a transparency and using an OHP pen they were asked to draw themselves on the map – wherever they learn. Bodies were placed and overlaid. This visual and physical layering drew attention to the connections between bodies, objects and spaces.

Awareness of the relationship of bodies, objects and maps of learning was further heightened when a small group of students was invited to draw where they like to learn at school. They used crayons and pastel and worked together on a large scroll of drawing paper. The bodies of the learners, the knowledge of the learning space, the paper, crayons and the open area are seen reaching out to each other in pedagogical interplays (see Figure 6.1 below). Images such as this one were not reduced through participant or researcher annotations. The images themselves made visible bodily engagements.

A pedagogical reading of the images such as in Figure 6.1 moves the understanding of the pedagogical relationship from a metaphorical one to a material pedagogical interplay. This reading invites the viewer to look without seeing borders, to look between bodies and objects. The young girls are seen in deep engagement with the large map they are making together. Their bodies are positioned alongside each other, reaching on to the map. They use the crayons and paper in the negotiation, collaboration and mapping of what they recognise as the learning sites in the school. Their bodies and the objects around them – paper, crayons, carpet, large open space – create a pedagogical engagement. In Figure 6.1, connections appear across physical bodies, presences and affected and affecting bodies. The body of each pedagogical participant extends beyond its material boundaries. It is not only that the learning and teaching are bodily but also the form of the relationship is bodily. In these extensions bodies reach out to the other.

Figure 6.1 Pedagogical interaction

Drawings, maps, images were laid out, rearranged and overlaid by researchers and students. This layered process was nuanced and generative of student perspectives not previously accessible through researcher observation, photograph or interview. It provided the opportunity for reflective work by individual students, collaborative work as students worked alongside each other, and multiple avenues of expression working across various researching styles. The image work evidences the physical presence of pedagogical engagements.

These extensions are felt by others and seen by others. For Deleuze the physical extension of bodies is embodied as 'matter-energy' (Deleuze & Guattari 1987, p. 408). Through a Deleuzian understanding of 'energies', Zembylas argues 'new affective and embodied connections' (2007, p. 20) are produced.

Numerical pedagogical representations and images

In Australia the public representation of pedagogy is largely constituted through statistical data of student learning outcomes. League tables of results and of schools are made available on a readily accessible, national website – *My School* (www.MySchool.edu.au). This website is managed by the Australian Curriculum, Assessment and Reporting Authority (ACARA). The *My School* website includes data on each Australian school regardless of the sector. These data include school demographics, class performance on national testing (NAPLAN, National Assessment Program – Literacy and Numeracy), school socio-economic data (ICSEA, Index of Community Socio-Educational Advantage) and school financial figures. ACARA suggests that the two main aspects of *My School* data – NAPLAN results and ICSEA – should be interpreted together. These tables of results and schools' data are the formatted images which are publicly available on the national website. The NAPLAN tests are carried out annually. The tables representing these test results have been made available since 2007. The data is intended to inform schools, policy makers and parents regarding the quality of each school. They are rendered through images constituted through tables with numerical data. The type of format used to show NAPLAN results is viewable by accessing the *My School* website and searching from the home page for any Australian school in the 'find a school' search box.

The viewable tables reveal how the average achievement of Year 9 students from an Australian school is compared to the average achievement of schools serving students from statistically similar backgrounds and secondly with all schools. In the instance of the case study school, the Year 9 at the project school performed below the average of similar demographic schools and significantly below the average of all schools. These on the screen images of pedagogical outcomes provide what are apparently truthful, accurate, scientific and meaningful renditions of the learning and teaching lives of participants in those classrooms. These images may have little effect on the community outside the school (Jensen 2013) but have significant effect on the teachers who, for example, can be judged for promotion on the basis of these results and for the students who are also judged four times over their schooling against national standards.

The very private performances of the young people on a literacy test or a numeracy test in their fourth year of schooling (named as Year 3 in Australia) is made public and compared with that of all Year 3 students from across the nation. These results follow the young person – attached to their bodies – moving through their school years to Year 5, Year 7 and Year 9 as they sit for the next level of testing (Wyn et al. 2014). The Year 3 teacher has the results for her class publicly available to her students, to the parents and families of her students, to her colleagues, to her principal. She is called to account for these results generated just four months into her work with these students (the national tests are carried out in May, four months after the beginning of the school year). These also serve as the public image/portrayal of her pedagogical work.

Alongside these images are similar renditions of the school socioeconomic data. The type of format used to show this data is presented in Table 6.1 below. To protect the privacy of the school, no actual data is given here. Rather a table has been created to convey the idea of the numerical image.

Table 6.1 presents how the demographic data of the case study school would be represented. The *My School* website advises these the literacy and numeracy and ICSEA tables need to be read together to appreciate the profile and comparative resources and performance of the school. In Table 6.2, the project school is identified as having a higher-than-average number of students with a lower educational advantage. The ICSEA data ranges from approximately 500, representing extremely educationally disadvantaged backgrounds, to about 1300, representing schools with students with very educationally advantaged backgrounds (ACARA 2015). The factors which are used to determine the social advantage are parents' occupation and parents' education together with school location and the number of indigenous students

Table 6.1 Type of data format: Index of Community Socio-Educational Advantage (ICSEA), Australian Curriculum, Assessment and Reporting Authority (ACARA), *My School* website

Student background 2014				
Index of Community Socio-Educational Advantage (ICSEA)				
School ICSEA value				
Average ICSEA value				
Data source				Parent Information
Distribution of students				
	Bottom quarter	Middle quarters		Top quarter
School distribution	$25+x$%	$25+z$%	$25-z$%	$25-x$%
Australian distribution	25%	25%	25%	25%

Note: Percentages are rounded and may not add to 100%.

at the school. The student population is also identified as having x% of its students having a language background other than English. The representation of these images (student performance on tests and socio-economic data) on the same site visually suggests a causal relationship between these disparate threads. They identify, in close visual proximity, the community and the performance of the students. The ownership by the public of these images provokes public response in the form of demand for increases in teacher 'quality' (Craven et al. 2014; Mockler 2013). This is often accompanied by an emphasis on teaching strategies which are as simplistic and reductionist as the data they convey – transmission strategies uninformed by the deep body of knowledge on pedagogy.

These graphical, tabulated snapshots of schooling, I argue, reduce the complex world of learning and of teaching to flat, comparative readings. Their repeated use in digital and publicly accessible form appears to render knowledge of teaching and learning accessible to all and reassure the community that schooling is manageable, controllable and ultimately simplistic, technical and should be easily improved (Lobascher 2011, p. 15–16). These readings also appear to lead to simple resolutions. This may be comforting for policy makers and the community at large. The 'answer' is as clear as the numerical image. In this way, these numerical and quick snapshots work at once as both portrayals and betrayals. Their promise of a clear resolution to a single, flat reading betrays the complex and nuanced lives which are captured in projects such as the one that is featured in this chapter.

In a recent review of public engagement with *My School*, Mockler (2013) examined thirty-four editorials in Australian newspapers focused on *My School*, published from October 2009 to August 2010. In her analysis she identified three key narratives in operation, those of distrust, choice and performance. She argued this public engagement promotes *My School* and its tables 'as the solution to problems of poor performance, "bad" schools and "bad" teachers' (Mockler 2013, p. 2).

These public portrayals cannot be dismissed, but the knowledge and beings they represent may be remade by the construction of a diverse array of pedagogical images that can then be made into public maps which do address complex relationships. It is timely to call to account the politics of representation in this hard data and ask what other images are needed or can be put to work to redress this portrayal. What could a critical cartography of classroom pedagogy offer? In the learning spaces project (Blackmore et al. 2011), the hard data from the *My School* website was a constituent in the pedagogical project which when juxtaposed against these data generated a wealth of soft pedagogical data in the form of images and student-created maps.

Merging data and new cartographies

Pedagogical readings of learning environments call upon us to read from the smallest intervals or moments of bodies reaching out to others to the wider surfaces of the classroom, to the school and to the community. A larger reading of the pedagogical images from the classrooms in the project is made available through the making of pedagogical maps. In the learning spaces project, students, teachers and researchers had photographed learning spaces. Students had also drawn a variety of maps of where they engaged in learning. This visual data of photographs and drawings is compiled here along with constructed examples of publicly available 'hard data' from Australian national testing (NAPLAN) and online school community profiles (*My School* and ICSEA) in this cartographic endeavour. The hard data images from national databases were not replaced in this cartographic work by soft data images as if a more real or more complex truth is now presented. Rather it is recognised that the hard data had already reconstituted the classroom and has its place on the map.

In assembling these data as maps, I put each piece of the data to work, plugging them in as cells creating maps which I term 'pedascapes' after

Appadurai's use of the term scape. Appadurai argued the use of the suffix 'scape'. He called up the imagined world of ethnoscapes, technoscapes, financscapes, ideoscapes and mediascapes (1990). Scapes allow us to point to the fluid, irregular shapes of landscapes which are not shaped through centre-periphery models. I call upon pedascapes to be added to our imagined worlds as deeply perspectival constructs, inflected by the historical, linguistic, and political situatedness of multiple sorts of actors in flows that are not bounded to the local or the subject but are carried within and across striated school spaces and oceans of smooth space – chaotic, undisciplined and turbulent.

The data mapping generated a series of pedascapes – one single pedascape is insufficient to engage the complexity of the pedagogical terrain and the wealth of the data. The pedascapes that are shown in this chapter are chosen to gesture towards the de/territorialisation (Deleuze & Guattari 1987, p. 142–145) that is working in and between the striated and smooth spaces of the school and of the classrooms. The pedascapes are constructed through the plugging in of hard and soft data. The plugging in of the data in a diffractive pattern does not map differences but rather maps where the effects of differences appear (Barad 2007). Following Deleuze and Guattari, the map that is discerned and evoked is 'always detachable, connectable, reversible, modifiable and has multiple entry ways and exits and its own lines of flight' (Deleuze & Guattari 1987, p. 21). The plugging in of images in maps termed 'pedascapes' provides generative mappings of classrooms which offer hope of redressing the portrayal/betrayal of current renderings. Pedascape 1, below, is offered as an introduction to the construction and format of a pedascape. A detailed explanation of the logic of a pedascape is then given in Pedascape 2.

The cells shown in Pedascape 1 (Figure 6.2) below have been chosen for their capacity to evoke the constant interchange between the striated school spaces (Deleuze & Guattari 1987) where everything is arranged and disciplined in closed systems and the smooth spaces of Amy's drawing act where everything is chaotic, sensate and undisciplined (Deleuze & Guattari 1987).

The assemblage of images and assessment data demands a reading which makes account of bodies, objects, spaces, performance and positioning. This geo-philosophical mapping calls on a pedagogical seeing which is understood through that epistemic eye after Eisner (1991), described earlier in this chapter.

I turn now to another pedascape from the case study school. In this instance I start with a discussion of each of the images and data I used to construct the pedagogical map. This pedascape provides a reading of the location of pedagogy in the school. The first data piece is a constructed table following the same format of the public image from striated spaces – data from the *My School* website.

This table is constructed to resemble part of the Index of Community Socio-Educational Advantage, as described earlier in this chapter. The profile positions the students in this school in the bottom half of the Australian community in regard to social and education advantage.

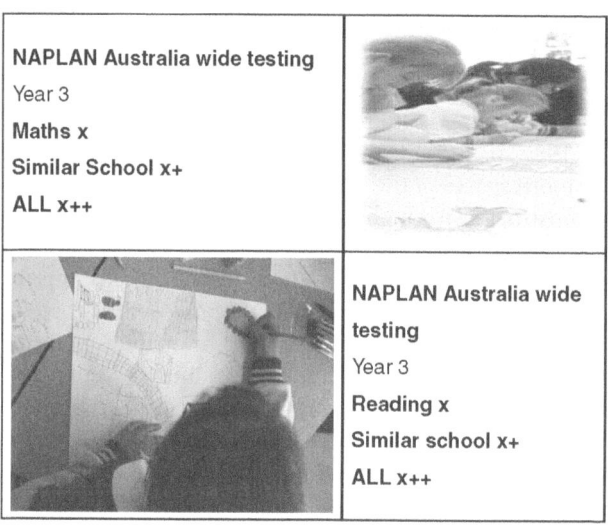

Figure 6.2 Pedascape 1: Amy's drawing, Amy's map of learning sites and constructed NAPLAN numerical image format assessment data

Table 6.2 Example of constructed table of socio-economic data

	Bottom quarter	Middle quarters		Top quarter
School distribution	$25+x\%$	$25+z\%$	$25-z\%$	$25-x\%$
Australian distribution	25%	25%	25%	25%

Note: Percentages are rounded and may not add to 100%.

The second data piece is an image of the new 'learning street' (see Figure 6.3 below). Innovative school designs often employ 'streets' privileging open massification of relationships. The streets call for bodies on the move, distanced from each other, in continuous movement. These spaces are designed for freedom of movement but also serve to facilitate surveillance. The space calls for pedagogical relationships which are en masse, moving, fleeting. On a principal-led tour of the learning streets, the principal claimed that in the street everyone can be seen and no one can hide. The design is reminiscent of a panopticon. Foucault (1975) argued that this design could be used for any group that needs to be kept under control. The image 'captures' the streets' relationships with bodies and objects.

In the third image plugged into the pedascape (see Figure 6.3), two students take themselves off to pods – intimate sites of pedagogical

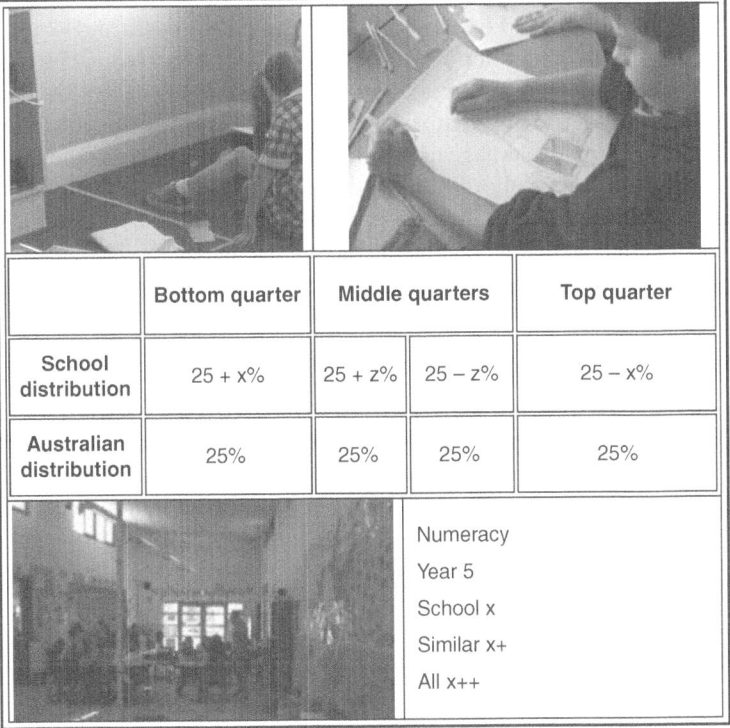

	Bottom quarter	Middle quarters		Top quarter
School distribution	25 + x%	25 + z%	25 – z%	25 – x%
Australian distribution	25%	25%	25%	25%
		Numeracy Year 5 School x Similar x+ All x++		

Figure 6.3 Pedascape 2

encounter – bodies reaching out. The action is in the middle – in the pod. The bodies, books and shelves reach out holding each other in pedagogical intra-actions.

Finally, I plug in Brody's map of learning sites of the school, which takes us out to the grounds with no rooms or streets but paths, ovals and trees. I take these images and plug them into a pedascape, mapping – not tracing – the pedagogical world of the school (see Figure 6.3).

Putting to work doubled consciousness (Mitchell 2005), the bodies and objects are read as reaching out to each other. The focus shifts from the buildings themselves. The rapid movement in the centre of action in the middle of the learning street draws attention from the walls surrounding the action and from the hard data representing the action. The school building is never a tabula rasa. It is not a passive surface on which life is played out. The spatial grammar of the school buildings needs to be read as a way of reading and writing the school body. The hard work and the many hopes of the building reform and the data on school body and student outcomes need to be read as they intersect with other pedagogical bodies – students, teachers, spaces and objects. The pedascape makes a double contribution. On the one hand, the hard data from the *My School* website does not give access to the lived experience of pedagogical engagements. Placing images from the classroom next to the numerical image makes this experience visible. On the other hand, the classroom photos alone do not evidence the constraints and the invisible presence of the national data comparisons. The classroom photos gain from being positioned next to those numerical images.

In these mapping moves, pedascapes call pedagogy to account, as it contemporaneously inhabits the public spaces of the school buildings, locations and national performances and the intimate and smooth space of bodies reaching out to each other. In these pedascapes the students are publicly located. In the cell in the lower left of the pedascape in Figure 6.3, the open learning streets with their surveillance mirror the clean, defined, striated data from national school websites. The maps perform the constant interaction between the striated school and classroom spaces, where everything is arranged and disciplined in closed systems; and the smooth spaces of a child's drawing time, where everything is chaotic, sensate and undisciplined.

Maps reveal the smooth and the striated spaces of the learning environments. For Deleuze and Guattari (1987, p. 492), the smooth space is occupied by intensities and events. It is haptic rather than optic. The striated space is a measured space created through the effects of technological mediation resulting in mathematical quantities as opposed to qualities. NAPLAN and *My School* are the most recent state machines in Australia on the already striated spaces of our official learning environments. The mapping analysis – with its identification of longitude and latitude of the striated spaces, its contours of smooth space and striated space, the circling of hot pedagogical spots, and the layering of mapping artefacts and images – reveals the flows between teacher, students, communities and policy makers.

Currently the pedagogical encounter is often reduced to outcomes evidenced by, at worst, school-based test results or, at best, tracking through images of classroom behaviour patterns. Generative pedagogical readings of learning environments in pedascapes call upon us to read from *the* smallest intervals or moments of bodies reaching out to others to the statistical reading of national test results. These readings must follow these flows capturing the bodily between. I have argued here that the readings of these images can be made, represented and communicated through the making of pedagogical maps. In an uptake of Appadurai's (1996) use of 'scape', I have termed these pedagogical maps as 'pedascapes'. In a Deleuzian (1987) reading, these flows are discernible within and across school spaces.

The creation of these pedascapes involved the use of photographs produced by researchers, by students and by teachers. I have zoomed in to one student's map of her school life, with 'street views' of her moments of her own mapmaking, moments with the other and then placed these against overhead maps with hotspots on images from the school gate travelling out to the neighbourhood. Mitchell's (2005) suggestions for reading images were taken up, and this question was kept in the forefront: has this work allowed us to maintain an imaginative state of awareness while at the same time a capacity to question their value and generative possibility? The analysis of images in this project insisted on a 'seeing' of pedagogical matter-energies between bodies. As the bodies of the learner and the teacher extend past their apparent boundaries, these pedagogical connections are felt by others and seen by others. In this reading, through Deleuze an emphasis on the interplay of the striated and smooth spaces of classrooms makes visible the relational pedagogy which is betrayed by attention to the instructional pedagogy complicit in striated spaces.

Pedascapes offer an alternative logic of pedagogical understanding and representation. As MacLure (2013) has argued about her cabinet of curiosities, this logic is 'one which allows for both the discernment of order and pattern, *and* is attuned to the lively excess that always exceeds capture by structure and representation, leaving openings where something new or something else might issue' (p. 229, original emphasis). These pedascapes are attempts to make pedagogy intelligible to the world. Images of both hard public data and soft classroom data have been used here to argue what cartographies made from these assemblages can do to address the pedagogical silences in the public portrayal of schools.

Note

1. These images are viewable as figures 13 and 14 at http://www.learningspaces.edu.au/schools/tlsm/ (CREFI 2011b)

References

ACARA (2015). Measuring Socio-educational Advantage. http://www.acara.edu.au/verve/_resources/Guide_to_understanding_ICSEA_values.pdf#search=guide%20to%20understanding%20icsea.
Appadurai, A. (1990). Disjuncture and Difference in the Global Cultural Economy. *Public Culture, 2*(2), 1–24.
Barad, K. (2007). *Meeting the Universe Halfway: Quantum Physics and the Entanglement of Matter and Meaning*. Durham and London: Duke University Press.
Blackmore, J., Bateman, D., Cloonan, A., Dixon, M., Loughlin, J., O'Mara, J., & Senior, K. (2011). *Innovative Learning Environments Research Study*. Victoria: Department of Education and Early Childhood Development.
Bloom, D. (2006). *Measuring Global Educational Progress*. Cambridge: American Academy of Arts and Science.
Clarke, D. (2009). Optimising the Use of Available Technology to Support International Collaborative Research in Mathematics Classrooms. In T. Janík & T. Seidel (Eds), *The Power of Video Studies in Investigating Teaching and Learning in the Classroom* (pp. 39–60). Münster, New York: Waxmann.
Craven, G., Beswick, K., Fleming, J., Fletcher, T., Green M., Jensen, B., Leinonen, E., & Rickards, F. (2014). *Action Now: Classroom Ready Teachers – Teacher Education Ministerial Advisory Group*. Canberra: Commonwealth of Australia.
CREFI [Centre for Research in Educational Futures and Innovations]. (2011a). Deakin University [Web portal]. Accessed May 15, 2015. http://www.learningspaces.edu.au/
CREFI. (2011b). Deakin University [Web page]. Accessed May 15, 2015. http://www.learningspaces.edu.au/schools/tlsm/
Deleuze, G., & Guattari, F. A. (1987). *A Thousand Plateaus: Capitalism and Schizophrenia*. Minneapolis: University of Minnesota Press.
Dixon, M. (2008). Images of Teacher and Student Positionings: From Speech Act to Body Act. In J. Moss (Ed.) *Researching Education – Digitally, Spatially, Visually* (pp. 87–106). Netherlands: Sense Publication.
Eisner, E. (1991). *The Enlightened Eye*. New York: Macmillan.
Foucault, M. (1975). *Discipline and Punish: The Birth of the Prison*. UK: Penguin Books.

Jensen, B. (2013). *The Myth of Markets in Schools*. Grattan Institute Report No. 20137. Melbourne: Grattan Institute.

Lobascher, S. (2011). What are the Potential Impacts of High-stakes Testing on Literacy Education in Australia? *Australian Journal of Language & Literacy 34*(2), pp. 9–19.

Luke, A., Freebody, P., Shun, L., & Gopinathan, S. (2005). Towards Research-Based Innovation and Reform: Singapore schooling in transition. *Asia Pacific Journal of Education, 25*(1), 5–28.

MacLure, M. (2013). The Wonder of Data. *Cultural Studies – Critical Methodologies, 13*(4), 228–232. DOI: 10.1177/1532708613487863.

Mazzei, L. (2013) Materialist Mappings of Knowing in Being: Researchers Constituted in the Production of Knowledge. *Gender and Education, 25*(6). DOI: 10.1080/09540253.2013.824072.

Mitchell, W. J. (2005). *What Do Pictures Want? The Lives and Loves of Images*. Chicago: University of Chicago Press.

Mockler, N. (2013). Reporting the 'Education Revolution': My School.edu.au in the Print Media. *Discourse: Studies in the Cultural Politics of Education, 34*(1), 1–16.

My School®. (2015). Profiles of Australian Schools. Australian Curriculum, Assessment and Reporting Authority. Accessed May 2015. http://www.My School.edu.au/

OECD [Organisation for Economic Co-operation and Development]. (2014). PISA-Program for International Student Assessment 2012 Results in Focus: What 15-Year-Olds Know and What They Can Do with What They Know. Paris: OECD.

Pinar, W., & Irwin, R. (Eds) (2005). *Curriculum in a New Key – The Collected Works of Ted T. Aoki*. Mahwah, NJ: Lawrence Erlbaum.

Roy, K. (2003). *Teachers in Nomadic Spaces: Deleuze and Curriculum*. New York: Peter Lang.

Stigler, J. W., Gonzalez, P., Kawanaka, T., Knoll, S., & Serran, A. (1999). *The TIMSS Videotape Classroom Study: Methods and Findings from an Explanatory Research Project on Eighth-Grade Mathematics Instruction in Germany, Japan and the United States* (No. NCES99–074). Washington, DC: US Government Printing Office.

Wyn, J., Turnball, M., & Grimshaw, L. (2014). *The Experience of Education: The Impacts of High Stakes Testing on School Students and Their Families*. Major Reports and Working Papers, Sydney, Australia, Whitlam Institute.

Zembylas, M. (2007). The Spectres of Bodies and Affects in the Classroom: A Rhizo-ethological Approach. *Pedagogy, Culture & Society, 15*, 19–35.

7
Using Film to Show and Tell: Studying/Changing Pedagogical Practices

Pat Thomson and Christine Hall

Many educational researchers want to do research which has an influence on practice. Much educational research is driven by a commitment to making a difference for children and young people, rather than simply making a contribution to scholarly knowledge (Griffths 1998). Such contributions can be, for example, analysis of what happens in educational settings and why, evaluation of interventions and innovations, and testing new approaches to teaching or new ways to understand educational practices. This chapter addresses another possibility – the development, through research, of websites and film intended to support teachers' learning.

This chapter reports on two research projects where film was used as the primary means of showing alternative pedagogical practices. The films are housed on project-based websites. The intended audience is teachers, both pre- and in-service, and artists who work with them.

The chapter discusses film in educational research and then provides snapshots of the two projects and the ways in which film was used in them. It then addresses the notion of pedagogical film and considers the kinds of intellectual resources that might be used to underpin their construction. The chapter concludes by suggesting that using film for pedagogical purposes means going beyond the visual methods literatures. It begins, however, by setting the context and explaining the motivation for pedagogically oriented visual research.

Teachers' work and learning: the English context

Since the mid-1980s, educational policy makers in England have undertaken a series of radical reforms. These are well documented and are generally understood to involve the transformation of a school system from being state-funded, -provided and -regulated to one which is marketised, privatised and contractualised (e.g. Ball 2008; Chitty 2014; Gunter et al. 2007; Tomlinson 2001; Whitty, Power & Halpin 1998).

Policy makers' concerns about the quality and equity of schooling have generally resulted in interventions which have increased the use of more prescriptive pedagogical approaches and reduced the possibility of teachers making decisions about content, methods and assessment (Gerwitz, Mahony, Hextall & Cribb 2009). This has played out in teacher education programs which have increasingly focused on 'delivery' of an existing national curriculum, rather than building a base of pedagogical content knowledge which can be used to both adapt and invent (Hulme & Menter 2012). Some schools, however, have been able to exercise more control over what they do than others (Ball, Maguire & Braun 2011; Hart, Drummond, Swann & Peacock 2012).

The rationale for these changes has been the continued gap in learning outcomes between students from wealthy homes and children and young people from low-income neighbourhoods. The policy problem is generally presented as one of poor teaching and school effectiveness rather than wider social structures and inadequate public policy (Thrupp & Wilmott 2003). 'Progressivism' is continually held up as a major blockage to reform. Researchers wanting to make a difference to the inequitable outcomes of schooling of these young people run the risk of significant political/media derision if their suggestions do not mesh with official directions (Jones 2003; Wallace 1993).[1]

In this context, it is crucial for educational researchers who go against the policy grain to offer 'evidence' for their proposals for alternative practice. We decided to work with film as a means of 'showing', not simply telling, what is pedagogically possible. Our aim was not simply to offer descriptions of alternative pedagogies, but to show what these looked like in and as practice. We wanted to offer rich descriptions and images of teachers, children and young people engaged in meaningful and challenging work that is also creative, innovative and pleasurable. We also wanted to avoid the common scenario of telling teachers what to do; instead, we offered them resources that they could use to do their own school-based curriculum innovation.

Using film in educational research

Our research was informed initially by visual research literatures.

Visual research is increasingly used in the education field, and it now has a place in education research methods textbooks. However, the focus is predominantly on still images. There is less methodological discussion about, and empirical reporting of, research using moving images. Those interested in film and video have to turn to more general visual studies literatures, and to anthropology, where ethnographers have been making films for as long as the discipline has been practised. However, the ways in which anthropologists have used and theorised film have changed significantly (Ruby 2000).

Early ethnographic film sought to produce 'truths' about cultures through 'factual' recordings. The films were both raw data to be watched and analysed, and also representations which could be used to illustrate and evidence 'findings' (Chaplin 1994). Today, social science ethnographers reject these premises and practices. Instead, filming is understood to be the product of a researcher's discursively positioned actions – material is selected, framed, emphasised, edited, sequenced and juxtaposed and manipulated. Analysis has already begun the moment the camera is turned on and the researcher begins to make decisions about what to shoot. This makes the use of professional film-makers particularly problematic, as researchers essentially hand over to another the responsibilities for making key analytic choices (Collier & Collier 1986). The separation of data from representation has also begun to collapse, as selection of shots and angles is also made with a view to an end product (El Guindi 2004; Emmison & Smith 2001; Harper 2013; Pink, Kurti & Afonso 2004). These understandings have also led to filming becoming much more integrated into sensory and embodied ethnographic processes of observing, participating, and making meaning (Pink 2006).

Ethnographers are highly aware of the need to be ethical in their practices and reflexive about their own positioning in order to take account of the implicit constructions they might bring to the process of 'seeing' (Jensson 2009). The considerable disquiet about the Othering capacities of the ethnographic gaze has radically changed practices related to moving image (Madison 2011). To counteract the tendency to exoticise their subject matter, many researchers now adopt participatory production approaches; decisions about what images to shoot and how to put them together are shared between researchers and research participants (Barbash & Taylor 1997).

Educational researchers interested in film have taken up these understandings (Prosser 1998; Thomson 2008). There are also now a handful of texts which offer approaches to participatory film-making in educational settings (de Lange, Mitchell & Stuart 2007). Haw and Hadfield (2012), for example, propose five video modalities while Mitchell and de Lange (2011) have perfected a one-day workshop which allows participants to shoot and make a film in order to produce a strong collective response to a pressing social issue.

Our research was concerned with how film, as research data/analysis/representation, might be used for pedagogic purposes. While film has often been used to communicate the 'results' of researcher analyses, recognition of both its limitations and advantages has been growing. Film tends to be a poor medium for showing generalisations and patterns, but it can provide unique insights into individual experiences and interactions (MacDougall 2012). It can represent bodies, and bodies in motion together, in ways that words cannot (Bates 2013). The ways in which it mobilises viewers' imaginations and senses allows film to convey aesthetic qualities and emotions that printed texts struggle to achieve (Jones 2006).

In this chapter, we are interested in how our aim to produce pedagogic resources for teachers shaped what we did throughout the research. We now report our two projects indicating key decisions we made related to this endpoint.

Project one: Signature Pedagogies

Creative Partnerships (CP) is an arts and educational reform program which ran in England from 2002–2011. Between 2002 and 2011, CP worked intensively with over 5000 schools, 90,000 teachers and over 1 million young people. Of the total funding, 70% went to support creative practitioners, primarily arts and arts-based organisations, to work with schools and teachers. This collaborative work was understood to have a range of benefits for students, including the growth of positive personal attitudes, behaviours which supported skills development and knowledge acquisition in 'creativity' as well as in other subject areas; and social benefits for groups of young people, classrooms, schools and communities, including the development of students' leadership and citizenship, and better attainment in the mandated curriculum (Parker 2013). Working with artists was also to provide new strategies for teachers to use and adapt (Galton 2010) – CP was intended to improve the quality of teaching and learning in schools. One of three 'legacy' projects funded to promote learnings from the program, the Signature Pedagogies project offered twelve case studies of creative practitioners at work with children and young people (Thomson, Hall, Jones & Sefton Green 2012).

About the project

The idea of Signature Pedagogies comes from research which explores how differing disciplines in universities educate doctoral students (Golde 2007; Guring, Chick & Haynie 2009; Shulman 2005). Researchers found some distinctive pedagogical disciplinary practices, such as the field trip in geography and studio practice in architecture. We would add the following examples to the list of specific arts-based practices: the workshop in creative writing, the 'crit' session in contemporary art, the vocal warm-up in singing and so on. These distinctive practices are intended to do more than inculcate knowledge; they also set out deliberately to teach 'habits of mind', the ways of *thinking*, *doing* and *being* a member of a disciplinary community. Signature pedagogies induct students into a 'profession' and its traditions, conventions and mores. Our aim was to ascertain the signature pedagogies of artists working in schools.

We selected twelve schools on the basis of their involvement in the CP-supported 'Schools of Creativity' network, assuming that in this way we would capture experiences of working with artists who were already embedded in the school. There were six primary and six secondary; in primary schools, we observed three story makers, one story teller, one dancer and one visual and movement artist. In the secondary schools, we observed work on radio, physical theatre, visual art, dance, media and creative activities such as problem-solving. We used observation and interview to develop rich descriptions of creative practice. Observation was conducted in two ways: (1) through researcher visits in which detailed field notes were kept, and (2) by filming two days when creative practitioners were working with students. Creative practitioners were interviewed both formally and informally.

Film was used in two ways in this project – as a means of generating data for analysis and as a way to communicate the research results.

Generating and analysing film data

The researchers worked in two teams, one based in London and the other in the Midlands: we were the latter. The Midlands team worked with professional film-makers, since our goal was to produce high-quality footage able to be used for professional development, as outlined earlier. They always used two cameras: one static camera on a tripod giving a wide-angle view and one handheld camera. They also had a handheld boom microphone. Sometimes the researchers would also use a flip video or digital camera to record small snippets of activity, particularly on days when the film-makers were not present. The London team worked with a young film-maker who used a range of borrowed equipment; he offered footage from a single, handheld camera.

The Midlands professional film-makers provided us with numbered, low-resolution DVDs of sustained footage of each session. They often missed with the handheld camera what we saw as key moments, but the wide-lens continuous footage meant that we generally had a view of what was happening in the class as a whole. The London young film-maker gave us a hard disc which contained over 700 short clips in a range of different formats. Our first task was to give this to the professional film-makers to get into a common format. However, as the short clips had already been pre-edited in the filming they were much less useful to us than the sustained footage; we were often mystified about why particular things had been filmed.

The film of artists at work allowed us to watch sessions repeatedly and was particularly good for capturing a range of non-verbal interactions which were more difficult to record in conventional field notes. It also allowed us to watch each other's field visits. However, we had over seventy hours of footage. While we could watch the film on our computers, this process was very time-consuming. We had to note key pedagogical strategies used during a session, referring to both field notes and film, compare these across artists to find commonalities, and then thematise and categorise the strategies.

We brought this analysis into conversation with our previous studies where we had also observed artists working and eventually arrived at our theorisation of signature pedagogies – an ontological and axiological platform underpinning a repertoire of strategies. We saw this as a heuristic.

Heuristics are not blueprints, instructions on how to do it, nor best practice. A heuristic is generally understood as an aid to learning and problem-solving. Because it is not a formula, the heuristic can be seen, by those seeking foolproof approaches, as being prone to error. However, a heuristic is intended to act as a stimulus to intelligent action and thus it is congruent with a view of teaching and learning which not only acknowledges but also relies on the thoughtful agency of the user. Thus, pedagogical heuristics are intended for teachers as capable professionals; their purpose is to show:

1. how particular principles can be made practical, and thus
2. act as a stimulus for adaptation, extension and re-design.

We wanted to check our heuristic with the artists before we embarked on building a website. We invited them to a workshop where we presented our theorisation of their work. The professional film-makers filmed the day's events and this footage also became available for use in the final publication.

Using film to communicate our 'results'

We pitched our project to CP as one which would produce materials for use in professional development. Their expectation, and ours, was always that we would produce a website which used film as illustrative material (www.signaturepedagogies.org.uk). But like many research websites, there was a significant time gap between the aim and its realisation. While we knew what we wanted to say on the website, and could work with a learning technologist to design a relatively straightforward architecture, we still had to select the exemplars of film which would go on it. With the help of a research assistant, a shortlist of over 200 clips was selected. The film-makers then provided these in a high-quality format, and they were all duly uploaded onto a Vimeo channel. We then spent two days watching and discussing the corpus of clips in order to make a final selection.

Our clips were designed to support and evidence the heuristic of signature pedagogies. We looked for clips which were not simply illustrations – ornaments for a written text which can stand without them. We wanted to find clips that were exemplars – moving images which related to our written text and showed how the practices actually occurred. We also hoped that some of the clips might act as mnemonics – they would encourage teachers to remember something similar that they had seen, read or experienced (see Elkins 2013, pp. 26–27, for a discussion of these three image types).

We have now worked with teachers using the website, as has Creativity, Culture and Education, the parent organisation of CP which now runs professional development programs around the world. It is also being used in pre-service and Masters-level courses in our own and other institutions. Our experience in using the materials suggests that while the overall signature pedagogies theorisation is available as both a report and as website sections, teachers benefit from having the framework explained face to face.

We have noted that many teachers are not used to watching film of children and young people to observe the finer details of what they are doing. While many researchers are accustomed to this kind of fine-grained observation, it is not something that busy teachers, with large classes and demands for pace and coverage of curriculum, have time to practice. While they are attuned to spot the child who is having difficulty, is off task, or who is likely to cause trouble, they are much less familiar with watching to see what learning is on offer and what is being taken up and how. We suspect that while a website can offer some pointers to what a clip might show, this does not come near what can be achieved through a shared 'live' viewing and face-to-face discussion.

Project two: Get Wet

The Get Wet project began at the invitation of the Papplewick Pumping Station Trust. Located on the rural outskirts of the city of Nottingham, Papplewick is a magnificent Victorian water pumping station.[2] The charitable trust that runs the station has decided that it does not want to simply be a museum but has ambitions to become a national centre for water education. Papplewick obtained funding[3] for a two-year project that would develop water literacy resources for schools.

Get Wet was a theoretical continuation of the Signature Pedagogies project. It took the learning from that project – the signature pedagogies – but added to it more substantive disciplinary knowledges and expertise in action research. The Get Wet research team consisted of two action researchers and two teacher educators from the University of Nottingham, five artists and the teachers of four classes from four Nottingham schools – two primary and two secondary. Some teacher education students were also involved and a PhD intern funded by the university conducted additional research. Like the Signature Pedagogies project the goal was not simply to design new curriculum in schools but also to provide website resources that would stimulate other teachers to do likewise.

Using film to document the process of action research

Action research typically uses cycles of action and reflection in order to generate new understandings. Rather than see action as end to a research process and using the results of research, action research generates data through action. That action is then the basis for critical reflection which informs the next action cycle (Kemmis & McTaggart 1993). Versions of action research are often used in school reform initiatives, and they can have a distinctly instrumentalist flavour, particularly at a time when policy is driven by the notion that all that needs to happen is to find out 'what works' and apply it more widely (McIntosh 2010). This was not the kind of action research in which we were interested. We wanted to use a process which was open-ended and which supported professional learning.

The first cycle of Get Wet action research began through engagement with an art installation; this encouraged children, university researchers, artists and teachers to ask and share questions about water. Teachers then worked with artists to design a set of activities around common questions. The water curriculum was interdisciplinary, always including art, literacy and another curriculum area. Both primary schools added science, geography and history, while one secondary focused on geography and the other on history.

The second action research cycle worked similarly to the first but placed more emphasis on systematic teacher planning. Our reflections on the first cycle suggested that while teachers were very familiar with planning a series of activities for children, they were less accustomed to thinking about planning using both macro- and meso-level concepts as their guide. This absence indicated that the teachers' initial teacher education and in-service learning had emphasised teaching methods at the expense of disciplinary knowledges. Our focus on school-based, thematic cross-curriculum work needed to both support and evidence challenging and robust student learning. We therefore developed an activity-theory-based conceptual mapping tool for this purpose.

Cycles of action research rely on good records of events and of ongoing reflection. We decided that using film and still images would be part of this ongoing documentation process. One of the artists working on the project was a film-maker, so he took on a dual role – working with teachers and students to use image and film as part of the curriculum development plus documenting the work using still images and film. At the end of each action research cycle, teachers, students and some of the artists worked together to make one narrative film from this footage about what they had done and achieved in the year. This was part of the end-of-cycle reflection process. Supplementary films focused on particular aspects of the project – for example, an analysis of student writing, or a report of the field trip to Papplewick to demonstrate the introduction of historical material through drama.

Film as a means of communication

As was the case with the Signature Pedagogies project, the films have become part of a website (www.getwet.org.uk). The website is intended to be both a record of the project and to act as a resource for teachers who want to visit Papplewick and/or to teach about water. We also hope that by showing examples of what some teachers have done with their classes, potential visitors will get the point that visits to the museum can be more than a day out and that they need to be built into a curriculum module.

The Get Wet films differ from the Signature Pedagogies clips in that they are digital stories. Get Wet films are all made with a voice-over; in many cases the images illustrate and evidence what the narrator is saying. The films also use captioned slides as a means of breaking up events and signalling their content. These films are deliberately constructed to guide the viewer and can be watched and understood without reference to the website.

We think about these digital films as being more than exemplars and mnemonics, although they are intended as both. Like the clips in the Signature Pedagogies project they are also intended to support an argument for an alternative approach to teaching, learning and assessment. We hope that the films might variously be:

- intelligent argument – images which add to a case being made
- interruptions – images which jolt us out of our everyday and force us to stop the usual flow of thinking
- reminders of an argument – images which do not in themselves contain, suggest, embody or propose arguments but simply prompt a memory of an argument
- prompts to slow argument – images that require us to stop to think about what is being put to us (Elkins 2013, pp. 32–50).

Our experience of working with these films is that they do encourage teachers to think about how they might either change their approach to teaching about water, or consider what is involved in planning, teaching and assessing cross-curriculum modules. Because of their narrative structure, which supports and strengthens the images, the films seem to be more persuasive than the Signature Pedagogies films: they appear to have more argumentative take by and in themselves, and they are less reliant on written text and on face-to-face discussion. However, like the Signature Pedagogies heuristic clips, they do appear to have greater effect when they are used in group discussions and in conjunction with written material.

Pedagogical film – beyond representation of results

Our two projects were not simply research to add to knowledge. They were both designed to also make a difference, by providing resources to change practice. As we explained at the beginning of the chapter, in times when policy agendas appear to close down opportunities for teachers to be activist professionals within an activist profession (Sachs 2003), exemplars, heuristics and stories of reform can act as reservoirs of hope and reasons for optimism (Wrigley, Thomson & Lingard 2011). This aim caused us to think beyond the question of representation, as it is most often discussed in the visual research methods literatures. We found ourselves going to other literatures in order to think about the kinds of choices that we had to make. We also enlisted a learning technologist to help us with website constructions.

Gillian Rose (2014) has recently addressed the question of the limitations of visual research methods literatures. She argues that discussions of visual research methods are unhelpfully separated from discussions of visual culture. These are not distinct, she suggests, but they converge. In order to make this case, Rose draws on the works of visual culture researchers, Actor Network theory, social semiotics and her own discipline of geography to argue that visual research methods make the social visible, that research participants are rarely constituted as already competent in visual cultures, and that the 'inscriptions' made through visual research are inherently unstable (p. 36). Rose argues that visual research methods in fact *perform* visual culture, producing images which

> may be representational tools that carry significant meaning; they may be tools for thinking with; they may invoke the ineffable; they may be sent as messages; remembered forever; deleted after a moment. (p. 41)

Rose suggests that advocates of visual research methods need to look to other literatures to help them focus on what their visual texts do in the world, how they are taken up, by whom and in what contexts. This is our orientation to thinking about the image-based work we have undertaken.

In this concluding section, we offer four initial contributions for a set of 'thinking tools' to ground and guide pedagogically oriented, image-based educational research.

The film-maker

We understand the process of producing 'exemplar and mnemonic' pedagogical research films to be both of the following:

- Authoring – we have responsibilities to those about whom we make texts, we bring our own positioning to the process, we make aesthetic decisions about the ways in which our texts are constructed (Geertz 1988). These are familiar concerns to visual researchers.
- Designing – we bring existing meaning-making resources and put them into new configurations in order to accomplish particular tasks. We note here the possible usefulness of Kress and Van Leeuwen (2006), social semioticians, who have developed a grammar of for multimodal texts. Visual and multimodal grammar is not widely considered in discussions of visual research methods; where it is considered, it is often restricted to questions of analysis, rather than seen as also being applicable to the production of texts. But questions of perspective, framing composition – where images are located in relation to others, the size of images, navigational choices for example – are important when considering how readers will encounter and use film.

The audience for the work

Making and using films on multimedia websites oriented to teacher learning is not the same as representing and communicating research results to a general public. We are making films for a particular audience. We are guided, therefore – in our choice of shot, selection of clip, inclusions and exclusions during editing, the addition of captions and voice-over, and what these say – by our understandings of the context in which they will be shown. In our case our choice of film was framed by our understandings of the positioning of teachers by current policy. We aimed to provide evidence, exemplars and heuristics that would 'speak back' to policy, and to offer not only hope but also directions that teachers might take up.

Teacher learning

Making film for pedagogic purpose must be underpinned by a theory of learning; in our case, teacher learning.

It is not particularly contentious to suggest that children-as-learners construct their own understandings through activities, texts, languages, experiences and narratives (Dewey 1938; Freire 1972; Vygotsky 1978). Children are active in the process. The task of the teacher is to design a curriculum in which knowledges and skills, texts, resources, activities and experiences are scaffolded, paced and sequenced in ways that allow learners to engage with them (Bernstein 2000). This can be seen as a linguistically and visually saturated, socially and culturally framed 'offer' with particular 'affordances' that learners have some agency in deciding what to take up, when and how (Carlson & Apple 1998; Leach & Moon 2008). This approach to learning is one which, inter alia, rejects the notion of the learner as tabula rasa, teaching as 'delivery' of content and skills from the teacher to the student, and learning as a cause-and-effect process (Gonzales, Moll & Amanti 2005; Hayes, Mills, Christie & Lingard 2005). However, in England, this approach is not always the one that is taken in relation to teacher learning; teachers are often on the receiving end of professional learning that consists of one-off didactic sessions, or scripted courses tightly associated with new policy or syllabus (Cordingley 2005). Thinking of the film as an 'offer' with 'affordances', as a 'resource' for professional activation, positions researchers to consider carefully both the content and narrative of their films. They/we aim to show and tell, but not to dictate. They/we want to encourage, provoke, inform and support teacher learning.

Film-making

Educational researchers making films also need to understand something themselves about the craft. It is, as we have suggested, insufficient to work with professional film-makers. In order to produce images, the researchers need already to be thinking about possible finished films. This requires some understandings of the production and reception of film texts.

It is non-contentious to argue that readers and viewers of texts construct their own meanings from their reading and viewing. A book, website or film can be understood as involving 'production, text and reception' (Holub 1984). Because texts do not have fixed meanings, it might be surmised that text producers cannot do anything to help their reception. No matter what the text producer intends, the reader/viewer will make what they want of it. However, writers, film-makers and artists do steer their audiences. They do this through their text design decisions – one only has to think of the ways in which point-of-view camera shots, music scores and sequencing are used in film to see how a textual 'offer' is made. These are the artistic equivalents to teaching choices about, for example, choice of texts, design of activities, pacing and sequencing.

Films for teacher learning then need to consider how to 'steer' their viewers using this artistic repertoire. However, while some discussions of film production can be found in the visual methods literatures, there is very little about artistic steerage in the educational visual methods literatures. There is a considerable body of work that can be called on here – from film production theory, to learning science, to data visualisation. We cannot claim to have engaged with all of this literature, but we know that we will need to if we want to keep working with film.

In conclusion

We have suggested in this chapter that knowing at the outset that the likely outcome of a research project is the production of pedagogic film positions the researcher throughout as simultaneously researcher and film-maker. This aim guides every aspect of data generation and analysis, as well as being important at the final stage of communication of results. Understandings of both pedagogy and moving image production must be harnessed in order to produce multimedia resources designed to support teachers' professional learning. We propose that there is insufficient discussion of these issues in the visual research methods literatures and this remains an area to be developed in the future.

Notes

1. For an example, see http://www.independent.co.uk/news/education/education-news/what-is-the-blob-and-why-is-michael-gove-comparing-his-enemies-to-an-unbeatable-scifi-mound-of-goo-which-once-battled-steve-mcqueen-9115600.html.
2. With its original gleaming brass James Watt beam engines, fully functional, coal-fired steam boilers, ornate filigree brass work and stained glass ornamentation, Papplewick is widely regarded as the finest water pumping station in Europe. See the architectural film of the station: www.getwet.org.uk
3. Get Wet was funded by Esmee Fairbairn and the Garfield Weston Trust.

References

Ball, S. (2008). *The Education Debate*. Bristol: Policy Press.
Ball, S., Maguire, M., & Braun, A. (2011). *How Schools Do Policy: Policy Enactments in Secondary Schools*. London: Routledge.

Barbash, I., & Taylor, L. (1997). *Cross-Cultural Filmmaking: A Handbook for Making Documentary and Ethnographic Films and Videos*. University of California Press.
Bates, C. (2013). Video Diaries: Audio-visual Research Methods and the Elusive Body. *Visual Studies, 28*(1), 29–37.
Bernstein, B. (2000). *Pedagogy, Symbolic Control and Identity* (2nd ed.). London: Rowman & Littlefield.
Carlson, D., & Apple, M. (Eds). (1998). *Power/Knowledge/Pedagogy*. Boulder, CO: Westview Press.
Chaplin, E. (1994). *Sociology and Visual Representation*. London and New York: Routledge.
Chitty, C. (2014). *Education Policy in Britain* (3rd ed.). London: Palgrave Macmillan.
Collier, J., & Collier, M. (1986). *Visual Anthropology: Photography as a Research Method*. Flagstaff, NM: University of New Mexico Press.
Cordingley, P. (2005). *The Impact of Collaborative Continuing Professional Development*. London: EPPI-Centre, Institute of Education.
de Lange, N., Mitchell, C., & Stuart, J. (Eds) (2007). *Putting People in the Picture: Visual Methodologies for Social Change*. Amsterdam: Sense Publishers.
Dewey, J. (1938). *Experience and Education* (1963 ed.). New York: Collier Books.
El Guindi, F. (2004). *Visual Anthropology*. Thousand Oaks: Sage.
Elkins, J. (2013). An Introduction to the Visual as Argument. In J. Elkins, K. McGuire, M. Burns, A. Chester, & J. Kuennen (Eds), *Theorising Visual Studies: Writing Through the Discipline* (pp. 25–61). New York: Routledge.
Emmison, M., & Smith, P. (2001). *Researching the Visual*. Thousand Oaks: Sage.
Freire, P. (1972). *Pedagogy of the Oppressed*. UK: Penguin.
Galton, M. (2010). Going with the Flow or Back to Normal? The Impact of Creative Practitioners in Schools and Classrooms. *Cambridge Journal of Education, 25*(4), 355–375.
Geertz, C. (1988). *Works and Lives: The Anthropologist as Author* (1994 ed.). Stanford, CA: Stanford University Press.
Gerwitz, S., Mahony, P., Hextall, I., & Cribb, A. (Eds) (2009). *Changing Teacher Professionalism: International Trends, Challenges and Ways Forward*. London: Routledge.
Golde, C. (2007). Signature Pedagogies in Doctoral Education: Are They Adaptable to the Preparation of Education Researchers? *Educational Researcher, 36*(6), 344–351.
Gonzales, N., Moll, L., & Amanti, C. (2005). *Funds of Knowledge*. Mahwah, NJ: Lawrence Erlbaum.
Griffiths, M. (1998). *Educational Research for Social Justice: Getting off the Fence*. Buckingham: Open University Press.
Gunter, H., Rayner, S., Butt, G., Fielding, A., Lance, A., & Thomas, H. (2007). Transforming the School Workforce: Perspectives on School Reform in England. *Journal of Educational Change, 8*(1), 25–39.
Guring, R. A. R., Chick, N., & Haynie, A. (Eds) (2009). *Exploring Signature Pedagogies: Approaches to Teaching Disciplinary Habits of Mind*. Sterling, VA: Stylus.
Harper, D. (2013). *Visual Sociology*. London: Routledge.
Hart, S., Drummond, M. J., Swann, M., & Peacock, A. (2012). *Creating Learning without Limits*. London: Open University Press.

Haw, K., & Hadfield, M. (2012). *Video in Social Science Research: Functions and Forms*. London: Routledge.
Hayes, D., Mills, M., Christie, P., & Lingard, B. (2005). *Teachers and Schooling: Making a Difference. Productive Pedagogies, Assessment and Performance*. Sydney: Allen & Unwin.
Holub, R. (1984). *Reception Theory: A Critical Introduction*. London: Methuen.
Hulme, M., & Menter, I. (2012). South and North – Teacher Education Policy in England and Scotland: A Comparative Textual Analysis. *Scottish Education Review, 43*(2), 70–90.
Jensson, T. (2009). *Behind the Eye: Reflexive Methods in Culture Studies, Ethnographic Film, and Visual Media* (P. Crawford, Trans.). Walnut Creek: Left Coast Press.
Jones, K. (2003). *Education in Britain: 1944 to the Present*. Oxford: Polity Press.
Jones, K. (2006). A Biographic Researcher in Pursuit of an Aesthetic: The Use of Arts-Based (Re)presentations in 'Performative' Dissemination of Life Stories. *Qualitative Sociology Review, 2*(1), 66–85.
Kemmis, S., & McTaggart, R. (1993). Critical Curriculum Research. In D. Smith (Ed.), *Australian Curriculum Reform: Action and Reaction* (pp. 125–142). Canberra: Australian Curriculum Studies Association.
Kress, G., & Van Leeuwen, T. (2006). *Reading Images: The Grammar of Visual Design* (2nd ed.). London & New York: Routledge.
Leach, B., & Moon, J. (2008). *The Power of Pedagogy*. London: Sage.
MacDougall, D. (2012). Anthropological Film-making. In E. Margolis & L. Pauwels (Eds), *The SAGE Handbook of Visual Research Methods* (pp. 99–113). Thousand Oaks, CA: Sage.
Madison, D. S. (2011). *Critical Ethnography: Method, Ethics, and Performance*. Thousand Oaks, CA: Sage.
McIntosh, P. (2010). *Action Research and Reflective Practice: Creative and Visual Methods to Facilitate Reflection and Learning*. London: Routledge.
Mitchell, C., & de Lange, N. (2011). Community Based Participatory Video and Social Action in Rural South Africa. In E. Margolis & L. Pauwels (Eds), *The SAGE Handbook of Visual Research Methods* (pp. 171–185). Thousand Oaks, CA: Sage.
Parker, D. (2013). *Creative Partnerships in Practice: Developing Creative Learners*. London: Bloomsbury.
Pink, S. (2006). *The Future of Visual Anthropology: Engaging the Senses*. London: Routledge.
Pink, S., Kurti, L., & Afonso, A. I. (Eds) (2004). *Working Images: Visual Representation in Ethnography*. London: Routledge.
Prosser, J. (Ed.) (1998). *Image-Based Research: A Sourcebook for Qualitative Researchers*. London: Falmer Press.
Rose, G. (2014). On the Relation between 'Visual Research Methods' and Contemporary Visual Culture. *Sociological Review, 62*(1), 24–46.
Ruby, J. (2000). *Picturing Culture: Explorations of Film and Anthropology*. Chicago: University of Chicago Press.
Sachs, J. (2003). *The Activist Teaching Profession*. Buckingham: Open University Press.
Shulman, L. (2005). Signature Pedagogies in the Professions. *Daedalus, 134*(Summer), 52–59.
Thomson, P. (Ed.) (2008). *Doing Visual Research with Children and Young People*. London: Routledge.

Thomson, P., Hall, C., Jones, K., & Sefton Green, J. (2012). *Signature Pedagogies*. London: Creativity, Culture and Education.
Thrupp, M., & Wilmott, R. (2003). *Educational Management in Managerialist Times: Beyond the Textual Apologists*. Buckingham: Open University Press.
Tomlinson, S. (2001). *Education in Post-welfare Society*. Buckingham: Open University Press.
Vygotsky, L. (1978). *Mind in Society: The Development of Higher Psychological Processes*. Cambridge, MA: Harvard University Press.
Wallace, M. (1993). Discourse of Derision: The Role of the Mass Media within the Education Policy Process. *Journal of Education Policy, 8*(4), 321–337.
Whitty, G., Power, S., & Halpin, D. (1998). *Devolution and Choice in Education: The School, the State and the Market*. Buckingham: Open University Press.
Wrigley, T., Thomson, P., & Lingard, B. (Eds) (2011). *Changing Schools: Alternative Approaches to Make a World of Difference*. London: Routledge.

8
Visual Language, Visual Literacy: Education à la Modes

Dawnene D. Hassett

I am writing about visual literacy and visual texts, and in doing so, I will share with you examples of children's 'picturebooks' where alphabetic print is no longer the primary carrier of meaning and where images and print often are symbiotic. Like Sipe and Pantaleo (2008), Arizpe and Styles (2003, p. 38), or Nikolajeva and Scott (2000), among others, I use the compound word *picturebook* to indicate my focus on how linguistic and image-based texts seamlessly integrate words and pictures. These books have various modes that carry meaning, and they may inspire children to use additional modes along with the picturebook to enhance meaning or even create new meaning. Examples of modes include speech, image, music, movement, facial expressions, colour, size, texture, and so forth. Bezemer and Kress (2008) define *mode* as a 'socially and culturally shaped resource for meaning making' (p. 171), and Serafini (2014) defines it as a 'system of visual and verbal entities within or across various cultures to represent or express meaning' (p. 12). These are just two definitions, but each implies in its own way that a mode operates within social and cultural understandings of possible ways to make sense. In other words, whatever the mode is (image, typography, colour), and whatever that mode signals or references, it is interpreted through socio-cultural lenses.

The picturebooks that I will be sharing always have more than one mode happening at a time, so they can be called *multimodal*. This chapter analyses multimodal children's picturebooks to propose an educational definition of visual literacy for the early grades. Drawing on social semiotics to push the boundaries of a print-based education, I begin with a definition of picturebooks that highlights the role of visual language and visual literacy in the texts I will share. Then I move to a discussion of several children's picturebooks to demonstrate a theoretical model for making meaning with visual texts (Hassett 2006, 2008, 2010a, 2010b) that I have combined with Rosenblatt's (1994, 1995, 2005) transactional theories of reading and writing. For educational purposes, this exercise is not only about the study of visual signs and how they might be interpreted, but also about the design of curricular environments where visual signs and representational modes can be played with freely and manipulated inventively. The chapter ends with a definition of visual literacy à la modes.

A poststructural caveat

Before we go on, I have a caveat that leans away from a structural understanding of textual interpretation, where it is assumed that the meaning lies in the text or the image, as if it is so structurally solid that it would have the same meaning no matter who opened the book or in which millennium. However, I am a poststructuralist at heart, with a few palpitations of the socio-cultural variety. As such, this chapter is a part of my larger research agenda, which is to investigate how the subject and the child of visual literacy are constructed socially, culturally, and educationally – including what counts as signs that mean something in their schooling. To this end, I agree with Smagorinsky (2001) when he writes, 'How a sign comes to mean is a function of how a reader is enculturated to read' (p. 137). He adds that '[a]t the same time, a sign can mean nothing to a reader for whom the configuration has no codified cultural significance, in which case it is not a sign' (p. 135). In other words, a sign means nothing, even if it means something to somebody else, unless the reader has been enculturated to recognise it as a sign of *something* in the first place. And like Smagorinsky (2001), I, too, 'will argue that attributing meaning to the text alone simply assigns to the text an officially sanctioned meaning, often one so deeply presumed that other interpretations inevitably are dismissed as wrong or irrelevant' (p. 137).

With this general position in mind, when I write about visual literacy and visual texts, I want to be very careful not to essentialise 'elements' of visual texts. I want to be careful not to do this because a visual text often may not have a language to describe it, especially for young children who are just discovering (or being enculturated into) ways to interpret meaning. My concern is that once the field of education hits the field(s) of visual literacy, somebody somewhere will generate lists of visual elements to teach, sorted neatly by grade levels, possibly followed by standardised tests and scripted interventions for the 'visually illiterate'. My concern is that having an essentialised and ahistoric list of visual elements to teach may end up looking an awful lot like teaching reading as if the image/print amalgam contains one literal meaning to decode, and how well you interpret a text depends on how closely (and possibly quickly) you get to that literal meaning. A few definitions may be in order here. By 'essentialised', I mean reducing something to its basic fundamentals, and it is problematic to reduce the open realm of visual language to a limited realm of essentials. By 'ahistoric', I mean acting as if meaning is static, timeless and without history. This becomes problematic if signs are taken too literally, and we are stuck outside of time and culture without the possibility of other interpretations. Finally, my parenthetical reference to how 'quickly' one can decipher a meaning corresponds to ubiquitous assessments that evaluate how quickly students are able to decode nonsense words or how quickly they are able to decode a passage (Goodman 2006). This is problematic, of course, when we value speed over understanding.

Furthermore, if visual language appears ahistoric and we essentialise elements of visual texts, then visual literacy, as a potentially open field, becomes a mere discourse to teach about referentiality (e.g. the colour red can be attached to a certain meaning such as danger or anger). This may not seem entirely bad or hurtful in any way, yet in this chapter, I suggest that visual educational research ought to be critical of social and cultural references that seem somehow universal or structurally fixed, when in fact they are contextualised historically and locally. Lyotard (1984) maintains that:

> [T]he society of the future falls less within the province of a Newtonian anthropology (such as structuralism or systems theory) than a pragmatics of language particles. There are many different language games – a heterogeneity of elements. (p. xxiv)

If a picture is worth a thousand words, then a picturebook is a heterogeneity of visual language particles, floating in the imaginations of viewers who play and invent games to capture the drifting elements. I suggest that an educational definition of visual literacy for young children ought to capture this type of play with possible meanings. Thus, I suggest that visual educational research ought to remain sceptical of referentiality as a form of truth-making in narratives, if for no other reason than to remain, like Lyotard, open to a heterogeneity of interpretations and steadfastly incredulous toward metanarratives (p. xxiv). Although everything we see, read, write, design or interpret is referential on some level (e.g. refers to something that is recognisable enough for interpretation), it is not referential in the sense that there is a grand narrative – or even an original reality (Baudrillard 1995) – to which we must all refer. After all, where is the playfulness in a visual language game that comes in its original packaging of predetermined and fixed metanarratives?

Social semiotics

In light of the social and cultural significance that I place on interpretation, I draw on social semiotics to study visual texts. Semiotics is the study of signs, including drawings, paintings, photographs, words, sounds and body language (Chandler 2002, pp. 1–2). Social semiotics is a branch of semiotics that studies how human beings make meaning in specific social and cultural contexts (Halliday 1978; Hodge and Kress 1988). Traditional semiotics itself is most closely associated with its founding father, Ferdinand de Saussure (1998, 2006), a Swiss linguist who defined the sign/signifier/signified relationship of communication in linguistic terms, but who also saw the importance of studying signs as a part of everyday social life (Chandler 2002, p. 6). Still, Saussure thought of semiology as a study of the laws that govern signs, and this kind of traditional semiotics focuses primarily on theorising unchanging semiotic systems through laws or linguistic structures.

Social semiotics expands Saussure's insights about signs in everyday life by exploring the fact that the 'laws' of language and communication are formed through social and cultural processes, which *do* change. So social semiotics is the study of the social and cultural dimensions of meaning making in practice, first brought up by Halliday (1978), but then later expanded on again by Hodge and Kress (1988), who think of social semiotics as the study of how people design and interpret meanings. They brought the study of texts as cultural artefacts into the field of social semiotics, as well as the study of how semiotic systems are adapted as societies change through social interests and relations of power.

Within social semiotics, we have specific 'socially and culturally shaped resources for making meaning', which is the definition of *mode* given by Bezemer and Kress (2008, p. 171) and cited at the beginning of this chapter. Alphabetic print is one of the sign systems (or modes) we use to make meaning, but resources for making meaning include visual, verbal, written, gestural, musical, aural, olfactory, tactile, gustatory, and so forth. We can think of the multiple modes available in a text as cultural artefacts that readers use as tools for interpretation and meaning production (Kress & van Leeuwen 2001). Social semiotics studies meaning making in all of these modes (Thibault 1991), and in terms of visual literacy and visual language in educational settings, the modes available for making meaning are a blend of linguistic and visual modes.

Challenging definitions: visual literacy, visual language and picturebooks

Definitions of visual literacy have proved challenging over time, most likely because visual literacy as a field of thought crosses many disciplines from photography to information technologies. In terms of educational definitions for visual literacy, sets of cognitive competencies laid forth by Debes (1968) and Fransecky and Debes (1972) in the late 1960s and early 1970s have morphed, at least in the United States, into today's sets of competencies as seen in the Visual Literacy Competency Standards (American Library Association 2014) as well as aspects of the Common Core State Standards (Center for Visual Literacy 2014). In the meantime, several authors from varying fields have (re)defined visual literacy as less about a set of skills and more about socio-cultural contexts and social negotiations (Serafini 2014, pp. 20–24). Bamford (2003), for example, discusses the teaching implications of visual literacy in terms of critical knowledge and creative thinking (p. 5). Most recently, Serafini (2014) defines *visual literacy* as 'the process of generating meaning in transaction with multimodal ensembles, including written text, visual images, and design elements, from a variety of perspectives to meet the requirements of particular social contexts' (p. 23).

Visual language, on the other hand, is challenging to define in its own right, especially if one is to go back to Cro-Magnon cave paintings as a form of visual language and storytelling. Kress and van Leeuwen (2006) have demonstrated the grammar involved in visual design, which helps to explain how the visual can be a language that communicates meaning through form and placement. Yet others, such as Horn (2001), are clear to add linguistic elements to define *visual language* as 'the tight integration of words and visual elements…. It has been called visual language although it might well have been called visual-verbal language' (p. 1).

This tight integration between words and visuals is reflected in the compound word picturebook, which retains the word 'book' even though e-books or digital books may have pictures, but not paper pages. Here, we can make a distinction between an e-book and a codex. The word *codex* is from the Latin *caudex*, which means *tree* or *trunk of a tree*, and a codex is a stack of papers or papyrus that are bound together to form one object. Digital books and e-books are 'books' in the sense that they are more or less closed circuits or single objects to read. Reading a digital book is not the same thing as reading a text on the Internet, which has links to an infinite amount of other texts and pieces of text. Instead, a picturebook, in either electronic or codex form, is an artefact of culture that provides an atmosphere for imagination and interpretation within a relatively closed circumstance for meaning making. In many ways, Bader's (1976) definition of 20th-century picturebooks still holds for either codex or digital forms:

> A picturebook is text, illustrations, total design; an item of manufacture and a commercial product; a social, cultural historical document; and foremost an experience for a child. (p. 1)

To this, I only would add that contemporary picturebooks contain multiple modes in their total design, and that the picturebooks I choose are ones where visual and verbal modes are more interdependent than in most of the traditional picturebooks reviewed by Bader (1976) and others. I am greatly influenced by Eliza Dresang (1999), who refers to the relationships between images and alphabetic print in contemporary picturebooks as providing a context for reading in which children must pay attention to more than linguistic elements (pp. 87–88), and who defines the integration of image and print as 'synergy' (pp. 87–92).

For visual literacy research in education writ large, the picturebooks available for study can come either in digital or codex form, and depending on one's research questions, the modes present in the picturebooks need not always be linguistic. For example, wordless picturebooks are virtual playgrounds for visual literacy studies, and digital picturebooks that are read aloud to students can leave more space available for students to focus on visual elements. However, my own research involves picturebooks where linguistic and visual modes are synergistic, and the closed circuit of the picturebook is open enough to allow for multiple modes beyond the visual and the verbal.

Multimodal picturebooks and models of comprehension

The type of multimodal picturebooks that I am interested in studying, whether in digital or codex form, are not always easy to spot. Just because a picturebook has pictures doesn't mean that the visual and the verbal are tightly intertwined (Nodelman 1988). While there certainly are magnificent children's picturebooks where the text largely supports the images and the images largely support the text, I spend my time finding and analysing picturebooks where the story could not be told *at all* without the images. These could not be books on tape (for they would make no sense without the images) or books that could be read aloud to a large group of students. Instead, they suggest a little more intimacy, a little more time spent looking, and a lot more conversation about the book's possible meanings. They suggest playing with visual-verbal elements.

Let me give you an example of the kind of picturebook that – while multimodal – is not the kind of picturebook I am interested in studying simply because the words and the images are not deeply intertwined, and the book itself does not suggest many possible meanings. Fairly recently as technology goes, Loud Crow Interactive (2011) produced an app for the iPad that interactively tells Beatrix Potter's (1902) classic, *The Tale of Peter Rabbit*. Mind you, I am not saying anything negative about this book or its tablet format, which is a delightful (re)creation of Potter's familiar story, including her original artwork. After the first screen where you can decide whether you want the book read to you and whether you want accompanying piano music, the book starts with the title page, as most traditional books do. Indeed, the images on the e-book look like an old-fashioned book with sewn binding. The title on the recto (right-hand side) is in its traditional 'Peter Rabbit' font with Potter's traditional image of a rabbit underneath, and the original publishing company's name centred under the rabbit. Pictures of the other animals (owl, mouse, squirrel and cat) are on the verso (left-hand side). Here, I am using the vocabulary (recto, verso) of a codex, but remember I am describing an e-book.

In this e-book, on the verso where the owl, mouse, squirrel and cat reside, the reader/viewer/player soon discovers that when you touch the owl, say, it will hoot and shake a bit, as will all of the other animals, birds, pies and teapots. A turned-up corner on the bottom of the recto signals that this is a place to touch or swipe to turn the page, and the next recto contains the print, with each word highlighted in green as the story is read, in synch with a British female voice. We can also go back and touch a word for it to be read to us again. On the verso is an illustration of Mother Rabbit with her four little rabbits: Flopsy, Mopsy, Cotton-tail and Peter. Leaves are falling everywhere, as in a movie, and the interactive element for the reader/viewer here is to play with the leaves that are falling: you can touch them and drag them up and down, around in circles, from verso to recto and back again. You also can touch any of the five rabbits, and they will wiggle and make sounds: squeaky giggles and such for the little rabbits, as the mother comfortably hums.

The illustrations, in this case, are something to play with, and the story is something to hear (if you choose to), with the bonus of tapping a word to hear it again. This picturebook is multimodal because it uses touch, movement, music, oral language, written language, and colour for highlighted words as well as images. Yet, I wish to emphasise that as charming and nostalgic as this story is, the words can exist without the images and the images can certainly exist without the words. In fact, children who play with this book seldom look at the words, and instead play with the interactive images that have little (if anything) to do with the story, no matter how much they swing, twist and turn. For me, then, this is an example of a picturebook that is definitely multimodal, definitely a playful experience, but continues to separate the role of the words (to tell the story) from the role of the images (to support the story and/or to be superfluous to the story).

An example of a picturebook that integrates words and images is *Meow Ruff*, illustrated by Michelle Berg and written by Joyce Sidman (2006). Every image on every page is made out of words that are photo-mechanically printed in different type faces, sizes, line lengths, colours and shapes. The typography itself creates the image, and it is an art form to convey meaning and emotion through the design of graphemes. The clouds look like clouds, and on each page, the words that make up the clouds change size or colour (e.g. from white to grey to black), which gives a new sense of meaning: from 'plump bright dome of sugary white sky-muffin' (p. 5) to 'thunder-plumped seething mass of gloomy fuming black bottomed storm brewing' (pp. 13–14). Items that may not typically change in their moods evoke a different sentiment from page to page, such as the picnic table, whose constructing words read differently from page to page: 'platform for picnics and crumbs and ants' (p. 14); 'platform for raindrops and puddles and winds' (p. 16); and when the cat and dog hide under it, 'platform as roofing for flooding and booming' (p. 20). Tiny ladybugs, present throughout the story, are under the picnic table too, saying, 'we are nice & cozy under here' in the smallest font size possible to remain somewhat readable. In the case of *Meow Ruff*, the images are integral to the story, and the story cannot be read without reference to the images. It is a codex picturebook that is multimodal because it uses font size, volume, colour, direction of flow, and nonlinearity in reading experience as resources for making meaning.

However, because this book cannot be read in a traditional way and because there are so many places to look for meaning, I have found that we need to update our model of the reading process, which was designed with traditional texts in mind. In some of my previous work (Hassett 2006, 2008, 2010a, 2010b; Hassett & Curwood 2009; Hassett & Schieble 2007), I have been updating and continually redrafting the traditional model of reading comprehension (Figure 8.1) to a model that involves visual texts and semiotics (Figure 8.2).

Visual Language, Visual Literacy   141

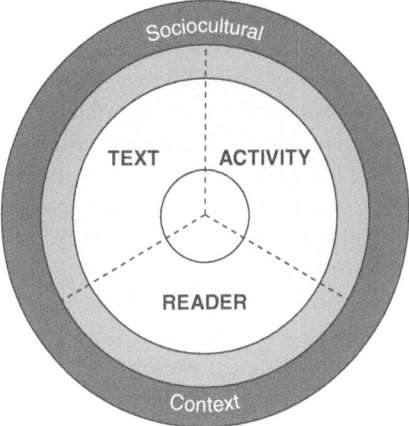

Figure 8.1 Traditional heuristic of reading comprehension
Source: RAND (2002).

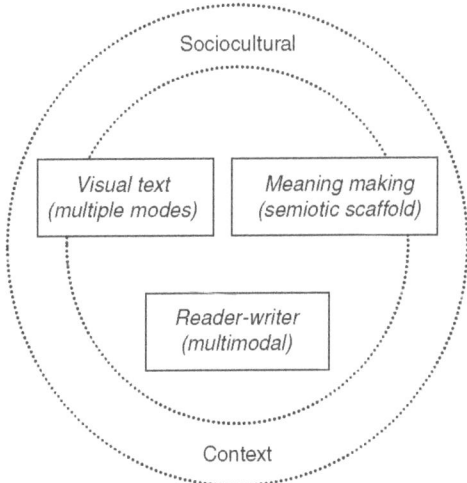

Figure 8.2 Model of reading/writing with visual texts
Source: Hassett (2010a).

The traditional model of reading comprehension involves an interaction between the reader, the text, and the activity (or purpose) of a lesson. In an updated model of visual literacy, the text to be understood is a visual text with a variety of modes for making sense. The reader from the traditional model becomes a reader-writer who uses semiotic resources within the text to make sense. And the activity (or purpose) of a reading/viewing is to construct meaning through a reflective recombination of the signs available (Siegel & Carey 1989).

In rethinking my current Figure 8.2, I wish now to add the word 'transactive' to the process of meaning making. I am never quite satisfied with any model for reading comprehension, and it occurred to me that the basis of these models, even my own revamped ones, relies on the *interaction* between the text, the reader and the context. However, Louise Rosenblatt (1995) makes the important distinction between *interaction* and *transaction*:

> *Interaction*, the term generally used, suggests two distinct entities acting on each other, like two billiard balls. *Transaction* lacks such mechanistic overtones and permits emphasis on the to-and-fro, spiraling, non-linear, continuously reciprocal of reader and text in the making of meaning. (p. xvi)

Leaning on Rosenblatt's (1994, 1995, 2005) transactive theories of reading and writing have helped me to understand that reading books like *Meow Ruff* involves more than information processing and an automatic reaction of looking at an image-text to mechanistically 'get' a particular meaning (as if two billiard balls hit each other). Rosenblatt (2005) explains further:

> Instead of trying to plaster over the distinction between the dualistic, mechanistic, linear, interactional view, in which the text, on the one hand, and the personality of the reader, on the other, can be separately analyzed...we need to see the reading act as an event involving a particular individual and a particular text, happening at a particular time, under particular circumstances, in a particular social and cultural setting, and as part of the ongoing life of the individual and the group....Instead of thinking of reading as a linear process, we have to think rather of *a complex network or circuit of interrelationships, with reciprocal interplay*. (pp. 42–43, emphasis added)

When thinking about the ongoing life of a classroom, I have come to realise that the complex circuits of interrelationships are present in any classroom – and they are exactly what are needed to make meanings out of books like *Meow Ruff*. The picturebook itself takes on a life of its own, with multiple stories to tell and multiple voices occurring on one page at a time. The picturebook becomes another player in the conversations that happen around it and through it as the readers and the text live transactively together in a particular social and cultural circumstance...such as the classroom.

Now, Rosenblatt was talking about adults making meaning from prose or poetry, but there are many examples of children's picturebooks that demand the transactive and 'continuously reciprocal influence of reader and text in the making of meaning' (Rosenblatt 1995, p. xvi). For me, there are many examples of highly visual and multimodal picturebooks that demand the continuously reciprocal influence *of many readers discussing meanings and interpretations together with their teachers*.

In the classroom: transactive instructional dynamics

If you are looking for lesson plans, you won't find that here because I cannot tell you who is in your classroom or what they are thinking, much less what they might be thinking if you and others in your classroom conversed and played together transactively with language-image particles. But I can give you some examples of picturebooks that provide multimodal fodder for reciprocally transactive conversations. From there, we can think about which one of us is best situated to offer advice about encouraging transactive storytelling, discussion and play in your own classroom. (Hint: it may not be me!)

Examples of multimodal picturebooks that are fodder for reciprocally transactive conversations include books with texture and three dimensions, such as *Meerkat Mail* (Gravett 2007), which includes all of the letters and postcards sent by a travelling meerkat back home to his family as he looks for better places to live. The postcards and letters lift out or turn over, and they include drawn images as well as written language to interpret together. *Open This Little Book* (Klausmeier 2013) is meant to be handled and opened on every page as each character opens a progressively smaller book folded into each other – and then progressively closes them. Picturebooks that offer three-dimensional facets can become springboards for writing (trans)activities, as children work together to use design techniques introduced by their favourite authors or characters.

144   Dawnene D. Hassett

Codex picturebooks, such as *My Map Book* (Fanelli 1995), as well as picturebooks that have many different formats, such as *Marcel the Shell* (Slate & Fleischer-Camp 2011), often capitalise on the affordances of different media. *My Map Book* absolutely demands to be in a 12x10 inch (when closed) codex because it contains many different child-like, illustrated two-page spreads (e.g. map of my family, map of my dog, map of my heart and a treasure map) that thoroughly fill whole pages with large images, large fonts, and large colours. *Marcel the Shell*, on the other hand, takes advantage of numerous formats: an e-book in an app for iPad or iPhone; movies on YouTube; online activities to do with Marcel; and a codex picturebook. The iPad and iPhone apps completely use the mode of sound to give Marcel a voice, to the point where I can barely read the codex to students without trying to read it in 'his' voice (because they know it). Meanwhile, the codex picturebook has the affordances of larger visuals to carefully look at for new discoveries, with the added bonus that teachers and/or children can pace themselves to carefully choose how to spend time looking, reading, thinking and discussing.

Many other picturebooks, such as *The Fantastic Flying Books of Mr. Morris Lessmore* (Joyce 2012) and *Arnie the Doughnut* (Keller 2003), come both in codex and e-book (or more) forms. William Joyce's *Morris Lessmore* comes in an animated iPad app, a movie, a codex picturebook and a surprising additional iPad app (for purchase) that allows the codex to become animated if you view it through your iPad's camera lens. If you are to do that, then you can see all of the animations from the movie coming 'out of' your codex and 'into' your iPad; plus at certain points, the program signals you to lift your iPad to see something happen, such as books flying around (from the app) in your own living room (as seen from the camera lens on your iPad). Of all the different *Morris Lessmore* formats, the codex picturebook is one I may have passed by in search of highly transactive picturebooks, mostly because the words tell a story and the pictures tell a story, but there is not necessarily a realm in between. And yet, with the combination of technologies, other transactive realities for the story occur, such as books flying around your own personal space.

Indeed, multimodal picturebooks demand a transaction with the text because the reader is integral to the image/word amalgam; he or she is necessarily involved in the plot. The picturebooks *Follow the Line through the House* (Ljungkvist 2007) and *We Are in a Book!* (Willems 2010), for example, both *require* the reader to take an active part in the story, or the story doesn't make sense. These changes mean that the socio-cultural context of the classroom relies not only on the reader, the text and the activity of reading (as is traditional) but also on the transactivities around the picturebooks. These could be designed by teachers but also left for happenstance, depending on the particular people and the particular visual texts.

Arnie the Doughnut is another picturebook that comes in both codex and e-book form, but the difference here is that the nuances and intricacies of smaller images/words are more difficult to see in the e-book, not only because of the size of the screen, but also because a close-up of any image (via a tap or two) only shows pieces of a larger whole that were originally (in codex) non-linear, circular, and irregular visual-verbal play and image-language art. In this particular case, as in others where the e-book is simply the book on a screen, it seems that our technologies have not caught up to the multimodalities in picturebooks yet. That may be satisfactory for a little bit longer, since many schools have not caught up with technological advances either. After all, to set up classroom environments that encourage transactive forms of literacy and dynamic forms of instruction, perhaps all we really need is a codex, a good library and the freedom to renovate our curriculum.

There are, of course, numerous semiotic elements teachers can point out to their students as picturebooks are read and discussed, whether in codex or digital form. I leave the decisions about which semiotic elements to teach to the particularities of the students, teachers, texts, and contexts, all of which change on a moment-to-moment basis. The most important thing a teacher can do, though, is to build and support a classroom environment that welcomes these picturebooks into an atmosphere of mindful curiosity.

To speak of *transactive instructional dynamics*, I am drawing, of course, on Rosenblatt's theories, but I also am drawing on a multi-dynamic literacy theory (Hassett 2008) that combines the best of what we currently know from early reading theory with the best of what we currently know from socio-cultural theories of language and literacy development. For example, if we decided we were going to build our classroom environments based on an understanding (no matter how fleeting) of transactive instructional dynamics, then we would choose to think of meaning making as 'a complex network or circuit of interrelationships' (Rosenblatt 2005, p. 43) that always responds to the socio-cultural constructions that are most relevant to us in a particular moment in time (Hassett 2008). To base our pedagogies on such a philosophy, then, we might actively choose to include picturebooks where visual and verbal modes intertwine, because we would always want to create a space for children to notice interesting textual elements and discuss possible interpretations together with their teachers.

In short, *transactive instructional dynamics* includes a knowledge that reading is not mechanical, but instead a product of relationships and interplay (Rosenblatt 2005, p. 43); and a commitment to treating literacy as multifaceted, socially constructed, and only relevant within the lived worlds of children (Hassett 2008). When it's all brought together, then, I suggest that visual literacy in education is absolutely without a doubt not mechanical, not rote, and not about information processing. Instead, it's a true-blue commitment to the multifaceted relationships that human beings have with each other, over moment-to-moment experiences that help us interpret visual language together.

Concluding remarks for beginning conversations: epistemological questions

At least in the United States, beginning literacy instruction is predominantly print-centric, with limited pragmatic use in a highly visual and image-based world. At the same time, 'visual literacy' as a field of thought crosses many disciplines: art history, mass media, information technologies, semiotics, philosophy, and so on. While all of these disciplines are highly educational at their roots, teaching reading and writing to young children may not need to delve too deeply into any one of these categories for us to understand how to read an image. Meanwhile, as we have seen, linguistic print itself can take on visual modes (e.g. colour, size, slant, shape), which portends meaning beyond the phoneme-grapheme connection, and which also means we can't throw out linguistic print altogether. Print, after all, is still visual, and is still a form of social semiotics: it just needs to be put in perspective on a larger landscape of communication, especially in the early grades.

Visual literacy research in education has a great potential for moving us away from those print-centric pedagogies. At the same time, in the spirit of taking a critical perspective on visual educational research and enlivening the debate about what constitutes 'the visual' in literacy, it should be noted that the signs that can mean something for children in their schooling today extend beyond visual (or even visual-linguistic) modes. So, in my concluding remarks, I would like to acknowledge that there are epistemological issues at hand having to do with visual literacy vis-à-vis multimodalities, and I have a few epistemological questions for future discussions.

1. Is it possible that visual educational research may not meet all of our needs, methodologically and pedagogically, because of multimodalities?
2. What are the theories that ground visual educational research, and have these theoretical foundations changed because of multimodalities? If so, what has changed, and what are the (positive, negative, neutral and unknown) repercussions?
3. Does naming it 'visual educational research' limit the modes we may research in education, or are there compelling reasons why visual education and visual literacy ought to remain their own research domains?

I won't be answering these questions today (unless you have already read something that I will have written in the future). However, I am looking forward to the animated discussions, YouTube videos, and apps that we'll share in the name of visual literacy and education à la modes.

References

ALA [American Library Association]. (2014). *ACRL Visual Literacy Competency Standards for Higher Education*. Retrieved August 25, 2014. http://www.ala.org/acrl/standards/visualliteracy

Arizpe, E., & Styles, M. (2003). *Children Reading Pictures: Interpreting Visual Texts*. London & New York: Routledge Falmer.

Bader, B. (1976). *American Picturebooks: From 'Noah's Ark' to 'The Beast Within'*. New York: Macmillan.

Bamford, A. (2003). *The Visual Literacy White Paper*. UK: Adobe Systems Incorporated, 28.

Baudrillard, J. (1995). *Simulacra and Simulation* (S. F. Glaser, Trans.). Ann Arbor: University of Michigan Press.

Bezemer, J., & Kress, G. (2008). Writing in Multimodal Texts: A Social Semiotic Account of Designs for Learning. *Written Communication*, 25(2), 166–195.

Center for Visual Literacy (2014). *Common Core State Standards Related to Visual Literacy*, online. http://www.vislit.org/common-core-visual-literacy/

Chandler, D. (2002). *Semiotics: The Basics*. London & New York: Routledge.

Debes, J. L. (1968). Some Foundations for Visual Literacy. *Audiovisual Instruction*, 13, 961–964.

Dresang, E. T. (1999). *Radical Change: Books for Youth in a Digital Age*. New York: H.W. Wilson Co.

Fanelli, S. (1995). *My Map Book*. New York: HarperFestival.

Fransecky, R. B., & Debes, J. L. (1972). *Visual Literacy: A Way to Learn, a Way to Teach*. Washington, DC: AECT Publications.

Goodman, K. (2006). *The Truth about DIBELS: What It Is – What It Does*. Portsmouth, NH: Heinemann.

Gravett, E. (2007). *Meerkat Mail* (1st U.S. ed.). New York: Simon & Schuster Books for Young Readers.

Halliday, M. A. K. (1978). *Language as a Social Semiotic: The Social Interpretation of Language and Meaning*. PA: University Park Press.

Hassett, D. D. (2006). Technological Difficulties: A Theoretical Frame for Understanding the Non-relativistic Permanence of Traditional Print Literacy in Elementary Education. *Journal of Curriculum Studies, 38*(2), 135–159.

Hassett, D. D. (2008). Teacher Flexibility and Judgment: A Multidynamic Literacy Theory. *Journal of Early Childhood Literacy, 8*(3), 295.

Hassett, D. D. (2010a). New Literacies in the Elementary Classroom: The Instructional Dynamics of Visual-Texts. In K. Hall, U. Goswami, C. Harrison, S. Ellis, & J. Soler (Eds), *Interdisciplinary Perspectives on Learning to Read: Culture, Cognition and Pedagogy* (pp. 87–100). New York: Routledge.

Hassett, D. D. (2010b). Technologies and Truth Games: Research as Dynamic Method. *Language Arts, 87*(6), 457–464.

Hassett, D. D., & Curwood, J. S. (2009). Theories and Practices of Multimodal Education: The Instructional Dynamics of Picturebooks and Primary Classrooms. *Reading Teacher, 63*(4), 270–282.

Hassett, D. D., & Schieble, M. B. (2007). Finding Space and Time for the Visual in K-12 Literacy Instruction. *English Journal, 97*(1), 62–68.

Hodge, R., & Kress, G. (1988). *Social Semiotics* (1st ed.). Ithaca, NY: Cornell University Press.

Horn, R. E. (2001). *Visual Language and Converging Technologies in the Next 10–15 Years (and beyond)*. Presented at the National Science Foundation Conference on Converging Technologies (Nano-Bio-Info-Cogno) for Improving Human Performance, Stanford, CA.

Joyce, W. (2012). *The Fantastic Flying Books of Mr. Morris Lessmore*. New York: MoonBot Books.

Keller, L. (2003). *Arnie the Doughnut*. New York: Holt.

Klausmeier, J. (2013). *Open This Little Book*. San Francisco, CA: Chronicle Books.

Kress, G., & van Leeuwen, T. (2001). *Multimodal Discourse: The Modes and Media of Contemporary Communication*. London: Arnold.

Kress, G., & van Leeuwen, T. (2006). *Reading Images: The Grammar of Visual Design* (2nd ed.). New York: Routledge.

Ljungkvist, L. (2007). *Follow the Line through the House*. New York: Viking, Penguin.

Loud Crow Interactive. (2011). PopOut! The Tale of Peter Rabbit. Retrieved August 26, 2014. https://itunes.apple.com/us/app/popout!-tale-peter-rabbit/id397864713?mt=8

Lyotard, J.-F. (1984). *The Postmodern Condition: A Report on Knowledge* (1st ed.). Minneapolis: University of Minnesota Press.

Nikolajeva, M., & Scott, C. (2000). *How Picturebooks Work*. Garland Publishing.

Nodelman, P. (1988). *Words about Pictures: The Narrative Art of Children's Picturebooks*. Athens: University of Georgia Press.

Potter, B. (1902). *The Tale of Peter Rabbit*. New York: Frederick War Co./Penguin Group.

RAND Reading Study Group. (2002). Reading for Understanding: Toward an R&D Program in Reading Comprehension. Retrieved November 14, 2008. http://www.rand.org/content/dam/rand/pubs/monograph_reports/2005/MR1465.pdf

Rosenblatt, L. M. (1994). *The Reader, the Text, the Poem: The Transactional Theory of the Literary Work*. Carbondale: Southern Illinois University Press.

Rosenblatt, L. M. (1995). *Literature as Exploration*. New York: Modern Language Association of America.

Rosenblatt, L. M. (2005). *Making Meaning with Texts: Selected Essays*. Portsmouth, NH: Heinemann.

Saussure, F. de. (1998). *Course in General Linguistics* (Reprint ed.). LaSalle, Ill: Open Court.

Saussure, F. de. (2006). *Writings in General Linguistics*. New York: Oxford University Press.

Serafini, F. (2014). *Reading the Visual: An Introduction to Teaching Multimodal Literacy*. New York: Teachers College Press.

Sidman, J. (2006). *Meow Ruff*. Boston: Houghton Mifflin.

Siegel, M. G., & Carey, R. F. (1989). *Critical Thinking a Semiotic Perspective*. Bloomington, Ind: ERIC Clearinghouse on Reading and Communication Skills, Smith Research Center, Indiana University.

Sipe, L. R., & Pantaleo, S. (2008). *Postmodern Picturebooks: Play, Parody, and Self-Referentiality*. New York: Routledge.

Slate, J., & Fleischer-Camp, D. (2011). *Marcel the Shell with Shoes On: Things About Me*. New York: Razorbill.

Smagorinsky, P. (2001). If Meaning Is Constructed, What Is It Made From? Toward a Cultural Theory of Reading. *Review of Educational Research, 71*(1), 133–169.

Thibault, P. J. (1991). Grammar, Technocracy, and the Noun: Technocratic Values and Cognitive Linguistics. In E. Ventola (Ed.), *Functional and Systemic Linguistics: Approaches and Uses* (Vol. Studies and monographs 55, pp. 281–305). New York: Moutin de Gruyter.

Willems, M. (2010). *We Are in a Book!* New York: Disney-Hyperion.

Part III
Power and Representation in Visual Educational Research

9
Repeat Photography and Educational Research

Amy Scott Metcalfe

Introduction

Qualitative research has been enhanced by the addition of visual methods (Banks 2007; Emmison & Smith 2000; Margolis & Pauwels 2011; Pink 2011; Rose 2007; Spencer 2010; Stanczak 2007; van Leeuwen & Jewitt 2001). Repeat photography, also called rephotography, entails the rephotographing of a visual phenomenon or a physical location in a specific temporal order to call attention to social or material change over time. Repeat photography derives from the natural sciences and has recently been applied to the social sciences, most notably in sociology (Klett 2011; Rieger 1996, 2011). It has not been widely used to date in educational research, although it has been applied pedagogically in the field of geography (Lemmons, Brannstrom & Hurd 2014). This approach can be considered the longitudinal analysis of visual methods.

I begin the chapter with a discussion of the disciplinary foundations of repeat photography, citing examples from sociology and the natural sciences (particularly geology). Then, I describe a shift occurring in the visual studies literature that encourages researchers to look deeper and theorise with more complexity. I distil these methodological considerations for repeat photography into a model. Next, I outline the key steps for repeat photography as described by Rieger (2011). Finally, I return to my model to describe examples of repeat photography from my recent visual analysis of academic science at a university campus.

Visualising sociology

Periodically, sub-fields need to 'check back in' with the larger disciplinary conversations in order to further develop theoretically and methodologically. As such, we see that the techniques and constructs of visual sociology are becoming more prominent in the sociology of education (Margolis & Pauwels 2011).

Foundational work in visual sociology questioned the role of the visual in the study of the sociological, but retained an emphasis on prevailing sociological theories (Grady 1991; Rieger 1991, 1996). Harper introduced visual sociology to the discipline in 1988, defining it as 'the use of photographs, film, and video to study society and the study of visual artifacts of a society' (Harper 1988, p. 54). As Holm stated in an essay titled 'Photography as a Research Method' for the *Oxford Handbook of Qualitative Research*, we should take care not to conflate the concept of imagery and image-making with the practice and phenomenon of photography (Holm 2014, p. 382). Yet, visual sociology has had a long-standing association with photography, which Harper ascribed to the relationship between sociology itself and this particular visual medium: 'Sociology came about as the result of industrialization and bourgeois revolutions in Europe; photography, too, was a child of the industrial revolution and had the effect of democratizing a new kind of knowledge' (Harper 1988, p. 55).

In an article titled 'Seeing Sociology', which appeared in *The American Sociologist*, Harper (1996) described the epistemological traditions of sociology, and then stated, 'Even though most sociologists are sighted, and even though much sociology depends upon observation, sociology has not derived from, nor has it reflected a visual record of the world. For many of us this has been unsatisfactory' (p. 69). Harper continued by recounting the early years of visual sociology, from meetings held since 1974 in conjunction with the American Sociological Association (ASA), and foundational scholarship that helped to legitimise the emerging field (e.g. Becker 1974). These developments resulted in the formation of the International Visual Sociology Association (IVSA) in 1980, and the formation of the journal *Visual Sociology* shortly thereafter.

In the decades since the IVSA's formation, visual sociology has been influenced by interdisciplinarity and a rise of the visual in popular culture. 'Visual literacy' is now an important component of criticality, as technological innovations constantly 'push' images and other digitised sensory content to our various electronic devices. Wyly (2010) noted, 'Overwhelmed by photographs, advertising, and moving images that move ever faster, people are losing the capacity for slow, careful contemplation' (p. 501). Pauwels articulated several key issues that, if not addressed, might impede the development of a more 'visually literate' research culture:

the indispensable awareness for the magnitude of types of visual representations and their distinct implications, the need for clarifying the role of aesthetics in a scientific discourse, the need for a more explicit visual methodology and theory, the crucial role of technology, the importance of staying tuned with our audiences, and of fostering a thoughtful eclecticism and interdisciplinary exchange. (Pauwels 2000, p. 7)

Pauwels concludes that researchers utilising visual methods would need to have a degree of 'visual competence' that permits them to understand the technical, social, aesthetic and epistemological consequences of their research. He stated, 'The absence of such a language to talk intelligibly about images – and visual parameters and practices more in general – is no doubt seriously hampering the development of a more visual science' (Pauwels 2000, p. 14).

To further aid in the development of a more visual literate research community, Pauwels (2010) developed a framework for visual studies. A simplification of this framework (Table 9.1) is useful here as a precursor

Table 9.1 Reframing visual sociology

Origin and nature of visuals	Research focus and design		Format and purpose
Origin/Production content • Pre-existing visual artefacts • Researcher-instigated visuals	Analytic focus • Image • Process • Response to imagery	Theoretical foundation • Visual theory • Theory with visual implications	Output/Presentation format • Academic publication considerations • Other dissemination
Referent/Subject • Object • Behaviour • Concept	Methodological issues • Competence • Data strategies • Validity • Participation • Contextualisation • Ethical considerations		Status of the visual • Explicative • Expressive • Relational
Visual medium/technique • Observation • Non-algorithmic (e.g. drawing) • Algorithmic (e.g. photography)			Intended and secondary uses • Scholarship • Policy • Practice • Advocacy

Source: Adapted from Pauwels (2010, p.549).

to a better understanding of the function and place of repeat photography within both visual sociology and visual studies, with implications for educational research. Pauwels (2010) suggested simultaneous consideration of the origin of visual data, the theoretical and methodological issues involved, and the dissemination of the research in which the visuals are analysed. In this sense, Pauwels' framework is not a step-by-step chart of the research process but a holistic impression of the contemporary state of visual sociology. A key element of the framework is that it acknowledges the influences of both technological change and interdisciplinarity on the modes and knowledge products of visual sociology. I will return to Pauwels' framework when discussing repeat photography in the next section.

Repeat photography as sociological method

Critical visual theory has taught us that images do not speak a thousand words. With widespread use of image editing software like Photoshop, context and content are often merged into disarticulated, manipulated images that present much more than they represent. In fact, as Wyly noted, there are many things that 'pictures don't tell us', because 'the invisible matters' (2010, p. 499). To aid in the understanding of our complex visual world through specific images, Wyly suggested three considerations: (1) conditions of possibility, (2) displacement, and (3) power and representation (Wyly 2010, pp. 505–507). *Conditions of possibility* refers to the unseen and therefore visually unknown contexts of the image and image-taking process. This entails the decisions made by the image maker and the material and social conditions that influenced those decisions. Wyly explains,

> Inevitably, people from different disciplines will ask different questions – a caricatured summary would be that sociologists ask 'Who' while historians ask 'When?' and geographers wonder 'Where?' But any thoughtful analyst will try to consider all of these perspectives in constructing a narrative to explain the conditions of possibility. (Wyly 2010, p. 506)

Displacement is the disposition of an image that has been removed from its contextual history. To recognise the implications of this, we as researchers need to displace ourselves, seeking to understand the conditions of possibility behind the image of interest. This might happen through interviews involving photo elicitation, document analysis of other contemporary materials and texts, ethnography, or visiting the site of the image itself. Attention to *power and representation* is necessary to understand the nature of selectivity in the visual record. Privilege affects technical acquisition of the means to create images, degrees of access to the subject matter, distribution of the images to preferred audiences, and stewardship of the images over time. Selection happens at many points along the lifespan of a visual artefact, even during the research process.

Repeat photography is a visual research method that fits well with Wyly's (2010) recommendations to consider conditions of possibility, displacement, and power and representation in image-based work. Smith defined repeat photography as 'a significant and particular kind of engagement with both a subject and a photograph, usually beginning with locating relevant archival materials (such as photographs, paintings, and drawings) and culminating in taking a photograph of the same scene from the exact original location' (2007, p. 184). Active engagement with archival materials, including relevant photographs, aids the researcher in considering alternatives that were possible for image-making at the time. Visiting the site of the original photograph(s) provides an opportunity for displacement of the self, to further consider conditions of possibility and to reflect on the power dimensions and modes of representation that influence the historical and present work.

Repeat photography derives from the natural sciences and specifically geology (Webb, Boyer & Turner 2010a), and it presents a compelling mix of science, policy advocacy and aesthetics. Repeat photography was inspired by the historic landscape photographs of Timothy H. O'Sullivan and William Henry Jackson, taken as part of the U.S. geological surveys in the 1870s, and which played a role in the legislative creation of America's western national parks such as Yellowstone. The contemporary geologist, artist and professor Mark Klett developed the visual research method of repeat photography in the 1980s, initially by capturing 'second sights' of natural landmarks a century or more after the original photographs by O'Sullivan and others were taken (Klett et al. 1984; Kumar 2014). Klett's work expanded to other landscape projects (Klett et al. 2004; Klett, Solnit & Wolfe 2005) and later evolved to urban 'rephotography', such as with *After the Ruins, 1906 and 2006: Rephotographing the San Francisco Earthquake and Fire* (Klett & Lundgren 2006).

A key element of Klett's work is his precision and emphasis on selecting the correct vantage point for the contemporary photography, following the historical image as exactly as possible. The technical considerations of vantage point and focal length are necessary for the purpose of 'an accurate evaluation of physical change over time' (Klett 2011, p. 116). This method permits comparative visual analysis, and if done precisely, can be used to measure geological or environmental change (Webb, Boyer & Turner 2010b; Zier & Baker 2006). Klett reflects on the utility and transdisciplinarity of the technique by stating, 'Common to many disciplines, there has been a need to visualize change, and the overall connection has been to gain a unique perspective on time related to place that is independent of discipline and challenges the observation of any single moment' (Klett 2011, p. 115).

The precision of repeat photography as it is used in the natural sciences is not as relevant for the social sciences (Smith 2007; Rieger 2011). Rather, the social implications of the juxtapositions of historical and contemporary views are more salient. However, careful attention to the vantage point and other technical aspects of the original photograph is useful for comparative purposes. Rieger emphasises the comparative aspects of the analysis, stating, 'The change, or lack of change, that the photographs reveal we then interpret in accordance with our theoretical expectations' (2011, p. 133).

To return to Pauwels' framework for visual sociology (Table 9.1), repeat photography begins with thoughtful reflection about (1) the origin and nature of the visuals, (2) the research focus and design, and (3) the format and purpose of the research. With regard to the first point, the visuals in repeat photography both derive from pre-existing visual artefacts and researcher-instigated images. The subject of the research might be a particular object, a behaviour, or a concept. The algorithmic process of photography would likely be the visual medium or technique of choice. With regard to the research focus and design, repeat photography is not that different from other visual research methods in that all of the items listed by Pauwels under the sub-headings 'analytic focus', 'theoretical foundation' and 'methodological issues' are important considerations. The format and purpose of the research are pertinent to the research design and should be determined prior to the start of the research rather than being left to the end of the process. The main reason for this is that many academic journals are not yet attuned to the presentation of photographs, so the dissemination venue should be considered up front. With this in mind, the researcher may want to reduce the number of visual elements in the analysis and/or the presentation, concentrating on a few representative images. With repeat photography, a relational (comparative) presentation makes sense, and can offer the opportunity to limit the number of images in the final publication to as few as two. Finally, the intended and secondary uses of the research may have a bearing on the images selected for analysis, the theoretical foundation and the various methodological issues encountered during the research process.

Taking the above into consideration, and drawing from methodological scholarship on the technique (Klett 2011; Rieger 2011; Smith 2007), the following table presents a methodological framework for repeat photography in the social sciences (Figure 9.1).

The framework shown in Figure 9.1 is intended to illustrate that the only linear aspect of the research process for repeat photography is the selection of two or more moments in time (two being the minimum, but three is not the maximum). The other elements are to be considered simultaneously or in relation to one another. For example, if policy advocacy is the chosen outcome, that will have a bearing on the theory selected as well as the research design. For each image in the time series, 'context and discourse' and 'technological aspects' of image-making and interpretation should be considered, as well as in contrast to the other images in the set. Context and discourse refers to the social, economic, political and environmental milieu in which the images were taken, and discourse references the dominant social narratives that pertain to or influence our interpretation of these visuals. Technological aspects include the mechanics of photography and the specific technologies

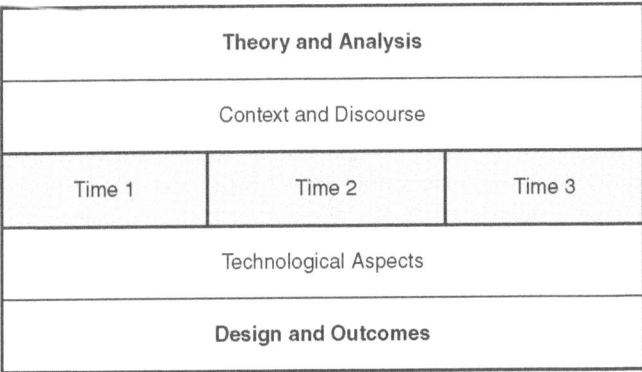

Figure 9.1 Methodological framework for repeat photography

used, as well as modes of representation that may affect later interpretation or distribution of these images.

The methodological work of Klett (2010, 2011), Rieger (2011) and Smith (2007) is useful to further clarify the technique of repeat photography. Rieger listed the following steps for researching change visually:

1. Selecting a subject that will become the focus of the research and developing a theoretical framework that suggests what changes might be expected.
2. Determining and identifying visual indicators to be recorded.
3. Finding existing documentation or creating such documentation for the initial (time 1) measurement.
4. Carrying out the follow-up (time 2) documentation when appropriate.
5. Analysing the accumulated evidence. (Rieger 2011, pp. 147–148)

Once a general topic and theoretical perspective are ascertained, the selection of images follows. Rieger (2011) notes that there are two ways to consider the temporal order of repeat photography: prospective and retrospective. *Prospective* studies begin at 'time 1' with researcher-initiated images and are followed up at specific if not predetermined dates for 'time 2' and beyond. This method provides the most control over the research process. *Retrospective* studies begin with 'time 1' in the past, and this moment may be determined by the existence of an archival image. Later images taken by the researcher at 'time 2' and so on are made in relation to the image that fixes 'time 1'. While offering less control over the entire research process, this method provides the added benefit of hindsight.

Many repeat photography projects are retrospective studies that begin with the archive (Smith 2007). For the *After the Ruins* (Klett & Lundgren 2006) project that rephotographed San Francisco in 2006, based on historic images of the great earthquake there in 1906, the selection process began by browsing several online archives (Klett 2010). The examination of these images prior to fieldwork was critical in order to have a larger understanding of the range of historic images available, and to determine which ones were suitable for the process of repeat photography. Some interesting images were unusable, for example, because they were taken from vantage points located in buildings that no longer existed a hundred years later. In addition, amateur photographers took most of the images found in the databases, and often there was no written record about the photographic equipment or technical specifications for each shot. In short, there was a great deal of missing information and unsuitable visuals in the archives, but each of these realities is actually part of the larger social and technical conditions that surrounded this catastrophic event. In fact, analysis of the scope of material in the archives and archival practices are useful if not necessary parts of understanding the 'conditions of possibility' mentioned by Wyly (2010) (see e.g. Margolis 1999).

In addition, a repeat photography project might entail efforts to understand a particular process, activity or function (Rieger 2011), which could influence the best timing for subsequent photographs. Once the timing is determined, repeat photography happens in the field, where the researcher becomes aware of the environmental conditions of the original photograph. This often leads to valuable insights, and can necessitate further data collection to seek alternative images, contemporary documents and archival materials, and interviews with research participants who have a connection to the images in question. Fieldwork for repeat photography in the social sciences can therefore have the dual purposes of documenting the specific location based on the first image and also of conducting a visual ethnography of the present (Pink 2011). Smith refers to this process of learning in situ as 'ground truthing'. She describes this in the following way: 'The person holding the photograph, repeating the photograph, realigns his or her body, and realigns the past, and thereby enables a new view of [the research site] to emerge through a particular, specific, and active engagement with a significant place' (2007, p. 191).

For researchers in the natural sciences, the analysis of repeat photography images is largely a scientific process of measurement and mapping, such as that which examines the retreat of glaciers due to climate change (Fagre & McKeon 2010). Yet even during the study of environmental phenomena the analysis can be narrative and qualitative. In recounting the process of image selection and analysis for *Yosemite in Time: Ice Ages, Tree Clocks, Ghost Rivers* (Klett, Solnit & Wolfe 2005), Klett discusses an 'embedded rephotograph technique' that combines historical and present-day images into a single panorama. This technique is artistic as much as it is scientific, and emphasises the narrative potential of the combined 'mash-up of images by three famous photographers [Eadweard Muybridge, Ansel Adams and Edward Weston]' and the researchers' own photographs (Klett 2011, p. 125). He remarks,

> Our desire for this project was to see Yosemite as a place that photographs had helped shape in the minds of viewers, whether they had

been visitors or not, and to revisualize the Park's iconic imagery as a layered mix of time, cultural representation, and personal stories. (Klett 2011, p. 125)

These rephotographic 'mash-ups' could be used as the basis for photo elicitation for qualitative interviews or memory work (Kalin 2013), as artistic prompts for art-based research methods or as a group analysis technique for collaborative research methods where photographs taken by individual participants are assembled into a collective whole (Monk 2014).

Repeat photography in practice

Repeat photography was the central method utilised in my research project titled 'Images of Academic Science: Photographic Evidence of Scientific Research at the University of British Columbia', undertaken during the five-year period of 2007–2012. The study site was the University of British Columbia (UBC), a large research-intensive, public university in western Canada. The site was selected for its historical development from a land-based, agriculturally focused university to its contemporary profile as a leading scientific research university, with associated medical school and proliferation of campus laboratories. Further, as my home institution, the site provided the added benefit of sustained engagement with the campus environment over the five-year period of the study.

Returning to the methodological framework for repeat photography (Figure 9.1, above), I present two sets of repeat photographs undertaken during the Images of Academic Science project. The next sections discuss the project's theory and analysis, context and discourse, technological aspects and design and outcomes.

Theory and analysis

The initial aim of the Images of Academic Science project was to understand how academic science was visually represented in the photographs housed in the university archive, from the foundation of the campus in the early 1900s to the present. The project was designed as an interdisciplinary project, drawing upon theories of visual representation from art history (Barthes 1982), critical theories of the relationship between the state, market and higher education such as academic capitalism theory (Slaughter & Leslie 1997; Slaughter & Rhoades 2004) from education, and theories of power (Foucault 1980) and representation (Butler

1990) from sociology. As the study progressed, it became apparent that critical theories of space and place were also useful, as the physical environment of the campus yielded rich analytic opportunities. Invoking a critical pedagogy of place (Gruenewald 2003) facilitated a change-based analysis that focused on critical reflection. Repeat photography proved useful as a structured, concretising method that would provide key points of reference across the large timespan of the study.

Context and discourse

Over the course of the research it became apparent that the agricultural sciences held a prominent position in the early years of the study site, and that the fields and farm buildings of UBC's foundational years formed a land-based legacy for the later development of large laboratories and scientific research facilities on campus. In fact, agricultural science was taught on the UBC Vancouver campus before it opened to the public in 1925, with the horticulture students even providing much of the technical expertise and physical labour necessary for landscaping the new campus. In this way, the size and design of the UBC campus was shaped by agricultural science. The visual archival record permitted a consideration of the agricultural fields as not only educational spaces but also as places of ceremonial value, where Deans of Agriculture stood for portraits and where groups of visitors might be greeted and shown the bounty of the day. Images from events in the 1930s and 1940s capture the fields and barns at the height of their social and pedagogical use. Subsequent photographs in the archive from the 1970s and 1980s depicted the creation of parking lots in former fields and the construction of large research buildings on the sites where students had once farmed on campus. As the student population of UBC grew sharply after the 1970s, the need for student housing, parking and research space outweighed the need for campus-based farming and fields. However, this shift also was marked by particular efforts to maintain and restore historic buildings that dated to the early days of the campus. This preservationist discourse was evident visually and textually in the archival materials.

Technological aspects

Photographic analysis requires an understanding of the photographic process and the context in which photographs are taken. For the Images of Academic Science project, many of the earlier photographs in the archive were devoid of technical notation. In many cases the photographer and equipment were not identified. Often the actual date of the photo was not known, although a year might be surmised through comparative analysis with other photos of specific events that were known through other source materials. Further, in some cases, the dates and place identifications associated with particular photos were later discovered by the research team to be incorrect, which often confounded or complicated the analysis.

A published photo essay proved to be invaluable for relational dating of the visual archival material. Early in the browsing process I found a publication by the University Extension Committee (UEC) that commemorated the opening of Vancouver's Point Grey campus site in 1925, which included photographs and textual descriptions of the extant campus facilities. This booklet, *Buildings and Equipment of the University of British Columbia* (UEC 1925), formed the 'visual base-line' for the study. The booklet contained a campus map from 1925, which was useful to understand the purpose and placement of facilities in the early days of the university. Further, the images of the booklet would form a visual marker for what could be seen on campus as it opened to the public. From this published set of images, I began searching for the facilities, both on foot and in the photographic archive.

In my fieldwork I found that the agricultural facilities of UBC have undergone some of the most dramatic changes of any group of campus buildings at UBC. Table 9.2 lists each agricultural building that appeared in the UEC booklet, the date built, and its status when the project began in 2007.

From this list of agricultural education facilities, only a few were still standing and in use in 2007. At the start of the project I assumed that these remaining buildings were the only ones available as data for the repeat photography project. However, I realised that I could compare a 'time 1' photograph from the archive with a 'time 2' photo of whatever stood on that site in the present day. In addition, I could also compare an archival photo of a building with a renovation or a replication of a building in the present day.

Design and outcomes

In addition to the university archives itself and the UEC booklet, sources of data were found in annual reports, budget documents, official campus maps, archived issues of the student newspaper and campus magazines, and public websites that discuss the history of the university and campus planning. Researcher-produced photographs formed a central part of the data collection process and subsequent visual analysis. In 2007 (the year the study began) and five years later in 2012, I took photographs

Table 9.2 Agricultural facilities listed in Buildings and Equipment of the University of British Columbia, UEC, 1925

Name in 1925	Date Built	Status prior to 2007	Status in 2007
Old Dairy Barn	1917	Demolished 1919	–
Horticulture Building	1917	Moved in 1924 Renovated in 1968 Renovated in 2006	The Barn Coffee Shop
Dairy Barn	1918	Demolished 1974	–
Dairy Building	1918–1920	Additions in 1930s and 1950s	The Cheeze Factory (abandoned)
Soldiers' Civil Re-establishment (SCR) Vocational Building	1918–1920	Moved in 1962	Stores Road Annex
Farm Cottages	1919–1920	Moved in late 1960s Demolished 1990s	–
Beef Barn	1919–1920	Demolished 1968	–
Horse Barn	1920	Demolished 2002	Design influence for Old Barn Community Centre
Agronomy Building	1921	–	Landscape Architecture Annex
Agriculture Building	1924–1925	–	Mathematics Annex
Piggery	1925	Demolished 1968	–

of specific campus buildings and building sites that existed in 1925, the year the campus opened.

Below I discuss the repeat photography of two locations on the UBC campus, and the related findings. First, I present a series of photographs of the Horticulture Barn, with an archival image from 1925 and repeat photographs taken in 2007 and 2012 (Figure 9.2). Second, I discuss another style of repeat photography using the example of the Horse Barn, as it was known in 1925. Demolished in 2002, a later building resembling the Horse Barn was erected in 2006, and the site was rephotographed as part of a visual ethnography (Pink 2011) conducted by the researcher in 2012 (Figure 9.3).

Figure 9.2 Horticulture Barn, 1925; Barn Coffee Shop, 2007; Owl at the Barn daycare, 2012

Sources: Photo at left reproduced courtesy of the University of British Columbia Archives [UBC 1.1/1360]; photos at centre and right taken by the author.

Figure 9.3 Horse Barn, 1925; Old Barn Community Centre, 2012

Sources: Photo at left reproduced courtesy of the University of British Columbia Archives [UBC 1.1/1358]; photo at right taken by the author.

The analysis of the images for the project drew upon the theoretical frameworks mentioned above. The changing needs of postsecondary students were understood through the lens of 'academic performativity' (Blackmore & Sachs 2007; Butler 1990). As the university expanded, demographic shifts in the student population motivated the university to build or repurpose facilities for student services. The research mission of the university grew, and more graduate students enrolled. The Horticulture Barn (Figure 9.2) was refashioned into a snack bar (the Barn Coffee Shop) in the late 1960s, and as the need for child daycare space on campus became a prominent student concern especially among graduate students, it was converted into a daycare facility in 2010, named The Owl at the Barn. Each change was precipitated by student demand; remodelling the barn was a response and 'performance' of concern for students on the part of the administration. Due to the small size of the facility, the university's services offered in each phase were so minimal as to merely demonstrate a symbolic commitment to the needs of students.

The Horse Barn (Figure 9.3) was not physically saved through renovation, but instead a new building resembling it was built on the same site, offering students and staff a new privately operated coffee shop and fee-based recreational facility. A plaque on the wall of the Old Barn Community Centre reads:

> The Old Barn Community Centre takes its name and architectural style from a barn that once stood on this spot. The Horse Barn, modeled after a Pennsylvania Dutch dairy barn, was built in 1920 at a cost of $13,000. The barn's first inhabitants were Clydesdale horses and it later housed cattle, pigs, and other animals. By the 1980s, most of UBC's agricultural buildings had made way for other campus facilities. The Horse Barn survived, however, and served as a storage facility from 1995 to 2000. Students asked the University to renovate the barn, but, when renovations proved to be too costly, the barn was demolished in 2003. Today, the Old Barn Community Centre provides the community with an exercise room, a coffee shop and other facilities. The Community Centre also houses the University Neighbourhood Association office and serves as a gathering place for the mid-campus community.

Theoretical perspectives of academic capitalism (Slaughter & Leslie 1997; Slaughter & Rhoades 2004) and the enterprise university suggest that we might consider the former fields that once surrounded the Horse Barn as a form of capital. When the Horse Barn was demolished, the land was leased to housing developers to generate much-needed university revenue through the sale and rental of market-based housing units for students, academic staff and non-university residents. These new housing units form a new type of public-private partnership for the university in question, with the Old Barn Community Centre at the heart of this semi-private residential zone on campus.

The preserved Horticulture Barn and the new Old Barn Community Centre evoke a sense of nostalgia for the years that the campus was renown for land-based education. Indeed, a university budget report speaks of the community centre barn as being an 'icon', using visual language to evoke a sense of history and transcendence. The grand opening of the Old Barn Community Centre in 2006 was heralded as an 'old-fashioned barn raising', metaphorically including the private-housing residents (who might *not* be faculty, staff or students) as full members of the campus community.

Ironically, if the barns and the surrounding fields had not existed as educational spaces for so long, the land might not have been available for large research laboratories and commercial housing developments. The currently visible architectural forms of The Owl at the Barn daycare centre and the Old Barn Community Centre pay tribute to more than just agricultural education; also to the legacy of public education in the province of BC itself. However, while referencing the visual discourses of preservation, the community centre, in particular, also masks the commercialisation of the activities therein and the market-orientation of the surrounding housing projects. The comparative perspective offered by repeat photography permits a sustained reflection on university strategic planning, student services and fiscal policy. The two buildings also offer opportunities for contrast as they capture the essence of publicly supported, fee-based student services (Owl at the Barn daycare) and privately funded, commercial amenities (Old Barn Community Centre).

Conclusion

As this volume illustrates, visual methods are integral to educational research (Fischman 2001; Prosser 1998). Innovations in visual research will be consistently drawn from the visual arts and other fields, as well as arising from educational research. Repeat photography, borrowed from the natural sciences, has the potential to provide another viewpoint from which to consider educational and organisational change. The challenge for future researchers is to situate these methods as part of critical educational policy studies (Ball 1993). For higher education researchers this will also mean increasing the awareness that place is a significant aspect of educational space (Gumprecht 2007; Marginson 2009), a concept that is already understood in the broader field of educational studies (Gulson & Symes 2007; Gulson 2011).

The work undertaken here is at the boundary of accepted practice and is offered as an innovative approach that might offer a new methodological opening for educational research. Repeat photography recalls the past as part of an ongoing present, and helps to 'ground' current educational policy and practice in place-based considerations. Repeat photography is useful to visualise how time and place are interconnected. The method is evocative, creative and can generate affective responses to change as seen in contrast, which may be useful to better understand shifts in the value and purpose of education as these relate to educational policy making and advocacy.

References

Ball, S. J. (1993). What Is Policy? Texts, Trajectories and Toolboxes. *Discourse: Studies in the Cultural Politics of Education, 13*(2), 9–17.

Banks, M. (2007). *Using Visual Data in Qualitative Research*. Thousand Oaks, CA: Sage.

Barthes, R. (1982). *Camera Lucida: Reflections on Photography*. Translated by R. Howard. New York: Hill and Wang.

Becker, H. S. (1974). Photography and Sociology. *Studies in the Anthropology of Visual Communication, 1*(1), 3–26.

Blackmore, J., & Sachs, J. (2007). *Performing and Reforming Leaders: Gender, Educational Restructuring, and Organizational Change*. Albany, NY: State University of New York Press.

Butler, J. (1990). *Gender Trouble: Feminism and the Subversion of Identity*. New York: Routledge.

Emmison, M., & Smith, P. (2000). *Researching the Visual*. Thousand Oaks, CA: Sage.

Fagre, D. B., & McKeon, L. A. (2010). Documenting Disappearing Glaciers: Repeat Photography at Glacier National Park, Montana. In R. H. Webb, D. E. Boyer, & R. M. Turner (Eds), *Repeat Photography: Methods and Applications in the Natural Sciences* (pp. 77–88). Washington, DC: Island Press.

Fischman, G. E. (2001). Reflections about Images, Visual Culture and Educational Research. *Educational Researcher, 30*(8), 28–33.

Foucault, M. (1980). *Power/Knowledge*. New York: Pantheon.

Grady, J. (1991). The Visual Essay and Sociology. *Visual Sociology, 6*, 23–38.

Gruenewald, D. A. (2003). The Best of Both Worlds: A Critical Pedagogy of Place. *Educational Researcher, 32*(4), 3–12.

Gulson, K. N. (2011). *Education Policy, Space and the City: Markets and the (In)visibility of Race*. London: Routledge.

Gulson, K. N., & Symes, C. (Eds) (2007). *Spatial Theories of Education: Policy and Geography Matters*. London: Routledge.

Gumprecht, B. (2007). The Campus as a Public Space in the American College Town. *Journal of Historical Geography, 33*(1), 72–103.

Harper, D. (1988). Visual Sociology: Expanding Sociological Vision. *American Sociologist, 19*, 54–70.

Harper, D. (1996). Seeing Sociology. *American Sociologist, 37*(3), 69–78.

Holm, G. (2014). Photography as Research Method. In P. Leavy (Ed.), *The Oxford Handbook of Qualitative Research* (pp. 380–402). Oxford: Oxford University Press.

Kalin, J. (2013). Remembering with Rephotography: A Social Practice for the Inventions of Memories. *Visual Communication Quarterly, 20*(3), 168–179.

Klett, M. (2010). Three Methods of Presenting Repeat Photographs. In R. H. Webb, D. E. Boyer, & R. M. Turner (Eds), *Repeat Photography: Methods and Applications in the Natural Sciences* (pp. 32–45). Washington, DC: Island Press.

Klett, M. (2011). Repeat Photography in Landscape Research. In E. Margolis & L. Pauwels (Eds), *The SAGE Handbook of Visual Research Methods* (p. 114–130). Thousand Oaks, CA: Sage.

Klett, M., Manchester, E., Verburg, J., Bushaw, G., Dingus, R., & Berger, P. (1984). *Second View: The Rephotographic Survey Project*. Albuquerque: New Mexico University Press.

Klett, M., Bajakian, K., Fox, W. L., Marshall, M., Usehina, T., & Wolfe, B. (2004). *Third Views, Second Sights: A Rephotographic Survey of the American West*. Santa Fe: Museum of New Mexico.

Klett, M., & Lundgren, M. (2006). *After the Ruins, 1906 and 2006: Rephotographing the San Francisco Earthquake and Fire*. Berkeley, CA: University of California Press.

Klett, M., Solnit, R., & Wolfe, B. G. (2005). *Yosemite in Time: Ice Ages, Tree Clocks, Ghost Rivers*. San Antonio, TX: Trinity University Press.

Kumar, N. (2014). Repetition and Remembrance: The Rephotographic Survey Project. *History of Photography*, 38(2), 137–160.

Lemmons, K. K., Brannstrom, C., & Hurd, D. (2014). Exposing Students to Repeat Photography: Increasing Cultural Understanding on a Short-Term Study Abroad. *Journal of Geography in Higher Education*, 38(1), 86–105.

Marginson, S. (2009). Making Space in Higher Education. In S. Marginson, P. Murphy, & M. A. Peters (Eds), *Global Creation: Space, Mobility and Synchrony in the Age of the Knowledge Economy* (pp. 150–200). New York: Peter Lang.

Margolis, E. (1999). Class Pictures: Representations of Race, Gender and Ability in a Century of School Photography. *Visual Sociology*, 14, 7–38.

Margolis, E., & Pauwels, L. (Eds) (2011). *The SAGE Handbook of Visual Research Methods*. Thousand Oaks, CA: Sage.

Monk, H. (2014). Intergenerational Family Dialogues: A Cultural Historical Tool Involving Family Members as Co-researchers Working with Visual Data. In M. Fleer & A. Ridgway (Eds), *Visual Methodologies and Digital Tools for Researching with Young Children* (pp. 73–88). Switzerland: Springer International Publishing.

Pauwels, L. (2000). Taking the Visual Turn in Research and Scholarly Communication: Key Issues in Developing a More Visually Literate (Social) Science. *Visual Sociology*, 15, 7–14.

Pauwels, L. (2010). Visual Sociology Reframed: An Analytical Synthesis and Discussion of Visual Methods in Social and Cultural Research. *Sociological Methods & Research*, 38(4), 545–581.

Pink, S. (2011). Sensory Digital Photography: Re-thinking 'Moving' and the Image. *Visual Studies*, 26(1), 4–13.

Prosser, J. (Ed.) (1998). *Image-Based Research: A Sourcebook for Qualitative Researchers*. London & New York: Routledge Falmer.

Rieger, J. H. (1991). Visual Sociology: A Practical Pedagogy. *Visual Sociology*, 6(1), 38–43.

Rieger, J. H. (1996). Photographing Social Change. *Visual Sociology*, 11(1), 5–49.

Rieger, J. H. (2011). Rephotography for Documenting Social Change. In E. Margolis & L. Pauwels (Eds), *The SAGE Handbook of Visual Research Methods* (pp. 132–149). Thousand Oaks, CA: Sage.

Rose, G. (2007). *Visual Methodologies: An Introduction to the Interpretation of Visual Materials* (Second edition). Thousand Oaks, CA: Sage Publications.

Slaughter, S., & Leslie. L. (1997). *Academic Capitalism: Politics, Policies, and the Entrepreneurial University.* Baltimore, MD: Johns Hopkins Press.

Slaughter, S., & Rhoades, G. (2004). *Academic Capitalism and the New Economy.* Baltimore, MD: Johns Hopkins Press.

Smith, T. (2007). Repeat Photography as a Method in Visual Anthropology. *Visual Anthropology, 20*(2), 179–200.

Spencer, S. (2010). *Visual Research Methods in the Social Sciences: Awakening Visions.* New York: Routledge.

Stanczak, G. C. (Ed.) (2007). *Visual Research Methods: Image, Society, and Representation.* Thousand Oaks, CA: Sage Publications.

UEC [University Extension Committee]. (1925). *Buildings and Equipment of the University of British Columbia.* Vancouver, BC: University of British Columbia.

van Leeuwen, T., & Jewitt, C. (2001). *Handbook of Visual Analysis.* Thousand Oaks, CA: Sage Publications.

Webb, R. H., Boyer, D. E., & Turner, R. M. (2010a). Introduction: A Brief History of Repeat Photography. In R. H. Webb, D. E. Boyer, & R. M. Turner (Eds), *Repeat Photography: Methods and Applications in the Natural Sciences* (pp. 3–11). Washington, DC: Island Press.

Webb, R. H., Boyer, D. E., & Turner, R. M. (Eds) (2010b). *Repeat Photography: Methods and Applications in the Natural Sciences.* Washington, DC: Island Press.

Wyly, E. (2010). Things Pictures Don't Tell Us: In Search of Baltimore. *City, 14*(5), 497–528.

Zier, J. L., & Baker, W. L. (2006). A Century of Vegetation Change in the San Juan Mountains, Colorado: An Analysis Using Repeat Photography. *Forest Ecology and Management, 228*(1–3), 251–262.

10
Children Framing Childhoods and Looking Back
Wendy Luttrell

Introduction

This chapter draws upon my longitudinal research, *Children Framing Childhoods* and *Looking Back*, which put cameras in the hands of thirty-six children growing up in working-poor and immigrant communities, inviting them to document their lives and schooling over time (at ages ten, twelve, sixteen and eighteen).[1] The research has generated an extensive audiovisual archive housed on a password-protected website: 2036 photographs; sixty-five hours of video- and audio-taped individual and small group interviews of the thirty-six participants talking about their images; and eighteen video diaries produced by a sub-set of participants from ages sixteen to eighteen.

Elsewhere I have written about specific analytic moves I think are necessary for understanding the children's meaning making through photography (Luttrell 2010). These moves include the following: (1) an inventory and analysis of the *picture content*; (2) a consideration of different *picture-viewing* contexts and audiences (e.g. what the children tell an interviewer and what they discuss among their peers); and (3) an examination of the conditions, limitations and affordances of the children's *picture taking* (ibid.). These three 'sites' of meaning making have often been pulled apart, as Gillian Rose writes (2001, p. 16). But in practice, these sites are interwoven through histories, ideologies, politics and theories that guide people's use of cameras, the pictures they take, the meanings these images hold and the experiences that bring particular photographs to life. In this chapter I want to reflect on my research process and identify some advancements in theory building that I offer to enrich what I consider an under-theorised approach to visual methods with children and young people that has burgeoned in educational research over the last twenty-five years (Clark-Ibanez 2004; Clark 1999; Cook & Hess 2007; Kaplan 2013; Luttrell & Chalfen 2010; Mitchell 2011; Orellana 1999; Prosser & Burke 2007; Thompson 2008; Tinkler 2008; Yates 2010;).

Sociology, photography, family and childhood

There is an important historical legacy that is too often neglected in discussions about photography as a form of educational research. Before describing my research process, I want to situate it and pay tribute to early-20th-century reform-oriented sociologists who used photography to study the plight of immigrants, industrial workers (Harper 1998), child labour (Jacob Riis & Lewis Hine) and African American childhood (W. E. B. Du Bois). Sociologist Howard Becker drew attention to this earlier tradition forty years ago (1974) when he noted that photography and sociology share the same birth date and a common agenda – the exploration of social life and individual agency/resilience. It was common in early issues of the *American Journal of Sociology* for photographs to be published as part of scholarly articles. But, as the split grew between those who saw photography as 'documentary' and those who saw it as 'art', sociology, in its drive to become more science-like, relied less and less upon photography. Becker was interested in bringing sociology and photography into conversation with each other again, but with careful attention paid to the theories (broadly defined) that guide people's particular use of photography. Becker encouraged sociologists to think about photography as a *social activity* in which the photographer's and the viewer's eyes and visions are guided by social institutions and organisations that support specific ways of seeing through specific codes and conventions; for example, to question why the same photograph is viewed as 'art' if it is housed in a museum but as 'news' if it is appears in a newspaper.

The rise of photography has also been associated with the creation of modern childhood. Penny Tinkler (2008, p. 255) quotes Robson (2001, p. 131) who writes, 'seeing the history of photography and the history of the child through the same view finder is not only possible, but inevitable'. Tinkler notes that photographs of children, dating from the 1850s through to the present, have attracted much scholarly attention. Depictions of children have evolved and continue to be contested to this day – from understandings of children as indistinguishable from adults; to the child as naturally sinful in need of discipline and correction; to being innocent in body and mind; to be in need of protection from or, alternatively, as threats to adult society; and finally to what Higonnet refers to as the contemporary image of the 'knowing child' (1998).[2] Indeed, Lewis Hine's photographs of child labourers were powerful precisely because they depicted scenes of hardship that defied the norms of what was considered acceptable for a good childhood.

W. E. B. Du Bois's pioneering attempt to re-create a theory of African American childhood through photography stands out in this regard. In 1923, Du Bois called for submissions of photographs 'of interesting children, not necessarily pretty and dressed-up, but human and real' ('Children's Number'). Michelle Phillips writes that Du Bois's effort was to build not only a 'more democratic imagery but a more democratic imaginary' of African American childhood and personhood (Phillips 2013, p. 597). In contrast to the 'many and singularly different ideas' of childhood at the time, from the child as 'bond slave', 'automaton', 'Item of Expense' and parental 'personal adornment', Du Bois sought to offer what 'few people think of': 'the child as Itself – as an Individual with the right and ability to feel, think and act; a being thirsty to know, curious to investigate, eager to experiment' ('Opinion' 250 in Philips 2013).

In light of this history, it is curious that so few 'giving kids cameras' studies consider the codes, conventions and theories that guide children's photography, or comment on the constructions of childhood that young people in these studies are reflecting, rejecting or inventing.[3] According to Sharples et al. (2003), many of these projects treat the children as 'apprentice adult' photographers thus carrying forward a view of children as simply learners of adult culture or adult ways of seeing.[4] Similarly, it is often hard to distinguish between children's own intentions or 'readings' of their photographs and those of the adult researchers who seek to represent them (Piper & Frankham 2007). In both cases, a form of 'adultism' (albeit sometimes unwittingly) underlies the practice. There is a nagging and hard-to-answer question when adult researchers give kids cameras: what imaginary of childhood and personhood is brought into focus, from whose perspective, and with what purpose in mind?

While I do not claim to fully answer this question in my project, I offer some strategies that allow for a fuller appreciation of what the children in this project were doing with their cameras, which I argue counters deficit and stigmatised visions of their childhoods, families and schools.

The research and analytic process for *Children Framing Childhoods*

Children Framing Childhoods began in 2003 and took place in a kindergarten through sixth grade (K–6) public elementary school in Worcester, Massachusetts. Worcester is the second-largest city in New England and has a legacy of being an immigrant, multi-ethnic, multi-linguistic, 'working-class' city whose labouring class dramatically diversified from 1880 to 1920 and then again from 1990 to present. In describing the school, the principal identified its racial, ethnic and linguistic diversity as a point of pride and challenge for her staff as they searched for strategies that would foster greater inclusion of immigrant children and their parents into the school culture. I saw this as an opportunity to join interests – the school's and mine – and designed a project that would bring the children's experiences and perspectives about immigration, social and cultural differences, and family-school relationships more fully into view.

The school enrolled 370 students, of whom 92% were eligible for free school lunch; 37% of students were White, 10% were Black, 18% were Asian, and 35% were Hispanic.[5] I was curious to know what role, if any, gender, race, immigrant status and economic (dis)/advantage would play in the children's representations of and reflections about school, family and community life.

The children who participated represented the linguistic, racial and ethnic diversity of the school. They were each given a disposable camera (now ancient technology) with twenty-seven exposures and had four days to photograph their everyday lives. The overarching prompt was: *You have a cousin moving to Worcester and attending your school. Take pictures that will help him/her know what to expect.* In addition to the prompt, the children brainstormed a list of more specific prompts, including *take pictures of what you do after school, where you feel comfortable, people you admire*, and so on. After the photographs were developed, either I or a research assistant met with each child to talk about the images and why he/she had taken them; whether there were any photographs they wished they had taken but couldn't; and which photographs they would want to show their peers, teachers and a larger public. Then we met in small groups with the children as they discussed each other's photos without adult direction. Both the individual interviews and small group discussions were audio and video recorded. The same process was followed when the children were twelve but with a single prompt: *Take pictures of what matters to you.*

At ages ten and twelve the children produced more family photographs than images of school or community life. These family snapshots revealed a choreography of people, possessions and activities – moms in kitchens, babies being cuddled, family members snuggled on sofas, intergenerational groupings of family members posing in living rooms, siblings and cousins playing, girls doing domestic work (laundry, child minding, cleaning), pets, home dwellings inside and out, furnishings and decorations, cherished belongings neatly displayed, birthday parties, and religious celebrations, to name a few.

Sociologist Erving Goffman would characterise these photographs as 'private pictures':

> The special properties of private pictures as part of our *domestic ceremonial life* are worth considering... [these properties] mak(e) palpable to the senses what might otherwise remain buried and tacit in the structure of social life. (1979, p. 10, italics original)

In one sense, it could be argued that the children embraced the prescription that 'cameras go with family life', reflecting what is said to be the earliest use of photography – the establishment of the 'family album' (Sontag 1977,p. 8). And, as Laura Wexler has argued, this history of the 'family album' has been politically fraught:

> A century and a half into the abundant store of photographic images of American domestic life, it is well to remember that the American family album was severely out of balance from the start. The paired questions of who takes the pictures and who is in the pictures are not the only issue. The evidence from slavery suggests that the formal principles of family photography can only evolve in relation to the political principles that govern the recognition of families in the first place. Who would gain control of the domestic signifier through photography has been an issue ever since the medium was invented in 1839. (2000, p. 3)

Taking control of domestic signifiers to represent their families with pride and dignity is a key feature of the children's use of their cameras. Their pictures and explanations communicate their place in communal webs of care (including their own and others' care work), revealing what otherwise might remain buried about the organisation of family life, including, for example, the value the children placed on their mothers' roles in 'feeding the family' (DeVault 1991). Of course their

Figure 10.1 Kendra: 'This is where I am comfortable and where I feel respect'

photographs can be read as evidence of familial ideology – presentations of harmony, togetherness, unity and happiness (Chalfen 1987); or as creating an illusion of family coherence set against a 'flow of family life' that does not match up with what the children imagined their viewers might expect or that they themselves wanted to represent (Hirsch 1997, p. 7). Indeed, the most common reason the children gave for taking a picture of a family photograph was to 'show my whole family' when parents (most often fathers) or other extended family members were unavailable to be photographed for numerous reasons ranging from the demands of shift work to incarceration, death, divorce and migration.

Kendra's photographs and discussion are a case in point, illustrating what I have come to call counter narratives of care and belonging expressed through the children's pictures of *homeplaces* – a term coined by bell hooks to speak about spaces that actively nourish rather than negate and devalue the knowledge, experiences and *very being of* people who traditionally have been marginalised or excluded (hooks 1990). Two-thirds of Kendra's pictures were taken of and inside her home, a powerful statement of what she chose to be identified with, what she wished to commemorate and, perhaps most important, what might be beyond expressing in words.

Kendra took a photograph of her apartment building, Terrace Gardens. During her interview, she explained to me, 'This is where I am comfortable and where I feel respect'.

But upon viewing the next photograph of her stuffed animals, Kendra changed her mind. 'Oh, this is where I feel comfortable' (*pointing to the photograph shown in* Figure 10.2).

She named each stuffed animal and doll, explaining that 'Tigger' (the bright-yellow striped tiger) is most recent – a Christmas gift from her mother. In the photograph, Kendra displayed these items to 'show my cousin' (following the photographic prompt to take pictures to show one's cousin what to expect), and then added, 'but they aren't usually lined up like that'.

Throughout our conversation about her photographs, Kendra established the emotional landscape of her surroundings, her comfort, sense of belonging and respect. She placed special value on her mother, whom she had photographed twice, and explained why she admires her mom – 'she's thirty-three, married, pretty and loves to read, I know that'.

Figure 10.2 Kendra's toys

Weeks after our interview, Kendra and five other children were looking through each other's photographs, saying what they noticed. Allison picked up Kendra's photograph of her stuffed animals and exclaimed that she, too, has Tigger. Kendra was grinning from ear to ear, as this was the photograph she had chosen as one of her five 'favourites' to share with her peers. Kendra said Allison was welcome to bring her Tigger to come play at her house after school. Allison said, 'But my mother won't let me go to Terrace Gardens. She says it isn't safe'. Kendra responded swiftly and matter-of-factly, 'That's not true; it is the safest place that I have lived', and grabbed the photograph from Allison's hand as if protecting her cherished possessions. Allison embraced this response just as quickly, saying, 'Good, then I will tell my mom that I can come to your house'.

Both girls' conversational agility to surmount the negative perception of Terrace Gardens, a public housing project, is noteworthy. Allison's view, spoken through her mother's voice, is a commonly held perspective among white, Worcester residents, and in many other urban settings. Allison's family lived in a 'three decker' building across from the school. 'Three decker' apartment buildings are common throughout New England, built during the late 19th and early 20th century to house large numbers of immigrants coming to work in factory mills. 'Three deckers' are typically light-framed, wooden structures with each floor serving as a single apartment, and sometimes two apartments. Allison, who is white, lived with her family of five on one floor, her grandparents lived on another floor, and her mother's sister's family lived on the third floor. Allison's extended family has resided in the 'three decker' building for all of her life. Kendra's family, who were African American, had moved five times in search of affordable housing. Terrace Gardens was the third public housing unit in which her family of four had lived. Both the spatial isolation and racial residential segregation of the Worcester public housing units (known as the 'blocs') served as axes of social difference to be navigated by the child participants. And this was one among many exchanges between the children where pictures of personal belongings – stuffed animals, games, toys, brand-name clothing – served as a means for them to both uphold and reject social differences between themselves and their peers (Buckingham 2011; Pugh 2009). In this case, both girls avoided the sting and scorn of difference (living in 'public housing'), with the trace of Tigger in the photograph serving as the valued social glue.

At ages ten and twelve, Gabriel's composite set of photographs, like Kendra's, featured his *homeplace* over school images. His first photograph was an exception (Figure 10.3), and 'show[ed] Spanish in my school that makes me proud'.

But the rest centred on life at home – his mom in the kitchen baking cupcakes; his mom and sister curled up together on the living room daybed; a photograph of a collection of family photos framed together hanging on the living room wall; his mother's parakeet brought from Puerto Rico; his video-game console and a photo taken by his mother showing him playing in the room he shared with his little sister. His interview about the photographs focused on his mother: 'I admire my mom cause she's creative with food'. He described 'cook day' at home when she taught him how to make chicken that was 'juicy from adding wine'. He gestured with his hands, describing her delicious food, tenderly stroking the photograph, and with palpable emotion, he said, 'I love her so much I could explode from too much'. He continued to declare, 'I love her very much because she helps me with a lot of things, teaches me things'. When asked what else she helped him with, he responded, 'She helps me with my homework but mostly she helps me with being a child. ... With momma's rules, do this, do that, clean up your room. But I don't mind because I love her'. Gabriel used his camera to communicate

Figure 10.3 Gabriel's school library

his love for his mother in another way as well. When speaking with the interviewer about a photograph he had taken of his church, ten-year-old Gabriel turned away from the interviewer and gazed into the video camera that was taping the conversation. He held up his photograph and spoke directly to his mother: 'Mommy, I took this picture for you, I'm sorry it is blurry'. He then turned to the interviewer and explained that he took it because 'it means so much to her'.

Elsewhere I have discussed the efforts the children, like Gabriel and Kendra, took to photograph their mothers and to extol their care-giving and educational value (helping with homework, being lovers of reading) as if to manage or protect their mothers' image in the face of others (school officials, teachers, researchers) who might judge them negatively (Dodson & Luttrell 2011; Luttrell 2011, 2012).

But in conversation with his peers, Gabriel emphasised that he had taken the picture of the church because it was where he went to 'hang with the teenagers' who invited him to join their activities, even though he was 'only in fifth grade', highlighting the dual worlds children inhabit as they seek belonging and status with peers.

I want to suggest that the children's family photography was far more complex and layered than at first glance and that the conversations in different picture-viewing contexts helped to draw these complexities out. I have called this distinctive feature of my approach 'collaborative seeing' through which the complex evocations of the children's images and their context-dependent meanings can be preserved (Luttrell 2010; Fontaine & Luttrell 2015). Theoretically speaking, collaborative seeing allows us to engage what Weis and Fine (2012) call 'critical bifocality', which links individual meaning making to larger discourses, public policies and conditions that 'come to be woven into community relationships and metabolized by individuals' (Weis & Fine 2012, p. 174). Allison and Kendra's conversation about Terrace Gardens is such an example of competing ways of seeing that can generate counter narratives of care and belonging from the children's lived experience and perspective.

I also want to suggest that these different picture-viewing contexts also help to fill out the 'embodied sense of seeing and feeling', and the 'emotional geography' of caring and 'togetherness', to use Gillian Rose's (2004) terms, of the children's photography. First, not only do the pictures and their content evidence the *theme* of care and belonging, but their pictures also embody this theme in terms of bodily proximity portrayed in the photographs, and just as important, the way the young people engaged their pictures through touch, gestures, and intensity, as if the photograph carried the presence of the person, cherished object, or activities shown. Rose's article about the relationship between mothering and photography prompted me to consider more closely the children's photographs of mothers in *homeplaces*. First, Rose suggests that to fully appreciate family photography, we must understand the everyday, embodied practices – the doing of things, like posing, developing, curating, framing, displaying, sharing with relatives, and so on, that are part of how family photographs are viewed and received. Second, Rose suggests that the taking of family photographs, especially photographs of young children, might serve to assuage the mixed feelings – the strain, guilt, and irritation as well as joys – that most mothers feel toward children, especially in a culture that valorises what Sharon Hays has called 'intensive mothering'. Indeed, Rose notes that children are photographed most often during the time they are most demanding of their mothers, and thus when mothers are most likely to experience ambivalence. For the mothers she studied, 'looking at photographs, then, may produce a proximal space in which the ambivalence of a certain kind of mothering can be encountered on its shifting ground' (2004, p. 561).

There is ample evidence of the children doing things related to care and caring in their photographic practice; for example, Kendra's 'lining up' her stuffed animals for the picture, or Gabriel taking a photograph for his mother. Their practice of picture taking was embedded in the very context of care and communal networks, including handing their cameras to others who asked to document important family events, and finding creative ways to represent the traces of people no longer in their lives. Insofar as the children's photographs symbolised and reiterated the integration of extended family units, it is important to recognise their own active participation in fashioning these units, including the directions they gave to various members about posing, what to wear (e.g. many children wanted to take photographs of their mothers in their 'work uniforms' to 'show they have good jobs'), where to stand, and what symbolic resources to use to convey extended kin relations (e.g. pictures of clothes and gifts given by loved ones) as well as showing themselves doing family chores. Similarly, perhaps the children's picture taking of moms served to assuage their mixed feelings – the strains and discomfort as well as the admiration, gratitude and pride associated with the demands placed upon their mothers, as well as themselves. Such mixed feelings have been documented in Marjorie Falstich Orellana's (2009) account of immigrant children's translation work for family members and by Linda Burton's (2007) discussion of children growing up in low-income communities who perform family duties otherwise associated with adults. My point is that the children made visible the 'emotional geography' of growing up in wage-poor families, and in a school culture that relies upon the hidden and unacknowledged work of mothers and children, and in fact, often punishes children for meeting these family demands, this is a critically care-conscious insight.

The children's photographs of *homeplaces* offer what 'few people think of' – the working-class, historically marginalised child who is caring and is cared for, and this defies deficit and stigmatising views about their lives.

The research process and analysis for *Looking Back*

In 2009, I was able to contact twenty-six of the thirty-six original participants, who were attending six different high schools in Worcester. All agreed to be interviewed about their childhood photographs and to reflect upon the ways in which they and their lives had and had not changed.

In looking back on his photographs taken at ages ten and twelve, Gabriel, who now had chosen a new pseudonym, as Juan,[6] was most drawn to pictures of his younger self, expressing both embarrassment as well as delight in his haircut, clothing and old video games. He carefully studied the blurry photograph of the church, reminiscing about when he had the time to go to church, a time of 'freedom' from 'grown-up' responsibilities. He did not remember why he had taken the photograph of his mother in the kitchen, or what he had said about his explosive love for her. What he did say was that he had framed and given the photograph to her: 'She still keeps it on her dresser'. He took notice of the 'togetherness' of his mom and sister on the daybed: 'They are still so close, like best friends'. The shifting ground of his relationship to his childhood, family and mother now included increased responsibilities and demands. Working two jobs after school hours in order to help make ends meet curtailed his participation in the next phase of the project.[7]

Twenty-two participants agreed to continue by taking photographs as they had in the past, and to also document their contemporary lifeworlds with a Flip camcorder. The decision to introduce video was based on the young people's own enthusiasm and preference. In the short span of time, technological advances had made taking photographs commonplace and disposable cameras were a relic of the past. Many, but not all, of the young people had cell phones with cameras and regularly posted photographs they took on Facebook. Nonetheless, we used disposable cameras because not everyone had cell phones, and for some, keeping up with their cell phone service bills was not guaranteed. Flip camcorders were new and exciting, and introduced the medium of 'our generation', in the words of one participant.

At ages sixteen and eighteen the young people took more photographs of school and work settings in almost the same proportion as the photographs they took at home. But as 'private pictures' the photographs continued to 'commemorate special occasions, relationships, achievements, and life-turning points, ... of a familial or organizational [in this case mostly school] kind'. (Goffman 1979, p. 10). The videos, however, generated a different kind of imagery, linked to different codes and conventions, and evoked different registers of feeling. Whereas the children used their cameras to produce family albums that communicated communal webs of care and belonging, the videos were linked to the imaginaries of social media and YouTube and the diversity of the spaces. As a participant named Danny put it, 'Well you have to understand, you're looking at a guy who grew up watching thousands of YouTube videos. So when I got a [video] camera – this was my first camera – I just thought well I guess I'll do what I saw'.

Like others studying youth and digital media, I found that the young people were using digital media that they had learned from their peers, not teachers or adults, and 'notions of expertise and authority ha[d] been turned on their heads' (Ito et al. 2009b, p. 2). Far from being introduced to new skills and technology through the research project, the young people were instructing *us*, the researchers, about their reconfigured contexts for communication, self-expression, and the performative and interactive quality of the kind of identity work they were doing online. Indeed, the young people were well versed in creating computer-mediated identities online, in ways Watkins has described as 'theatrical and aspirational' (2009, p. 42). They crafted flattering personas, often sexualised and gender specific,[8] and, at times, exaggerated aspects of their lives – their incomes, social statuses, ages and activities. As one participant said of his video, 'I didn't just want to show my normal life because it's pretty boring'. Asked what parts of his video were out of the ordinary, he replied that going to the arcade was very unusual for him. He said that most people would be surprised to see him there because usually he is at home with family, doing homework (Luttrell et al. 2012). Whereas the children's family albums depicted their place in communal webs of care and support, the young people's videos featured mediated friendships and forms of emotional support that were linked on- and offline (Boyd 2014; Ito et al. 2009a; Lange

2014); I argue that these serve as their updated communal webs of care and belonging.

There is much to unravel in the layers of meaning making that the young people were doing through video. A discussion of their 'critical bifocality' and the 'emotional geography' of teenagehood portrayed by their videos needs to be grounded in the codes and conventions that guide digital photography and its uses: ways of seeing and interpreting moving images compared to photographs, the young people's different levels of access to and participation on- and offline, and media constructions of urban 'teenagers' and their prior experience in the *Children Framing Childhood* project, to name but a few. The hard-to-answer question is what imaginary of racialised, immigrant, 'urban' teenagehood and personhood is brought into focus by the young people in the *Looking Back* project?

Concluding thoughts

I undertook visual research with young people for three compelling reasons: because of what visual images can communicate about human values and social conditions; because this approach is known to introduce topics that might otherwise be overlooked or poorly understood by 'outsiders' and can surface local knowledge – in this case, children's knowledge; and because I wanted the research to build and support young people's agency, to give them maximum control, authority and say over their self-representations. Offering the young people multiple opportunities to make meaning of their own and each other's images in different contexts, and over time, generated both individual and collective insights that challenge a reigning discourse of deficit and blame and showcased their efforts to navigate dual worlds and differences. My goal for this chapter has been to deepen the dialogic, reflexive and theoretically informed analysis that guides visual research with children and youth so that we can more fully see their *homeplaces* as they see them – as more than material shelter, but also as shelter for the people, things and activities that make their lives meaningful and worthy. In the context of the current schooling regime, 'the child of school' (Popkewitz 1998) is understood to be an object to be targeted, labelled, blamed, explained, worried about, remediated and fixed so it can perform to expected standards. It is perhaps all the more striking then that the children's photography went beyond this imagery and brought attention to things unseen and unrewarded in school about 'being a child' and growing up in wage-poor households.

Notes

1. See Luttrell (2010, 2012, 2013); Lico & Luttrell (2011); Luttrell et al. (2011); Luttrell et al. (2012); Fontaine and Luttrell (2015).
2. Higonnet contends that for the first time in the history of art, children are being endowed 'with psychological and physical individuality at the same time as they [are] recognize[d]...as distinctively child-like'. (1998, p. 12).
3. See Wagner (1999) for his introduction to a special issue about how childhood is seen by children through photography that set the stage for doing visual research *with* not just *about* children.
4. See Cavin (1994) for a compelling exception to this rule.
5. These are the labels and percentages provided by the school; they do not publish records of the immigrant status of the children. Students are eligible for 'free and reduced lunch' in U.S. schools if their family income is at or below 185% of the federal poverty line. The percentage of students in a school receiving free and reduced lunch is an indicator of the socio-economic status of a school.
6. One of the challenges of doing longitudinal research and giving young people as much authorial control over their representations has included their desires to rename themselves. Gabriel/Juan is not the only young person who wished to do so.
7. This was the case for three other youth participants.
8. Girls visual self-representations often 'reinforce many of the strict codes of femininity in popular media culture', and boys often 'subscribe to tried and true notions of masculinity' (Watkins 2010, pp. 43–44).

References

Becker, H. (1974). Photography and Sociology. *Studies in Visual Communication, 1*, 3–26.
Boyd, D. (2014). *It's Complicated: The Social Lives of Networked Teens*. New Haven & Boston: Yale University Press.
Buckingham, D. (2011). *The Material Child: Growing Up in Consumer Culture*. Malden, MA: Polity Press.
Burton, L. (2007). Childhood Adultification in Economically Disadvantaged Families: a Conceptual Model. *Family Relations, 56*, 329–345.
Cavin, E. (1994). In Search of the Viewfinder: A Study of a Child's Perspective. *Visual Studies, 9*(1), 27–41.
Chalfen, R. (1987). *Snapshot Versions of Life*. Bowling Green, OH: Bowling Green State University Popular Press.
Clark, C. D. (1999). The Autodriven Interview: a Photographic Viewfinder into Children's Experiences. *Visual Sociology, 14*, 39–50.
Clark-Ibanez, M. (2004). Framing the Social World with Photo-Elicitation Interviews. *American Behavioral Scientist, 47*(12), 1507–1527.
Cooke, T., & Hesse, E. (2007). What the Camera Sees and from Whose Perspective: Fun Methodological in Engaging Children in Enlightening Adults. *Childhood, 14*(1), 29–45.
DeVault, M. (1991). *Feeding the Family: The Social Organization of Caring as Gendered Work*. Chicago: University of Chicago Press.

Dodson L., & Luttrell W. (2011). Families Facing Untenable Choices. *Contexts*, *10*(1), 38–42.
Fontaine, C., & Luttrell, W. (2015). Re-Centering the Role of Care in Young People's Multimodal Literacies: A Collaborative Seeing Approach. In M. Hamilton, R. Heydon, K. Hibbert, & R. Stooke (Eds), *Negotiating Spaces for Literacy Learning: Multimodality and Governmentality*. Bloomsbury Books.
Goffman, E. (1979). *Gender Advertisements*. New York: Harper and Row.
Harper, D. (1998). Visual Sociology: Expanding Sociological Vision. *American Sociologist*, (Spring), 54–70.
Higonnet, A. (1998). *Pictures of Innocence: The History and Crisis of Ideal Childhood*. London: Thames and Hudson.
Hirsch, M. (1997). *Family Frames: Photography, Narrative and Postmemory*. Cambridge, MA: Harvard University Press.
hooks, b. (1990). Homeplace: A Site of Resistance. In *Yearning: Race, Gender, and Cultural Politics* (pp. 45–53). Boston: South End Press.
Ito, M. et al. (2009a). *Hanging Out, Messing Around, and Geeking Out: Kids Living and Learning with New Media*. MIT Press.
Ito, M. et al. (2009b). *Living and Learning with New Media: Summary of Findings from the Digital Youth Project*. MIT Press.
Kaplan, E. B. (2013). *'We Live in the Shadow': Inner-city Kids Tell Their Stories through Photographs*. Philadelphia, PA: Temple.
Kuhn, A. (1995). *Family Secrets: Acts of Memory and Imagination*. London: Verso.
Lange, P. (2014). *Kids on YouTube: Technical Identities and Digital Literacies*. Walnut Creek, CA: Left Coast Press.
Lico, S., & Luttrell, W. (2011). An Important Part of Me: A Dialogue about Difference. *Harvard Educational Review*, *81*(4), 667–686.
Luttrell, W. (2010). 'A Camera Is a Big Responsibility': A Lens for Analyzing Children's Visual Voices. *Visual Studies*, *25*(3), 224–237.
Luttrell, W. (2012). Making Boys' Care Worlds Visible. *Thymos: Journal of Boyhood Studies*, *6*(2), 185–201.
Luttrell, W. (2013). Children's Counter-Narratives of Care. *Children and Society*, *27*(4), 295–308.
Luttrell, W., & Chalfen, R. (2010). Hearing Voices: An Introduction to Dilemmas in Visual Research. *Visual Studies*, *25*(3), 197–200.
Luttrell, W., Restler, V., & Fontaine, C. (2012). Youth Video-Making: Selves and Identities in Dialogue. In E. J. Milne, C. Mitchell, & N. deLange (Eds), *Participatory Video Handbook* (pp. 164–178). AltaMira.
Luttrell, W., Dorsey, J., Hayden, J., & Shalaby, C. (2011). Transnational Childhoods and Youth Media: Seeing with and Learning from One Immigrant Child's Visual Narrative. In J. Fisherkeller (Ed.), *International Perspectives on Youth Media: Cultures of Production & Education* (pp. 192–208). New York: Peter Lang Publishers.
Mitchell, C. (2011). *Doing Visual Research*. SAGE Publications.
Orellana, M. F. (1999). Space and Place in an Urban Landscape: Learning from Children's Views of Their Social World. *Visual Sociology*, *14*, 73–89.
Orellana, M. F. (2010). *Translating Childhoods: Immigrant Youth, Language and Culture*. New Brunswick, NJ: Rutgers University Press.
Phillips, M. (2013). The Children of Double Consciousness. From the Souls of Black Folk to Brownies' Book. *PMLA*, *128*(3), 590–607.

Piper, H., & Frankham, J. (2007). Seeing Voices and Hearing Pictures: Image as Discourse and the Framing of Image-Based Research. *Discourse Studies in the Cultural Politics of Education, 28*(3), 373–387.

Popkewitz, T. S. (1998). The Culture of Redemption and the Administration of Freedom as Research. *Review of Educational Research, Spring, 68*(1), 1–34.

Prosser, J., & Burke, C. (2007). Childlike Perspectives through Image-Based Educational Research. In J. G. Knowles & A. Cole (Eds), *Handbook of the Arts in Qualitative Research: Perspectives, Methodologies, Examples and Issues*. London: Sage.

Pugh, A. J. (2009). *Longing and Belonging: Parents, Children, and Consumer Culture*. Berkeley: University of California Press.

Robson, E. (2001). *Men in Wonderland: The Lost Girlhood of the Victorian Gentleman*. Princeton, NJ: Princeton University Press.

Rose, G. (2001). *Visual Methodologies: An Introduction to the Interpretation of Visual Materials*. London; Thousand Oaks, CA; Delhi: Sage.

Rose, G. (2004). 'Everyone's Cuddled Up and It Just Looks Really Nice': An Emotional Geography of Some Mums and Their Family Photos. *Social and Cultural Geography, 5*(4), 549–563.

Sharples, M., Davidson, L., Thomas, G. V., & Rudman, P. D. (2003). Children as Photographers: An Analysis of Children's Photographic Behavior and Intentions at Three Age Levels. *Visual Communication, 2*(3), 303–330.

Sontag, S. (1977). *On Photography*. New York: Anchor Books, Doubleday.

Thompson, P. (Ed.) (2008). *Doing Visual Research with Children and Young People*. London: Routledge.

Tinkler, P. (2008). A Fragmented Picture: Reflections on the Photographic Practices of Young People. *Visual Studies, 23*(3), 255–266.

Wagner, J. (1999). Seeing Kids' Worlds. *Visual Sociology, 14*, 1–5.

Watkins, C. (2009). *The Young and the Digital: What the Migration to Social Network Sites, Games, and Anytime, Anywhere Media Means for Our Future*. Boston, MA: Beacon Press.

Weis, L., & Fine, M. (2012). Critical Bifocality and Circuits of Privilege: Expanding Critical Ethnographic Theory and Design. *Harvard Educational Review, 82*(2).

Wexler, L. (2000). *Tender Violence: Domestic Visions in an Age of us Imperialism*. Chapel Hill & London: University of North Carolina Press.

Yates, L. (2010). The Story They Want to Tell, and the Visual Story as Evidence: Young People, Research Authority and Research Purposes in the Education and Health Domains. *Visual Studies, 25*(3), 280–291.

11
On 'Gods' and 'Kings' in the Tutorial Industry: A 'Media Spectacle' Analysis of the Shadow Education in Hong Kong

Aaron Koh

Introduction

There is something spectacular about the visual ecology of tutorial centre advertisements that is circulating in the mediascape of Hong Kong. It is difficult to miss these scintillating, attention-grabbing advertisements. They are everywhere in the public spaces of Hong Kong. Not only do they appear as huge billboards erected on well-trafficked avenues, and public transport such as MTR and double-decker buses, they are also circulated in social media platforms like YouTube and more traditional media formats, such as TV commercials and full-page newspaper advertisements.

Called 'shadow education', these tutorial centres are multimillion-dollar industries. According to Mark Bray and Chad Lykins (2012, p. 20), the market size of the tutoring industry is estimated to be around HK$1.984 billion (US$255 million). The sheer size of the industry invites many curious questions about this thriving enterprise. The analytic focus of this chapter is, however, limited to the analysis of multimodal tutorial centre advertisements.

This chapter is situated within a growing body of research on the global phenomenon of shadow education (see e.g. Manzon & Areepattamannil 2014; Aurini et al. 2013; Mori & Baker 2010; Lee et al. 2009). Specific to the private supplementary education in Hong Kong alone, there has been a sudden surge of research interest indicated by numerous recently published literatures (see Koh 2015; Bray et al. 2014; Chan & Bray

2014; Kwo & Bray 2014; Bray 2013; Zhan et al. 2013). In the literatures, considerable knowledge about the consumption of tutorial services has revealed patterns and demography, and why students attend tutorial centres and their perception of the effectiveness of private tutoring when compared with mainstream schooling. These are important areas of research. Yet given the proliferation of tutorial advertisements in the mediascape of Hong Kong, there is, surprisingly, no research that forays into the production of the tutoring industry. By 'production', I am referring to the visual economy of tutorial advertisements as a form of direct marketing.

In this chapter, I set up 'media spectacle' (Kellner 2003) as a theoretical apparatus to frame the study of the mediascape of multimodal tutorial centre advertisements. Indeed, I argue that the media spectacle of tutorial advertisements has become an endemic feature closely associated with the culture of education in Hong Kong.

The overall aim of this chapter is to fill the void in the literature of shadow education on the 'production' of the tutoring industry featuring a close-up, multimodal discourse analysis of the ideological work of media spectacle of tutorial advertisements. Theoretically, it also reinvigorates Kellner's notion of media spectacle by drawing on two bodies of knowledge – namely, marketing semiotics (Oswald 2012) and emotion studies (Ahmed 2004) – to derive an analytical framework to analyse two multimodal tutorial centre advertisements.

Media spectacle: a theoretical framing

'Media spectacle' is developed out of Guy Debord's (1977) seminal work *Society of Spectacle*. The crux of his theory is that consumption has become the culture of everyday life encouraged by a dazzling array of advertising images. Referring to news, propaganda, advertising and entertainment as examples of 'spectacles', Debord theorises that 'all that once was directly lived has become mere representation' (p. 12). Put simply, the scintillating images of commodities are a defining feature of contemporary society *mediating* a reality of the world.

Writing in the late 1960s, Debord (1988) was critical of the 'the excesses of the media' (p. 7) in generating false needs. He repeatedly acknowledged the persuasive power of the media in producing 'waves of enthusiasm for particular products' (p. 44). Comparing 'old religious fetishism, with its transported convulsionaries and miraculous cures' to commodity fetishism, Debord argues that 'the fetishism of the commodity also achieves its moment of acute fervor' (p. 44). What is conjured up here is the overpowering influence of commodities to the extent that people are hypnotised and seduced by multimodal advertising to consume, although 'multimodal' would not be the lexicon used in Debord's time.

However, where Debord's consumption theory becomes problematic is when he asserts that 'the spectacular *subjects* living human beings to its will to the extent that the economy has brought under its sway' (p. 16, emphasis mine). In other words, he is suggesting that the consumer is powerless, passive and easily succumbs to the relentless propaganda of goods. This assumption has since been critiqued by audience study and reception theorists who proposed the theory of active consumption and readership (see Hall 1980; Ang 1985; Fiske 1990; Hall 1993). This limitation aside, Debord's sociological observation of an image-commodity society aided by the pervading influence of media advertising is even truer in our contemporary multimodal world where sophisticated advertising images arrest our attention online and offline.

While retaining the theoretical essence of Debord's 'society of the spectacle', Douglas Kellner (2003) expands this theory with concrete examples of contemporary media spectacles. This includes branding in corporate culture, celebrities culture, and fashion, film, and television industries where the spectacular display of visuality and visual practices work to mobilise consumption, thought and action (ibid). Kellner's extension of 'media spectacular' is helpful in that it explores how the 'society of the spectacular' can be applied to contemporary mediascape. He adds clarity to Debord's abstract theorising with generous examples. But this is not all. There is a critical slant to his coinage of 'media spectacle'. The term is meant to provoke critical analysis of 'what media culture discloses about contemporary society, as well as carrying out ideological critique of the specific politics of a text or artefact' (Kellner 2003, p. 14).

The media spectacle of tutorial advertisements in Hong Kong

In reference to the phenomenon of tutorial advertisements, 'media spectacle' appositely applies to the visual landscape of attention-grabbing advertisements. As mentioned, these advertisements can be seen everywhere in the mediascape of Hong Kong, even on moving double-decker buses.

For something to reach a phenomenal level, not only does popularity count but there must be a huge crowd of followers. In some instance, its consumption reaches a frenzy level closely sought after by its fans. Not unlike the flash and glitz of popular culture, I am referring to the media marketing of tutorial advertisements as a local cultural phenomenon unique to the Hong Kong education landscape. One could easily mistake these ads for some celebrity event or Asian pop megastar endorsing some product. The media images of celebrity-looking tutors, stylised in designer clothes and cool hairdos, with their model-like posturing is familiar enough for one to recognise that its 'genre' is heavily borrowed from the fashion and style of pop idols in the entertainment industries (see Figure 11.1 and 11.2). A more thorough analysis will follow in the latter part of the chapter. Indeed, these ads are quintessential 'media spectacles'. The cost of investing in these advertisements is enough to take the *production* of the tutoring industry seriously for analysis. One source reveals that the more established tutorial centres spend between HK $900,000 to HK $1.3 million in advertising alone each year (Brenhouse 2011).

Applying the lens of 'media spectacle', these multimodal advertisements invite the reader/viewer to ask questions that extend beyond the aesthetic appeal and surface meaning of the advertisement. For example, what do these visual texts disclose about education in Hong Kong, and the wider Hong Kong society? What social normative messages are conveyed by these advertisements? While obvious, it is nevertheless important to ask, *who benefits* from the production of these ads? These are *critical* questions a media spectacle analysis invites, which I will return to answer in the analysis section of the chapter.

However, conceptually, 'media spectacle' does not adequately attend to the affordances of the multimodal composition of these advertisements and the emotions they generate. My premise is that tutorial advertisements belong to the semiotic economy of signs which deploy culture-specific modes of meaning representation to generate a register of emotions to persuade prospective consumers. As an expansion to Kellner's theory of media spectacle, I turn to theories of marketing semiotics and emotion studies to develop an analytic framework to analyse the visual *production* of the tutorial industry.

Theorising the visual production of the tutorial industry

Marketing semiotics is the amalgamation of two bodies of knowledge, 'semiotics' and 'marketing' for effective branding. It involves 'a strategic reorganization of the brand-building hierarchy that moves semiotic research to the front of the planning process' (Oswald 2012, p. 1). This entails applying the knowledge of semiotics to the full spectrum of the branding process. In order to target prospective consumers, the semiotising of the branding process pays close attention to the meanings associated with the brand, the consumer and the cultural context of the product advertised (ibid).

Marcel Danesi (2013) further explains that the process of semiotising at work in brand creation 'involves semiotizing a product by assigning it a name, a visual sign (logo), a system of language forms (slogan, taglines, etc), and then textualizing the brand by creating appropriate ads and commercials for it' (p. 1). Although Danesi does not use the language of multimodality to explain how marketing semiotics works, his explanation alludes to the way different modes (i.e. visual and language systems) work to create meanings. In the language of semiotics, 'mode is a socially shaped and culturally given semiotic resource for making meaning' (Kress 2010, p. 79). Whether it is the language system or visual sign, the choice of semiotic inventories 'must reflect a deep and nuanced understanding of the multiple cultural categories in which the brand is embedded' (Oswald 2012, p. 46). This is also to say that marketing semiotics places importance on knowing the cultural and social context for effecting branding of a product.

The theory of marketing semiotics offers a few insights to the visual production of tutorial advertisements. First, these ads can be powerful to persuade because the semiotic inventories of the advertisement synergises with other elements of the culture are already in play (Arend 2014). In other words, a nuanced reading of tutorial advertisements requires some understanding of the culture of education in Hong Kong because these advertisements are essentially social texts that tell stories about the wider culture of Hong Kong. Second, to understand the brand discourse of tutorial advertisements requires an exploration of the intersemiotic relationship between the selection of signs and linguistic resources and their affordances. As modes are loaded with culture-specific meanings, every aspect of the textuality of the advertisement such as the choice of fonts, colour, layout and so forth are treated as part of a complex sign system used to represent meanings and position the reader/viewer.

There is, however, more to the semiotising of tutorial advertisements. Often glossed over in the analysis are the accompanying emotions that these advertisements evoke and circulate. The scholarship on emotion studies is particularly useful as a theoretical resource to understand the emotional associations of tutorial advertisements. I extract a few theoretical points primarily from Sarah Ahmed's (2004) seminal work on emotions relevant to my theorising of the visual production of tutorial advertisements.

Drawing on Descartes, Ahmed's (2004) theoretical point that 'feelings...take the "shape" of the contact we have with objects' (p. 5) is illuminating as it implies the consequent effect of the frequent exposure to the attention-grabbing tutorial advertisements. That is to say, 'objects' like tutorial advertisements produce and evoke a whole register of emotional responses; they are full of affective value and 'they involve (re)actions or relations of "towardness" or "awayness" in relation to such objects' (p. 8). In the case of the tutorial advertisements, their visual salience and glossy appeal attract more than repel. This is where, I argue, the potency of the affect of tutorial advertisements resides.

Of significance, trenchant to the theorising here is Ahmed's point that emotions do things to people: 'emotions work by working through signs and on bodies to materialize the surfaces and boundaries that were lived as worlds' (p. 191). I therefore argue that the semiotic sentiments of emotion 'are mobilizing as they motivate people to act' (Kenway & Fahey 2011, p. 169). This argument points to the central tenet of my theoretical premise about the visual production of advertisements in the tutorial enterprise which is mobilised by the semiotising work of advertisements and the accompanying emotions.

In sum, Ahmed's theorising of emotions – in particular, her pointed argument that emotions are attached to things and that they move and do things to people – as well as the combinatory theory of marketing semiotics bear insights into the visual production of the tutorial industry where intensive and extensive advertising continue to cast their magical spells on Hong Kong students. My analysis of the advertisements later will include an analysis of the emotional contour of the advertisements. At this juncture of the chapter, I provide a brief context of the education system in Hong Kong and its culture of schooling. This contextual information is necessary in order to appreciate the semiotic and ideological work of the advertisements.

The social context and culture of education in Hong Kong

Like most East Asian societies, education in Hong Kong is a serious endeavour that involves parents planning for their children's education as early as kindergarten. This navigation is never a straightforward process because the education policies in Hong Kong have inevitably created a 'market of schools' for parents to 'shop' and 'choose', conditioned by how well a child performs academically and at admission interviews. Its language policy, for example, has created two types of schools, known as English Medium-of-Instruction (EMI) schools and Chinese Medium-of-Instruction (CMI) schools. The former is more popular than the latter because parents believe an education in English will have more economic purchase for their child. Thus, EMI schools are highly regarded, and competition for places is very keen. In my research in one elite EMI Direct Subsidy School (DSS) in Hong Kong, for example, the school received well over 800 applicants for 120 places in Form 1 (Grade 7) in 2011.

While there isn't an official ranking for secondary schools in Hong Kong, it is common knowledge for the locals that secondary schools are differentiated into Band 1, 2, and 3 schools based on the calibre of students they admit. Band 1 schools are schools with high-achieving students, and are therefore the most prestigious; whereas Band 2 schools have middle achievers. Finally, Band 3 schools take in students from the bottom end of the spectrum. In addition to local government schools, existing within the different bands of schools are also the Direct Subsidy Schools. These schools charge fees while also receiving a smaller subsidy from the Hong Kong government. But they have more leeway with their curriculum and also hiring of their staff. The last category of schools is the international schools operating in Hong Kong. These are full-fee paying schools meant for children of expatriates working in Hong Kong, but increasingly these schools are also attracting local students.

An understanding of the 'market of schools' in Hong Kong is important because the competition to enter top EMI schools has come to define the broader culture of education in Hong Kong. Many middle-class parents believe that sending their children to top-performing schools will increase their chances of entering the local universities. The competition to get into good schools, as well as doing well in the exam of their lives – the Hong Kong Diploma in Secondary Education (HKDSE) examination – which determines if students qualify for the local universities, has come to embody the educational frenzy that shapes the sentiments of the culture of education in Hong Kong. It is precisely this educational frenzy that is propelling the popularity and thriving tutorial industry. According to Ora Kwo and Mark Bray (2014), a survey conducted in 2011–2012 revealed that 61.1% of sampled Grade 9 and Grade 12 students had received private supplementary tutoring.

The knowledge of the local, socio-cultural context of education in Hong Kong will be useful in the analysis of the production of multi-modal tutorial advertisements, as Gillian Rose (2012) appositely states: 'The seeing of an image ... always takes place in a particular social context that mediates its impact. It also always takes place in a specific location with its own particular practices' (p. 15). Given the idiosyncratic culture of education in Hong Kong, of analytic interest is how the semiotics of the media marketing of the tutorial industry work in relation to the emotional geography of its education landscape. I shall answer this question in the analysis section.

A *situated* visual methodology

This chapter sets out to examine the visual *production* of the tutorial industry and the commodification of education. The two photo images selected for analysis are deliberately chosen to reflect the mediums in which tutorial advertisements commonly appear in the public domain of Hong Kong: Figures 11.1 (Billboard) and 11.2 (Flyer). The photographs were taken in situ using my iPhone during my trips to Hong Kong between 2011 and 2013 to do ethnographic fieldwork in an elite school for a project I was involved in. I did not go to a specific location or set up a plan to take photographs of these advertisements. Wherever I came across a tutorial advertisement, I took a shot to add to my visual data bank. In visual methodologies, such an approach would be considered as 'researcher-generated photography' (Tinkler 2013, p. 124) or as 'photo-documentation' (Rose 2012, p. 298) with a view to analysing the visual phenomenon.

Featuring these images for analysis, however, poses some ethical dilemmas. The issue of consent to reproduce the advertisement and the thought that the respective tutorial centres featured in the photo images here in this book are getting free 'advertising space' troubled me. I flipped the pages of books on visual methods for answers to address this ethical dilemma, but none were found, understandably so because every visual-related research project works with different kinds of visual texts. Nevertheless, I took on the advice of Emmison et al. (2012) 'to justify your decisions based upon your context' (p. 10) when considering ethics in visual research.

In reproducing the photo images of tutorial advertisements, my purpose is to treat these advertisements as 'social text' for analysis. However, the ethical issue of naming specific tutorial centres led me to crop off all references to the name of the tutorial centre. As the motivation of the analysis is to understand how education is packaged as a commodity semiotically by media marketing, I clarify that the photo images reproduced here should not be seen as receiving free publicity or thought of as reputable just because they are found featured in a scholarly work. I also do not think consent needs to be sought from the tutorial centres because these advertisements are essentially everyday texts seen everywhere in Hong Kong. Furthermore, my research has no direct bearing to the operations of specific tutorial centres, as the focus of my research is on the phenomenon of visual spectacles of tutorial advertisements.

One analytic aspect this chapter explores is the intersemiotic relationship between text and image identified as a salient modal affordance in the advertisements. To do this analysis would require some translation work, from Chinese to English, as the linguistic texts of the advertisements are in Chinese. Whilst I know some Chinese, to ensure the accuracy and the essence of meanings conveyed by the Chinese text, I enlisted the help of two former Hong Kong students,[1] who are 'insiders' and native speakers of the language, to do the translation so that meanings are not lost in translation. Only the main caption in each advertisement is analysed, as some of the fine prints are too small to read.

Deriving a multimodal discourse analytical framework

There are many analytic frameworks available on multimodal analysis such as those inspired by the systemic functional grammar and social semiotic multimodal analysis framework formulated out of the Multimodal Analysis Lab at the National University of Singapore (e.g. O'Halloran 2004; Lim & O'Halloran 2012; Feng & O'Halloran 2012), the extension of Gunther Kress and Theo van Leeuwen's (2006) 'visual grammar' analytical framework applied to multimodal analysis (Machin 2007), and the merging of Critical Discourse Analysis with Multimodal Analysis called Multimodal Critical Discourse Analysis (MCDA; Machin & Mayr 2012; Machin 2013). Other frameworks, such as a multimodal framework for analysing websites, are also developed by Luc Pauwels (2012) and an eclectic multimodal framework featured in Maiorani and Christine (2014).

These frameworks, however, cannot be duplicated wholesale and applied to the photo images. To do so would impose an analysis that would yield up a contrived analysis that does not serve the purpose of inquiry into the media spectacle of tutorial advertisements. Taking into consideration the theoretical underpinnings of media spectacles, marketing semiotics and emotion studies, I drew up an analytical framework mobilising an assemblage of analytical tools borrowed from multimodality (Machin 2007), visual grammar (Kress & van Leeuwen 2006),

Table 11.1 A multimodal discourse analytical framework

Media spectacles	Analytic categories	Semiotic affordances
How are 'star tutors' represented?	Visual representation of social actors	Age; facial expressions (gaze); hairstyle; fashion; poses; angle
How is the reader/viewer positioned?	Aesthetics	Associative meanings of colour, typography, composition/layout
What emotions are invoked? That is, 'emotionality of texts' (Ahmed 2004, p.12)?	Intersemiotic relations of image and text	Lexical items and their connotations; metonymy and (visual) metaphor; image-text relation
How is the reader/viewer affected emotionally by the text?	Emotional effect of aesthetics	Colour; size of typography, typographic profile and salience

semiotics of cinema (Lotman 1976) and critical visual methodologies (Rose 2012).

To analyse and interpret how education and teacher identities are packaged and commodified, and the emotional appeal of the media spectacles of tutorial advertisement, a framework for analysis is proposed (see Table 11.1). In all the tutorial advertisements that I collected, there is an apparent format to them; the portrait of a star tutor is featured, sometimes in pairs or in a group. The images of these star tutors are striking enough to grab the reader/viewer's attention because they look like fashion models or pop stars. Borrowing from Theo van Leeuwen's (2008) 'visual representation of social actors' (p. 136) framework, my analysis is directed at the image of the star tutor because it stands out strikingly as a *signifier* loaded with semiotic meanings, enhanced by the semiotic affordances of the 'gaze', 'fashion', 'hairdo', 'poses' and 'angle'.

Clearly, these advertisements are designed with a particular audience in mind. How then does the visual representation of the star tutor connect and 'speak' to the reader/viewer? Here the aesthetics of the advertisements are not arbitrarily chosen but ideologically shaped to position the reader; recall that in the economy of semiotics, all signs are motivated (Kress 2010). Therefore, the analytic category of 'aesthetics' picks on relevant semiotic inventories and analyses the associated meanings that semiotic resources such as colour, typography and composition/layout carry.

To find out how emotions are constituted in tutorial advertisements and the specific emotions generated, the analytic category of 'intersemiotic relations' of image and text is the focus of analysis. Carey Jewitt (2009) defines 'intersemiotic relations' as 'the relationship across and between modes in multimodal texts' (p. 17). In the proposed framework, the modes of (Chinese) linguistic text and image are explored as affordances of meaning production, although it is the former that has more salience. Specific to the tutorial advertisement, I adulterated Ahmed's notion of 'emotionality of texts', in which she refers to only 'figures of speech' (p. 12) to include the analysis of lexical items used and the *emotional* connotations they evoke.

Next, the proposed framework also considers how the texts position the reader/viewer emotionally. Ahmed (2004) posits that emotions can move through the circulation of objects such as advertisement. This aspect of the analysis is examined in relation to the semiotic resources of 'colour', 'size of typography', 'typographic profile' and 'salience'. In essence, 'the emotionality of texts' (Ahmed 2004, p. 12) is semiotically produced through framing strategies such as the choice of aesthetic designs as well as the deployment of visual metaphor and the associated meanings of the Chinese linguistic texts.

Analysis of tutorial advertisements

There is a distinct reading path that is set up for the reader/viewer in Figure 11.1. This reading path is organised by the visual salience of the image as 'Dr Koopa Koo' is positioned in the nucleus of the text. However, his formal wear and hairstyle are dull and do not seem to measure up to his iconic 'star tutor' status. Furthermore, the colour coordination of his fashion serves to enhance his rather serious demeanour. The overall colour scheme of the advertisement further accentuates the aura of seriousness as if demanding the reader/viewer to be in awe of him. While there is a direct gaze at the viewer, the visual demand of the image is less than friendly. In fact, there is an aura of austerity in his countenance, which could be explained by the linguistic text. Yet the frontal angle and mid-shot suggest otherwise. In visual semiotics, the size of frame signifies social distance, whereas the angle from which we see the image connotes social relation (van Leeuwen 2008; Marchin 2007). The mid-shot and frontal angle of the image in this instance construct Dr Koopa Koo as a relatable teacher who wants to be involved in teaching his prospective students.

200 Aaron Koh

Figure 11.1 A tutorial billboard advertisement in an MTR station

However, in this advertisement, the linguistic text presides over the meaning of the image. In other words, the intersemiotic relationship between the text and image is not one where the verbal and visual mode is mutually reinforcing the meaning potential of the multimodal text. Instead, the represented image feeds on the modal affordance of the verbal mode and its associated meanings for a wholesome interpretation.

The use of a verbal metaphor together with the metaphorical association of the typographical profile of 數神 is not to be discounted for its semiotic affordances and meaning potential. The literal translation of 數神 is 'Math God'. While 數神 is linguistically a noun phrase, it functions metaphorically to 'name' the identity of the image as an expert in Math. The verbal metaphor 數神 elevates Dr Koopa Koo to a deity, a God of Math or what we would commonly say in English, a Math Wizard. Furthermore, the sheer size of the linguistic text 數神 affords greater visual weight and therefore directs our reading path. The bold font signifies substance and confidence while the Chinese calligraphy typeface suggests tradition and a sense of history as the tutorial centre has been around since 1998.

All these work to position the reader/viewer to be in awe of Dr Koopa Koo who is elevated to a God-like status because he is a Math expert. Now this also explains why he does not smile, although his visual demand is not threatening but one that demands that we give him due respect. The dull colour scheme also blends in to create an atmosphere of mystic around this 'God-like' character.

Yet there is more to the ideological operation of the modal affordances of the verbal text and colour. They evoke emotions. I am, however, not suggesting that emotions reside in the text. Rather, the emotionality of text must be read against an external stimulus, which is the wider emotional climate of the culture of education in Hong Kong. This will help us to understand 'how texts are "moving", or how they generate effects' (Ahmed 2004, p. 13). Given the educational frenzy around getting into a good EMI school and getting good grades for the public exam (i.e. the HKDSE exam), tutorial advertisements sell 'hope' and 'confidence' in an overriding emotional climate of fear and panic. I turn now to analyse the verbal text, which is translated below – in particular, paying attention to the connotation of lexical items and associated emotions.

Table 11.2 Translation of Chinese texts in Figure 11.1

Chinese text	Literal translation
全球Top Five	Global Top Five
壓倒哈佛	Defeats Harvard
華盛頓大學	Washington University
數學博士	Mathematics doctorate

My analysis earlier established that Dr Koopa Koo is constructed as a 'Math God' by the naming of the noun phrase, 數神. But this 'title' surely needs justification. The four phrases above, translated into English, are discourses related to credentials. Indeed, the claim that he is a 'Math God' is backed by Dr Koopa Koo's credentials. He has a doctorate from Washington University, which is a Top Five institution known for its strength in Mathematics, even beating Harvard. Notice that the typography used in Figure 11.1 is Arial. Because these are texts presenting credentials, the credibility and seriousness are the associated meanings suggested by the typography. The ranking of Washington University is validated by the Times Higher Education source in a footnote.

Figure 11.2 A tutorial advertisement flyer

It is uncommon to find Hong Kong school teachers possessing a doctorate in Mathematics. This is why the 'Math God' metaphor and his title evoke a sense of awe and confidence. To be called a 'Math God' is also to suggest that he will be able to help those who are weak in Math and/or those who are 'praying' for a better grade in the subject. Such positive emotions target prospective students seeking help in the educational frenzy in the Hong Kong education landscape. Instead of highlighting the glamour of this star tutor through a more snazzy portrayal of the image, and a more generous splash of bright colours and aesthetic design, this advertisement, however, capitalises on Dr Koopa Koo's credential to sell 'confidence'. And as a 'Math God', the 'emotional temperature' (Machin 2007, p. 70) of composition of the advertisement must be sombre and serious in synch with the image of a God.

Leaving the analytical framework aside for the moment, I begin the analysis of Figure 11.2 by focusing on two striking semiotic inventories in the flyer because they arrest the attention of the reader/viewer. The first is the colour scheme, and the second is the modal affordance of the verbal text. Intuitively, the visual salience of the colour gives a good 'feel' to the text. But semioticians do not follow intuition; they have a language for colour (Kress & van Leeuwen 2002; van Leeuwen 2011).

According to Kress and van Leeuwen (2000), colour has two direct kinds of value. The first value has to do with the impact of colour on viewers, and the second value is the associative meanings that colour carries. Machin (2007) suggests that to analyse colour as a semiotic mode, it is important to consider the dimensions of colour. Relevant to this flyer are the semiotic affordances of 'brightness', 'saturation', 'purity', 'modulation', 'differentiation', and 'hue' – all aspects of colour dimensions are considered as meaning potentials that also contribute to the 'emotional temperature' of the advertisement.

The emotional appeal of the advertisement is conveyed by the semiotic choice of strong colours, with red and blue at the background. But these primary colours are no ordinary colours. They are used as a visual metonymy for the Union Jack, which also takes on symbolic values. This level of reading is derived by the verbal text which cues us to interpret the symbolic use of Union Jack in the background. Jeffrey Lau is an English teacher. But he is no ordinary teacher. The Chinese text is bold (literally and figuratively). Notice a differentiation of colour used for the Chinese text *碩士級英文系才子*句構學權威*碩士級文法專家*寫作之神* underscoring his credentials and also suggesting his confidence – that he holds a Master's degree in English and has exceptional talents. The visual metonymy of the Union Jack is clearly deployed as a sign to symbolise Jeffrey Lau's high standard of (British) English Language proficiency and the implied British English that students will learn in the tutorial centre.

The emotionality of this advertisement is strongly conveyed by the working of the semiotic affordances of the dimensions of colours used. The brightness and use of saturated colours enhance the 'emotional temperature' to convey a sense of optimism, high energy and confidence. The deployment of this semiotic inventory and the associated meanings are, of course, transported onto the star tutor whose teaching and classroom are strongly suggested to be lively, vibrant and fun.

Attention needs to be drawn to the typography 'Jeffrey Lau', however. A reading path is set up by the verbal text 'Jeffrey Lau' because of the font size and bold, capital letters used. Spread across diagonally and superimposed on the image, the text jumps at us, demanding attention. While obvious that the text functions to give the image a name and identity, the associative meanings of standing tall and confidence are suggested by the strong vertical lines and bold fonts. Colour differentiation is used to underscore his credentials and expertise in teaching syntax and composition while the associated meanings of his energy and creativity are also suggested by the solid font and colour differentiation.

At this point of the analysis, it is necessary to clarify that while the semiotic affordances of colour are important, as a semiotic resource, colours do not stand alone as a semiotic inventory; they work together with other modes to produce meanings. In other words, the intersemiotic relationship between the two modes, texts and colours, are 'mutually enhancing' (Unsworth & Cleingh 2009) in producing meanings. A translation of the Chinese texts is provided in Table 11.3 below to analyse the centrality of how texts are used in relation to other modes to construct the star tutor Jeffrey Lau.

Table 11.3 Translation of Chinese texts in Figure 11.2

Chinese texts	English translation
碩士級英文系才子	Master's in English
句構學權威	Best in teaching syntax
碩士級文法專家	Master's level in grammar
寫作之神	God of writing

There are a few operative characteristic discourses that are used to construct the identity of Jeffrey Lau. First, discourses of credentials are used to position him in the market of the tutoring industry with the legitimacy and the credibility to teach English. Furthermore, he uses the discourse of niche marketing by 'selling' his expertise as the best of the best in teaching syntax and a distinguished grammar expert at Master's level. Above all, he is a 'God of Composition/Writing'.

Despite his admirable credentials and titles, he is portrayed as a friendly and approachable teacher from the visual demand that he performs. His friendly smile is to be read as an extension of friendship. Indeed, the smile and bright lighting on his face softens his countenance to feature a friendly persona. The use of a frontal and close-up shot are symbolic semiotic affordances that reinforce the construction of his image as a personable, warm, likeable teacher.

Furthermore, his fashion sense and hairdo give a preppy look that resembles that of a pop icon who teens can relate to. Indeed the modal resources of the advertisement work to construct a cool, hip and 'modern' teacher who is an endearing 'model' to look up to.

Conclusion

Advertising, as Raymond Williams (1962/1993) theorised, is a 'magic system' that transforms commodities into glamorous signifiers. Indeed, my analysis of the media spectacle of tutorial advertisements also reveals 'a system of organized magic' (Williams 1993, p. 423) presenting 'star tutors' as 'Gods' with the power (that comes from knowledge and credentials) to change the fate of students for the better in a culture of education where performing well in exams matters. While these 'Gods' are not presented as deities to be feared, the semiotic design and (multi)modal affordances of the advertisements tell us otherwise. They are portrayed as the 'modern' teacher who is 'cool' and 'funky' in outlook (in particular Figure 11.2), knowledgeable in their subject area yet knowing how to customise knowledge for exam success. Therefore, as a 'magic system', these advertisements sell messages of hope and confidence in an emotional educational climate where fear and anxieties characterise the education landscape.

The media spectacle of tutorial advertisements is symptomatic of the marketisation of education where the provision of education is now commodified as services bought and sold in the educational marketplace. However, what is to be noted is that increasingly the shadow (private) education in Hong Kong has become closely entwined with the public education system as both systems offer 'a diffuse, expanding, and sophisticated system of goods, services, experiences and routes' (Ball & Youdell 2008, p. 98). As my analysis of the tutorial advertisements has demonstrated, these tutorial advertisements are selling a different kind of learning experience 'serviced' by the 'Gods' and 'Kings' of learning who know best how to help students score in exams. Indeed, these advertisements feed on the emotional insecurities that the culture of education in Hong Kong has generated. Students turn to supplementary, private, after-school tutorial centres to seek what their schools cannot provide, 'the magical potion' (Koh 2015) to win in the academic race.

The use of 'media spectacle' as a critical lens to understand the phenomenon of the production of tutorial advertisements in the urban spaces in Hong Kong has been generative. While useful to a point, I addressed the inadequacy of 'media spectacle' as a framework for conducting the textual analysis of tutorial advertisement by pulling together the theories of marketing semiotics and emotion studies to develop an analytic framework for doing the kind of textual analysis required of multimodal tutorial advertisements. While media spectacle points to a wider contextual understanding of the culture of education in Hong Kong, the framework developed enabled an analysis that unveils the way 'the system of organized magic' (Williams 1993, p. 423) works – a system organised around semiotic modes and the emotional affordances – will continue to cast its magical spell on Hong Kong students.

Note

1. I thank Gideon Kian and Jeffrey Lau for verifying and cross-checking the translation.

References

Ahmed, S. (2004). *The Cultural Politics of Emotion*. London: Routledge.
Ang, I. (1985). *Watching Dallas: Soap Opera and the Melodramatic Imagination*. London: Routledge.
Arend, P. (2014). Gender and Advertising. In A. Trier-Bieniek & P. Leavy (Eds), *Gender & Pop Culture: A Text-Reader* (pp. 53–79). Rotterdam, The Netherlands: Sense Publishers.
Aurini, J., Davies, S., & Dierkes, J. (Eds) (2013). *Out of Shadows: The Global Intensification of Supplementary education*. Bingley: Emerald.
Ball, S. J., & Youdell, D. (2008). *Hidden Privatisation in Public Education*. Brussels: Educational International.
Bray, M. (2013). Benefits and Tensions of Shadow Education: Comparative Perspectives on the Roles and Impact of Private Supplementary Tutoring in the

Lives of Hong Kong Students. *Journal of International and Comparative Education*, 2(1), 18–30.
Bray, M., & Lykins, C. (2012). *Shadow Education: Private Supplementary Tutoring and Its Implications for Policy Makers in Asia*. Hong Kong, Comparative Education Research Centre, Faculty of Education, University of Hong Kong.
Bray, M., Zhan, S., Lykins, C., Wang, D., & Kwo, O. (2014). Differentiated Demand for Private Supplementary Tutoring: Patterns and Implications in Hong Kong Secondary Education. *Economics of Education Review*, 38, 24–37.
Brenhouse, H. (2011). The Glamorous Celebrity Tutors of Hong Kong. *Slate Magazine*. accessed, http://www.slate.com/articles/double_x/doublex/2011/08/meet_the_glamorous_celebrity_tutors_of_hong_kong.html, March 8, 2013.
Chan, C., & Bray, M. (2014). Marketized Private Tutoring as a Supplement to Regular Schooling: Liberal Studies and the Shadow Sector in Hong Kong Secondary Education. *Journal of Curriculum Studies*, 46(3), 361–388.
Danesi, M. (2013). Semiotizing a Product into a Brand. *Social Semiotics*, 23(4), 1–13.
Debord, G. (1977). *The Society of Spectacle*. New York: Zone Books.
Debord, G. (1988). *Comments on Society of Spectacle*. London: Verso.
Emmison, M., Smith, P., & Mayall, M. (2012). *Researching the Visual* (2nd Edition). London: Sage.
Fiske, J. (1989). *Reading the Popular*. Boston: Unwin Hyman.
Feng, D., & O'Halloran, K. L. (2012). Representing Emotive Meaning in Visual Images: A Social Semiotic Approach. *Journal of Pragmatics*, 44, 2067–2084.
Hall, S. (1993). Encoding, Decoding. In S. During (Eds), *The Cultural Studies Reader* (pp. 507–517). London: Routledge.
Jewitt, C. (2009). An Introduction to Multimodality. In C. Jewitt (Ed.), *The Routledge Handbook of Multimodal Analysis* (pp. 14–27). London: Routledge.
Kellner, D. (2003). *Media Spectacle*. London: Routledge.
Kenway, J., & Fahey, J. (2011). Public Pedagogies and Global Emoscapes. *Pedagogies: An International Journal*, 6(2), 167–179.
Koh, A. (2015). The Magic of Tutorial Centres in Hong Kong: An Analysis of Media Marketing and Pedagogy in a Tutorial Centre. *International Review of Education*. DOI: 10.1007/s11159-014-9460-y.
Kress, G. (2010). *Multimodality*. London: Routledge.
Kress, G., & van Leeuwen, T. (2002). Colour as a Semiotic Mode: Notes for a Grammar of Colour. *Visual Communication*, 1(3), 343–368.
Kress, G., & van Leeuwen, T. (2006). *Reading Images*. London: Routledge.
Kwo, O., & Bray, M. (2014). Understanding the Nexus between Mainstream Schooling and Private Supplementary Tutoring: Patterns and Voices of Hong Kong Secondary Students. *Asia Pacific Journal of Education*, 34(4), 403–416.
Lee, C.-J., Park, H.-J., & Lee, H. (2009). Shadow Education Systems. In G. Sykes, B. Schneider, D. N. Plank, & T. G. Ford (Eds), *Handbook of Education Policy Research* (pp. 901–919). London: Routledge.
Lim, F. V., & O'Halloran, K. L. (2012). The Ideal Teacher: An Analysis of a Teacher-Recruitment Advertisement. *Semiotica*, 189(1/4), 229–253.
Lotman, J. (1976). *Semiotics of Cinema*. Translated by Mark E. Suino. Ann Arbor: Michigan Slavic Contributions.
Machin, D. (2007). *Introduction to Multimodal Analysis*. London: Bloomsbury.

Machin, D., & Mayr, A. (2012). *How to Do Critical Discourse Analysis: A Multimodal Introduction*. London: Sage.
Maiorani, A., & Christine, C. (Eds) (2014). *Multimodal Epistemologies: Towards an Integrated framework*. London: Routledge.
Manzon, M., & Areepattamannil, S. (2014). Shadow Educations: Mapping the Global Discourse. *Asia Pacific Journal of Education, 34*(4), 389–402.
Machin, D. (2013). What Is Multimodal Critical Discourse? *Critical Discourse Studies, 10*(4), 347–355.
Mori, I., & Baker, D. (2010). The Origin of Universal Shadow Education: What the Supplemental Education Phenomenon Tells Us about the Postmodern Institution of Education. *Asia Pacific Education Review, 11*(1), 36–48.
O'Halloran, K. I. (Ed.) (2004). *Multimodal Discourse Analysis: Systemic Functional Perspectives*. London: Continuum.
Oswald, L. R. (2012). *Marketing Semiotics: Signs Strategies, and Brand Value*. Oxford University Press.
Pauwels, L. (2012). A Multimosal Framework for Analysing Websites as Cultural Expressions. *Journal of Compoter-Mediated Communciation, 17*, 247–265.
Rose, G. (2012). *Visual Methodologies: An Introduction to Researching with Visual Materials* (3rd Ed.). London: Sage.
Tinkler, P. (2013). *Using Photographs in Social and Historical Research*. London: Sage.
Unsworth, L., & Cleirigh, C. (2009). Multimodality and Reading: The Construction of Meaning through Image-Text Interaction. In C. Jewitt (Ed.), *The Routledge Handbook of Multimodality Analysis* (pp. 14–27). London: Routledge.
Van Leeuwen, T. (2008). *Discourse and Practice: New Tools for Critical Discourse Analysis*. Oxford: Oxford University Press.
Van Leeuwen, T. (2011). *The Language of Colour*. London: Routledge.
Williams, R. (1962/1993). Advertising: The Magic System. In S. During (Ed.), *The Cultural Studies Reader* (2nd Ed.) (pp. 410–423).
Zhan, S., Bray, M., Wang, D., Lykins, C., & Kwo, O. (2013). The Effectiveness of Private Tutoring: Students' Perceptions in Comparison with Mainstream Schooling in Hong Kong. *Asia Pacific Education Review, 14*, 495–509.

12
The Abductive Leap: Eliding Visual and Participatory in Research Design

Elaine Hall and Kate Wall

This chapter seeks to problematise some of our assumptions about visual methods and their role in relation to participatory design and ethics in educational research. We make use of abductive reasoning (Peirce 1878, 1903) to explore the ways in which other researchers, but most specifically the ways we, have attributed causality and connection in this area. Our experience in exploring these assumptions to write this chapter suggests that the use of greater precision and transparency in framing the relationship between the researcher's intent and the use of visual methods is a vital first step, which can set the context for a more reflective data collection process as well as a more reflexive discussion of intent, design and process.

Things that will not be appearing in this chapter

This is the place in an article where we would say something like, 'Visual methods are increasingly popular in social science research', and then we would re-work some of the overview of the field, historical description paragraphs that we have included in some of our other work (e.g. Wall et al. 2013, 2012). However, in a book like this, that is a complete waste of everyone's time: you are likely to be reading this having already encountered many of the key texts (e.g. Prosser 1998; Banks 2001; Pink 2007; Thomson 2008; Margolis & Pauwels 2011; Karlsson 2012; Rose 2007/2012), and if not, this by no means exhaustive list is presented as a separate section in the references.

The motive for undertaking this chapter was to challenge, both in public discourse and in our own thinking, the casual and increasingly frequent elision of 'visual' and 'participatory' in discussions of research design. To illustrate this point, we originally intended to take a cross-section of recent papers in visual research to perform a qualitative hermeneutic enquiry into how the place of the visual in relation to the participatory has been presented. This posed a number of problems for us; most crucially that when we looked at our own writing on visual methods and other methodological and research design issues, we noticed that we have always concluded that what should be privileged is the researcher's *intent* (Baumfield et al. 2013; Lofthouse & Hall 2014; Wall et al. 2013; Woolner et al. 2010). In trying to construct explanatory frameworks through what would essentially be a tertiary analysis, we might be able to demonstrate that the discourse around these ideas is ambiguous and problematic, but we would have little if any warrant for saying anything about intent. Chastened, we realised that this chapter instead needed to be more reflexive, so we have opted to challenge the assumptions we carried into our own empirical work using visual methods and to 'come clean' about where we have found ourselves on a continuum of approaches to participation.

What was the immediate appeal of visual methods?

This section presents the evolution of appeal from the personal, to the interaction with participants and the experience of analysis, and back again to the personal. We have found visual methods rather motivating for us as researchers, in part because we viewed them as intrinsically more fun than traditional methods like interviews, focus groups, questionnaires or observations. In our discussions, we used

attractive, engaging, novel, distracting, relaxing

and it would be disingenuous to pretend that this was not the immediate cause of our taking up visual methods. All the claims that we subsequently made for visual methods and visual data have to be filtered through this first level: we worked in this way because it sounded fun; we carried on working in this way because it **was** fun. It is important to note that the majority of our team had backgrounds in schools and were naturally comfortable working with concrete and playful activities. We can argue that because we were engaged and enthusiastic, this might have some positive impacts on the quantity and quality of the data collected, but we cannot make a utilitarian argument about efficiency in relation to our intent. If, as it sometimes turned out, we collected data that could not have been generated by other means, we can go on to conceptualise the visual method or tool as a secondary artefact (Miettinen & Virkkunen 2006); however, we cannot pretend that we knew this was going to happen. There is a terrible temptation to write about research as if more was known in advance and less was a series of happy accidents, and this operates less consciously when the research process is a brief description in a paper that privileges the presentation of the data. However, much of what we discovered was the result of exploration, not of design.

As we engaged with groups of participants (ranging from three- and four-year-old children to adults, encompassing different cultures, varying social, communication and literacy abilities), we began to collate our impressions about the process of visually focused or mediated data collection compared to traditional methods. Key common ideas from across the team (of eight researchers):

Participants volunteer more readily.
Participants stay longer.
Participants report finding the experience less intrusive than interviews.
Methods themselves encourage creative and unexpected responses to the enquiry.

Claims have been made that a key aspect of visual methods' accessibility has to do with avoiding text (e.g. Lorenz & Kolb 2009) and while this may be an element, it could equally be argued for interviews. Since our normal practice had been to ask creators for explanations of visual data (in the encounter) or alongside (in data collection at one remove), we felt that we were placing similar cognitive or social burdens on our participants to articulate their ideas through talk or writing as traditional research methods. The challenge level was similar; it was rather something about the visual activities themselves that was the root of the attraction.

Our own sense that the activities were more fun appears confirmed by the ease of recruitment and length of engagement, though of course the social desirability bias inherent in all research encounters may have produced a degree of mirrored enthusiasm. The positive feedback led us to theorise about the mediating properties of visual activities in interviews and to speculate that they might encourage wider and more authentic participation (Woolner et al. 2009). This, of course, provided additional motivation to use visual methods with more heterogeneous research groups both to continue to test the attractiveness of the methods and to test the creative flexibility that we thought we had identified.

212 Elaine Hall and Kate Wall

As a research group, we came from a number of initial disciplines (History, Geography, Classics, Education, Psychology, Mathematics and Criminology) and had absorbed the cultural expectations of those disciplines in terms of what constituted high-quality research data. Research design that reflected these different paradigmatic expectations had been quite challenging, particularly in terms of generating data that might lend itself to multiple analyses, so instead we developed a form of methodological pluralism that, had we known Onwuegbuzie and Leech's (2006, p. 453) terms, we might have considered mostly *correlational* with occasional excursions into *comparison* (see Figure 12.1 below). Therefore, we welcomed the potential of visual data to be analysed in a number of ways. That visual methods generate large quantities of data facilitates quantitative analysis, particularly in terms of descriptive statistics exploring iconic images and themes

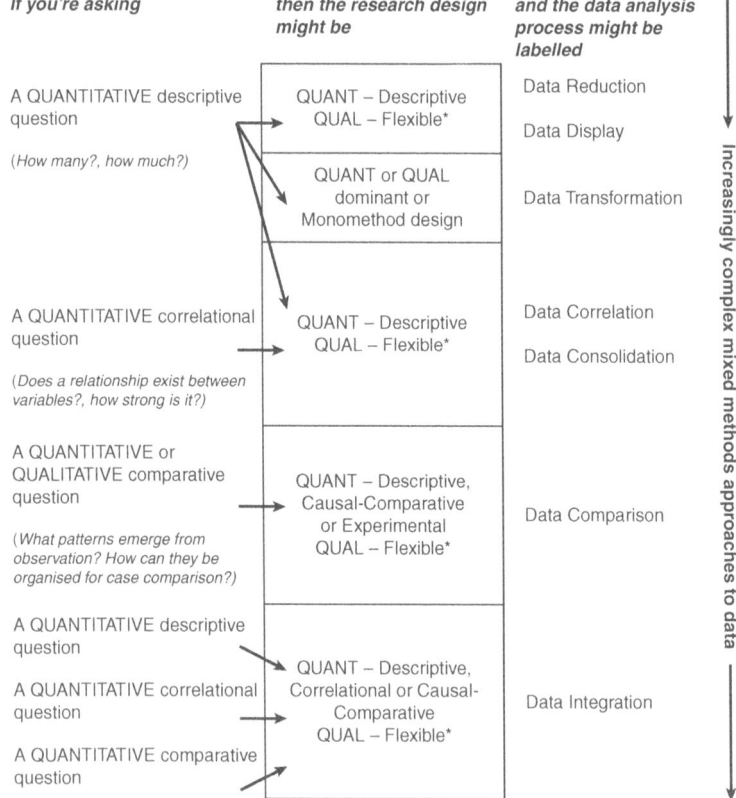

Figure 12.1 Models of mixed methods use from Onwuegbuzie and Leech, 2006

(Wall & Hall 2008); that they produce data that is not over-structured allows for a grounded thematic analysis, with the potential to disrupt the assumptions of the researchers (Towler et al. 2009), and at the same time, they produce a group of artefacts that can be treated as a rich data set, accessible to multi-method analysis (Wall et al. 2013). In addition, visual representations can offer what we refer to as crystallisation: the capture ('when the shutter falls' in photography, for example) of complex experience in a single piece.

We expanded our repertoires to include the visual/spatial in tools and analysis (Woolner et al. 2010; Hall et al. 2011), all the time becoming more convinced by the epistemic and catalytic qualities of visual methods. Engaged and content (albeit daunted sometimes by the practical challenges of large ambiguous datasets: Wall et al. 2013; Hall & Wall. 2009), it is perhaps not surprising that we began to aggregate the personal and relational positives with the methodological ones.

The positive observations – the richness and diversity of the data; the potential disturbance in the researcher's frame of reference; the crystallisation of thoughts, emotions and experience into an image or series of images – were interpreted by us as *visual methods offer unique meaning-making opportunities*, distinct from that offered by interviews, questionnaires or observations. The range of potential uses for visual data appears to offer *both* a complexity that reflects the epistemic nature of the research enquiry (Knorr Cetina 2001) *and* a simplification that allows for wider participation, ease of analysis and communication across audiences. This was interesting both in terms of data and the research relationships, actual and potential. We were increasingly framing our work supporting practitioner enquiry as a form of practitioner enquiry, nested within a more reflexive partnership where expertise and learning belonged to all participants. The *unique opportunities* seemed to extend beyond data to encompass open-ended and crystallised perspectives on researcher and participant positionality. Working collaboratively on analysis necessitated clear communication about roles and expertise (particularly in repairing when things had gone awry), while reframing research encounters as less bounded and certain challenged some of our safe assumptions about one another while making space for richer, more complex relationships in our research partnerships. The difficulty for this analysis is that these relationships were developing organically within ongoing projects, so we are cautious in attributing all the catalytic quality to the visual elements. It did all seem to fit together: we were developing new methodological and positional possibilities and they seemed, to us, to be part of a coherent whole in which better data was emerging from more authentic relationships.

We imagine (because no one has said explicitly why they think this) that it is following experiences like these that researchers make claims for visual method as being *inherently* participatory, of being *necessarily* more democratic and inclusive – and therefore ethically more robust – or that the data produced will be *more likely* to be disruptive to prevailing cultural dominance. We certainly found this framing of our work seductive, but over time, we began to question: could any method be this multifaceted? If visual methods were so fantastic, what was the nature of our evidence that they were, and could we go beyond a felt sense of this virtuous cycle to construct a logical framework to support these kinds of claims?

The use of reasoning to unpack the visual process

Using a form of mathematical reasoning from Peirce, we will explore the logical underpinnings of these claims. Therefore, a brief digression into forms of logic which draws on the excellent summary provided by de Waal (2013).

Researchers are familiar with the concepts of deductive (necessary inference from a principle) and inductive (drawing general conclusions from particular cases) reasoning and with their inherent limitations (deduction relies upon the principle being correct; induction relies on both a broad enough experience and an accurate analysis of it). However, Peirce demonstrates a third form, abductive reasoning, which explains how we incorporate new data swiftly and almost instinctively.

> Upon finding himself confronted with a phenomenon unlike what he would have expected under the circumstances, he looks over its features and notices some remarkable character … which he at once recognises as being characteristic of some conception with which the mind is already stored, so that a theory is suggested that would **explain** (that is, render necessary) that which is surprising. (Peirce, *Baldwin's Dictionary*, 2:427; cited by de Waal 2013,p. 63, emphasis in original)

The use of abductive reasoning allows us to begin to theorise about the new and surprising where deductive reasoning might reify the principle and encourage us to reject the data as an error and inductive reasoning might delay the development of a theory until more evidence from experience has accrued. The three forms of reasoning support and challenge one another: abduction provides the hypothesis, deduction provides the logical framework by which it can be tested and induction provides the experiential testing. However, whilst researchers make use of the three kinds of reasoning, Peirce directs our attention to the complex relationship between instinct and reason, which coexist in the *logica utens*[1]: 'a rather haphazardly formed but seasoned grab-bag of modes of inference' (de Waal 2013, p. 55). Since reflection on how we make use of the *logica utens* is necessarily a conscious act, it is inevitable that most of the time we do not question our reasoning. However, whilst unquestioned, our (for example) abductive reasoning can be mislabelled as inductive and subsequently the modes of enquiry we select to test our reasoning will be incongruent.

In this case, if we considered our experience as researchers using visual methods as an example of inductive reasoning, we are drawn to defend a position that we have undertaken our visual methods encounters with a broad and systematic method of gathering data about the characteristics of visual methods *as* methods, allowing that data to accumulate as a way of building up a theory of what the properties of visual methods are. We did not do that. We used visual methods initially as research tools, driven by a combination of attraction to the novelty and a pragmatic sense that they were at least as efficient as other data collection tools, and as we did that, we met with pleasant surprises as the visual methods appeared to do more than we had intended. Our development of theory about visual methods was essentially abductive, allowing us to weave the surprising elements in and continue with our work without having to pause and interrogate our reasoning. It is only as claims for visual methods (our own and others') seem to outstrip the weight of experience that we realise, faintly, that our reasoning has not been inductive and it is time to stop and think.

In order to make our reasoning available for reflection, Peirce suggests the use of structures and symbols that demonstrate the basis for the argument and the relationships between them, in particular the conscious deployment of *illative transformation*: 'therefore', 'causes' and 'leads to'. When accurately and faithfully employed, this technique produces a system for assessing the strength of an argument, up to the point of satisfaction for the individual researcher and, in the long run, to the point of completeness: 'a complete argument is one that is structured such that, if the premises are taken to be true, the conclusion cannot be said to be false without violating the system's rules' (de Waal 2013, p. 59). To this end, therefore, we have constructed a number of premises and relationships derived from our experience using the notation in Table 12.1 below.

When these arguments were first presented to an audience of doctoral students, we were asked why, in a lecture about visual methods, there were no pictures. Our response is that these arguments are in themselves a form of visual crystallisation, in which the complexity of assumptions and arguments are rendered a simple, static form, amenable to analysis. If the underlying logic of the argument is felt to have sufficient warrant, then data (pictures, drawings, diagrams, maps and sculptures) can be introduced to test the argument, but the data themselves being used as primary evidence would be another good example of an abductive leap masquerading as induction.

We began with the premise that visual methods are attractive:

$$V = A$$

We can confidently draw on our inductive experience, triangulated amongst the team and given greater validity by repetition in different contexts as described earlier, to confirm that *we* find visual methods attractive. In order to feel confident about the strength of the more global argument, we would have to examine how we understand the label 'attractive'. When we say that George Clooney (please feel free to substitute your personal favourite here) is attractive, we do not mean that everyone is attracted to him, merely that many people are and many of those who are not would acknowledge his theoretical attractiveness;

Table 12.1 Notation for the arguments

A	Attractive		
O	Open-ended data		
C	Crystallised data	=	Equals, is the same as
R	Range of responses	→	Leads to, causes
D (*D*)	(*potential*) Disturbance	↑	Increases, makes more likely
I (*I*)	(*potential*) ease of Interpretation	↓	Decreases, makes less likely
p	participation in terms of engaging in the activity	∵	Because
P (*P*)	(*Potential*) democratic Participation	∴	Therefore
Q	Quality of the data collected	[ ][ ]	Different, coexisting groups
W	Warrant for inference based on the data		

we do not mean that the attraction is sexual, merely that 'being attractive' contains responses made up of one or all of desire, admiration, approval and a positive predisposition towards the attractive person. The argument *George Clooney is attractive* does not appear to be threatened by the unarguable fact that some people have neutral or negative reactions to him; perhaps because the number of positive reactions are more numerous or the negative ones not strong enough to impact on the sales of movies or magazines. If we are going to make use of this (relatively weak but recognisable in an everyday sense) standard, the global argument would need to run as follows: *Visual Methods are attractive in that most people have some form of positive response to them and the negative or neutral responses of the minority do not impact on the success of the research encounter.*

This is where we run into trouble, since we have not collected systematic examinations of non-participants, so we do not really know whether the visual elements repelled some potential participants or whether their contribution to the research in some other form would have materially altered our understanding of the study. Moreover, since a lot of our research has been conducted in schools, we cannot be sure about the nature of the consent given, and high response rates may just reflect the power relationships inherent in the situation; while we as researchers always offer participants the choice of whether or not to join in – and we offer multiple opportunities to withdraw – schools are places in which it is expected that everyone will join in (Dockett et al. 2009). When visual methods are offered, we have informally noted (particularly from adults, who presumably feel less constrained to express these) a number of negative reactions, which can be categorised as *technical, structural and emotional* (see examples in Table 12.2).

Table 12.2 Examples of negative reactions

Technical	[*when given a camera*] 'I've never used one of these ones, the photos might not be very good.'
	[*when asked to draw*] 'I don't like doing this, I'm rubbish, I'm not the creative type.'
Structural	[*when asked to make a map*] 'Should I use a scale, or particular symbols? How will I know I've got it right?'
	[*when asked to select photos for a diamond ranking*] 'Why can I only have nine? What if I need more?'
Emotional	[*when modelling with plasticene*] 'I'm remembering how I felt then, I was really worried.'
	[*when offered a fortune line, pointing to the sad face*] 'I'm not sure I want to get in to that.'

Technical objections to visual tasks tend to focus on the unfamiliarity of the media or on the intrinsic ability of the participant, but they always centre on the additional demands of the visual methods, compared to traditional verbal inquiries. By inviting participants to *show* us their responses as well as tell, an anxious response is likely to occur alongside or instead of the interest and enthusiasm we hope for. Structural reactions are very common and are linked to the open-ended or crystallised nature of the task, though what is particularly important to note is that sometimes different participants *in the same task* appear to feel that there is either not enough or too much structure. While that can be attributed to individual desire for or resistance to structure, it may also come from a lack of clear intent from the researchers about the interpretive goal, and we will address this later on. Emotional reactions are especially difficult to examine critically since when participants become distressed we shift into managing and containing that distress and we are unlikely to learn whether the activity itself has triggered the emotion. We note, however, that in psychotherapy the use of visual and creative techniques is deployed to provide access to buried emotion and to heighten clients' awareness and experience of these feelings (see e.g. Carey 2006). What is clear, from this limited and unstructured evidence, is that there is a distinct possibility that visual methods have attributes of technical and creative challenge, of structural looseness or tightness, and of evoking feeling that some participants experience as negative. The best that we can advance as an argument is that visual methods are attractive to *some people* about whom we know more than those who do not find them attractive.

[V = A] *[V ≠ A]*

So we proceed with caution: some people (including us) find visual methods attractive. What do we hypothesise is the reason for this attraction? In exploring what we had written about our data, we noted two apparently contradictory characteristics that we liked: that it was *open-ended* and that it was *crystallised*.

[V = O] [V = C]

As we've already noted, it is unlikely that the explicit intent of the researcher is to produce both kinds of data in the same research encounter, though, if unquestioned, there may be problems of communication with participants about what the goals are. The production of either kind of data is predicated on certain assumptions about their role in the research process, so what are the underlying characteristics of open-ended or crystallised data implicit in the arguments? In this discussion we quickly come up against measures of quality, which in turn are linked to underlying and often implicit, epistemological assumptions. We have tried to be explicit about the ways in which we have understood quality, since as Wittek and Kvernbekk remark:

> it seems to us that even in the absence of an agreed-upon, unified definition of quality, we all (think we) recognize quality when we see it...We can tell the difference between good and poor student papers when we see them, even if we cannot pinpoint exactly the basis of our judgment. Art experts agree that one painting is better than another, even if they can point to no objective criteria. This is interesting, given the lack of a clear definition of quality. We still (think we) know what it is. (2011, p. 675)

We can propose the argument that visual methods produce open-ended data because they are capable of eliciting a range of responses, including those not anticipated.

$$V = O \therefore \rightarrow \uparrow R$$

Some researchers might, therefore, actively choose visual methods and deploy them in this open-ended manner in order to produce *disturbance*, to challenge their premises and to refine their research questions and iterative design. From an epistemological perspective, this use of visual methods fits with an interpretivist standpoint, and the claims for quality that might be made for visual methods in this context would be those of authenticity (since a range of real-world responses are gathered) and trustworthiness (since incorporating the range of responses requires the researchers' ideas to be made explicit). We might argue that open-ended approaches therefore increase the potential for disturbance.

$$V = O \therefore \rightarrow \uparrow R \therefore \rightarrow \uparrow (D)$$

If the attraction of visual methods is instead because of crystallisation, this seems to be linked to simplification through a reduced range of responses. It is easier to explain the structure of the task; the interpretation and analysis of the data is simplified because categories and themes are more explicit and these clear units of analysis can also potentially be explored quantitatively. This crystallised perspective aligns with more positivist and realist epistemologies, so quality claims rest on the validity of the framing of the task, and the categories that emerge from it, and the reliability with which that task is used across groups and time. If this potential for easing interpretation is realised, the researchers can enjoy the subsequent benefits when communicating the findings both within and beyond the research project.

$$V = C \therefore \rightarrow \downarrow R \therefore \rightarrow \uparrow (I)$$

These are both 'best case' scenarios, and we have no warrant for suggesting that disturbance or ease of interpretation necessarily follow on from open-ended or crystallised intent: hence the tentative italics and parentheses. What they do indicate, however, is the importance of researcher intent in directing the process of all aspects of an enquiry. If we set out consciously to use a visual research method to produce crystallised data, then the recruitment and framing of the research encounter will be very different from using the same method to produce disturbance. There will doubtless be high-quality ethical and professional standards underpinning the member-checking in the research in both cases, but the nature of the conversations will differ; since in the first case, the goal is to *converge* on a number of clear categories for understanding the data whilst the goal for the second case is to create more and more *divergent* perspectives. In both cases, there will be paradigmatic expectations shaping the researchers' sense of *how many categories is enough*, although these are unlikely to be explicit success criteria; rather they are an instinctive sense held in the *logica utens*.

We have therefore set up a logical relationship that states that visual methods are attractive for at least two potentially contradictory reasons, linked to researcher intent.

$$V = A, \therefore \quad [V \rightarrow \uparrow R \therefore \rightarrow \uparrow (D)] \quad [V \rightarrow \downarrow R \therefore \rightarrow \uparrow (I)]$$

These different approaches can make epistemologically appropriate claims to quality and therefore, can claim warrant for the findings in their enquiry based on meeting those quality criteria.

However, the abductive leap that prompted us to write this chapter is the claim that research projects that make use of visual methods are of a higher quality, with findings that carry greater warrant because visual methods are inherently participatory; and it is this participatory element, in combination with the disturbance or crystallisation, that creates the quality and the warrant.

$$\uparrow Q \rightarrow \uparrow W \therefore V = P$$

This is a much more complex argument because it is not reliant merely on the operations of one or other of the different approaches but on an intrinsic element of visual methods themselves and on an implied relationship between participation and quality (Torrance 2012). Torrance makes the argument that participation drives quality through both the disturbance and crystallisation mechanisms, either by participants being able to expand the frame of reference for the enquiry or to co-construct and validate the units of analysis. However, given that quality itself is a normative judgement based on Wittgenstein's 'family resemblances' between instances of experience and 'Thus understood, quality becomes a concept that does not yield to the ideal of precision and the demand for an essence' (Wittek & Kvernbekk 2011, p. 683), we have to examine the 'family background' of participation to assess whether it is (or could be) a predictor of or mechanism for quality.

Torrance asserts,

> Similar ideas are widely debated across the social sciences in discussions about new forms of knowledge production and knowledge transfer. It is now widely recognized from many different perspectives, including that of the empowerment of research subjects on the one hand, and also policy relevance and social utility on the other, that other voices must be heard in the debate over scientific quality and merit, particularly in applied, policy-oriented fields such as health and education. (2012, p. 119)

For these many voices and multiple perspectives to be accessed, we have to recruit as many different people to our research encounters as possible, and one of the ways to do that is to make the activities in the encounter attractive. From a recruitment perspective, therefore, we can draw on our tentative conclusion that visual methods are attractive (to some) and, therefore, we can encourage 'small p' participation, where more people take part, or stay longer, or contribute more freely, within the confines of the research activity. There are a number of problems to iron out here: 'small p' participation is based often on an implicit contract that involvement will not take very much time or be burdensome – often it is predicated on a single research encounter – so either the analytic categories have to be already in place and explicitly shared with participants to ensure that 'real time' member-checking takes place or the researchers have to share with the participants the uncertainty – essentially asking them to hand over their ideas to an interpretation process that is only just beginning. Both of these positions are ethically defensible, provided they are explicitly stated, and thus it is open to participants to choose not to engage or to challenge the position.

Testing the association of the visual with participation and quality

Our abductive hypothesis was that visual methods are linked to participation which is linked to quality. The hypothesis appears to be resting on a 'more is more' belief that, while persuasive, crucially fails to get to grips with the meaning of non-participation. For example, I may be asked to stop on my way home tonight by a cheery person with a clipboard to discuss my views, and given the lateness of the hour and the call of my supper, unless I have strong feelings on their product or policy, I will just get on the bus. I might get the next bus if I am invited to engage in something active or fun. Getting more people to join in because the activity is attractive carries the risk that relative indifference will falsely present as strong positive or negative views. Of course, this is more likely within a traditional research paradigm where researchers decide what the question is before spending time with their participants. Could the link from participation to quality rest on the ability of the participants to edit the question?

This implies that it is possible to set the bar higher: there is an explicit use of democratic values as a marker of quality in Torrance's argument, where he offers a critique of 'participant member-checking' being subordinated to 'expert analysis' in mixed methods research, and this begs the further question of the degree and timing of participation (Arnstein 1969 Hart 2013). 'Big P' Participation would include (at least) a degree of member-checking but might also include roles in analysis of the data, refining and challenging the categories, and reflexively assessing the utility of the research tools or indeed re-framing the research questions themselves, at which point we are at the apex of the ladders where participants are co-researchers and democracy is the leading principle. To explore this further and in order to ask a number of questions simultaneously, we have used an analytic matrix (see Table 12.3).

As Table 12.3 implies, the visual methods themselves are subject to the researcher's intent, both in terms of the kinds of data sought and

Table 12.3 Analytic matrix

	Researcher Intent	
	Data sought	
Participatory process	Intent to converge	Intent to diverge
Taking part ('small p' participation)	Visual methods are attractive and through this relationship appear to engage participants $$V \to A \to p$$	Argument
	Visual activities likely to be more highly structured. $V \to C (\uparrow I) \to \uparrow Q \to \uparrow W$	Visual activities likely to be more loosely structured. $V \to O (\uparrow D) \to \uparrow Q \to \uparrow W$
Member-checking (Participation)	Visual methods produce *crystallised meanings*, which are easy for researchers to interpret and easy to member-check.	Visual methods produce *open-ended data*, which because of its unexpected qualities, *requires* member-checking.
Collaboration in analysis and meaning making (democratic participation)	So interim findings can be analysed and critiqued by participants and disseminated widely. $\therefore V \to C (\uparrow P + I)$	And this dialogue creates the potential to disturb the frame within which the research is understood. $\therefore V \to O (\uparrow P + D)$
	Accuracy	Authenticity	Claim for Quality and Warrant

the framing of the research encounter in terms of the participation that might be invited or permitted. The same photo-elicitation task could be used with equal warrant for convergent or divergent purposes, though it is likely that how that task is introduced to participants will differ significantly and that these differences will be magnified by the type of participation that the researchers are consciously or unconsciously inviting. A 'small p' divergent research encounter might involve a very loosely framed engagement with a set of photographs, multiple forms of response (e.g. written comments, responses through drawing, verbal report, symbolic – by attaching stickers) which would then be interpreted by the researchers using appropriate qualitative analysis techniques. In contrast, Democratic Participation convergent research would involve a number of structured and iterative agreements about meaning and interpretation: of the set of photographs chosen, of the modes of response offered, of the guidance given to participants, of the coding and analysis of the data and of the meaning(s) generated by the activity. Each of these would have to address their specific issues of rigour, transparency and ethical strength in order to make knowledge claims that have sufficient warrant but neither is inherently superior. The table therefore lays bare some of the mechanisms through which visual methods *could be* made more or less participatory and brings into the researcher's awareness what some of the issues of quality will be.

Unpacking the abductive hypothesis has meant a dismantling of the attractive elision of visual methods, participation and quality data. Visual methods may be more attractive (to some), but the attraction itself is not necessarily unproblematic. Where this attractiveness leads to more data, we cannot be sure that it is 'better'; indeed, we cannot engage meaningfully in a discussion of quality without considering how we have understood the visual encounter in terms of intent to produce crystallised or open-ended data. The roles of all the players in participation are shaped by the goal of convergence or divergence, the more so as aspirations towards more democratic research relationships enter the field (Nind 2011). The questions researchers are faced with about the nature of their enquiry, how this shapes the data and the participatory possibilities are actually *generic* to all research encounters, rather than particular artefacts of working with visual methods.

However, to come full circle, we return to our own and others' experience in the field: there is something about visual methods, a catalytic quality (Baumfield et al. 2009) that recruits, that engages, that extends the encounter, that has the potential to facilitate agreement and to disrupt fixed ideas. Since we only partly understand how this works, the ethical priority is to be clear about our intent and to gather more than felt sense impressions about discomfort and non-participation.

Acknowledgements

An early version of this chapter was presented as a lecture entitled (with hopefully obvious irony) *Nicer, Fairer, Better: Visually Mediated Participatory Research for Validity and Social Justice* at the ESRC Doctoral Training Conference on Visual Methods held at Newcastle University, UK, in July 2014. We would like to thank the participants for their critical engagement and questions which have contributed to these arguments.

Note

1. Logic in use, contrasted by Peirce with *logica docens*, or logic studied.

References

Arnstein, S. R. (1969). A Ladder of Citizen Participation, *Journal of the American Planning Association*, 35(4), 216–224.

Banks, M. (2001). *Visual Methods In Social Research*. London, Sage.

Baumfield, V., Hall, E., Higgins, S., & Wall, K. (2009). Catalytic Tools: Understanding the Interaction of Enquiry and Feedback in Teachers' Learning. *European Journal of Teacher Education*, 32(4), 423–436.

Baumfield, V., Hall, E., & Wall, K. (2013). *Action Research in Education: Learning Through Practitioner Enquiry*. London: Sage.

Carey, L. (Ed.) (2006). *Expressive and Creative Arts Methods for Trauma Survivors*. London: Jessica Kingsley.

De Waal, C. (2013). *Peirce: A Guide for the Perplexed*. London: Bloomsbury.

Dockett, S., Einarsdottir, J., & Perry, B (2009). Researching with Children: Ethical Tensions. *Journal of Early Childhood Research*, 7, 283–298.

Hall, E., & Wall, K. (2009). *Dealing with Data Overload in Visual Methods: Cartoons about Learning*. 1st International Visual Methods Conference, September 15–17, 2009, Leeds University, UK.

Hall, E., Wall, K., Thomas, U., & Higgins, S. (2011). 'This Is My Kind of Network': Beyond Age, Stage and Subject Groupings for Developing Innovative Professional Learning. Paper presented in Network 15 Research Partnerships in Education at ECER 2011 'Urban Education', Berlin, Germany, September 13–16.

Hart, R. A. (2013). *Children's Participation: The Theory and Practice of Involving Young Citizens in Community Development and Environmental Care*. New York: UNICEF/Earthscan.

Karlsson, J. (2012). 'Visual Methodologies'. In Arthur, J., Waring, M., Coe, R. & Hedges, L.V. (Eds.) *Research Methods and Methodologies in Education*. London: Sage.

Knorr Cetina, K. (2001). Objectual Practice. In T. R. Schatzki, K. Knorr Cetina, & E. von Savigny (Eds), *The Practice Turn in Contemporary Theory*. Abingdon: Routledge.

Lofthouse, R., & Hall, E. (2014). Developing Practices in Teachers' Professional Dialogue in England: Using Coaching Dimensions as an Epistemic Tool. *Professional Development in Education*, 40(5). http://www.tandfonline.com/doi/full/10.1080/19415257.2014.886283

Lorenz, L. S., & Kolb, B. (2009). Involving the Public through Participatory Visual Research Methods. *Health Expectations*, 12(3), September, 262–274.

Margolis, E. and Pauwels, L. (Eds.) (2011). *The SAGE Handbook of Visual Research Methods*, London: Sage.

Miettinen, R., & Virkkunen, J. (2006). Learning in and for Work and the Joint Construction of Meditational Artefacts: An Activity Theoretical View. In E. Antonacopoulou, P. Jarvis, V. Andersen, B. Elkjaer, & S. Hoerup, S. (Eds), *Learning Working and Living: Mapping the Terrain of Working Life* (pp. 154–169). London: Palgrave Macmillan.

Nind, M. (2011). Participatory Data Analysis: A Step Too Far? *Qualitative Research*, 11(4), 349–363.

Peirce, C. S. (1878). Illustrations of the Logic of Science VI. *Popular Science Monthly*, 13(August).

Peirce, C. S. (1903). Pragmatism – The Logic of Abduction. *Collected Papers*, 5, 195–205. Cambridge, MA: Harvard University Press.

Pink, S. (2007) *Doing Visual Ethnography* Second Edition. London: Sage

Prosser, J., Ed. (1998). *Image-based Research*. London: Routledge Falmer

Rose, G (2007; 2012) *Visual Methodologies*. London: Sage

Thomson, P. (2008) *Doing Visual Research with Children and Young People*. London: Routledge

Torrance, H. (2012). Triangulation, Respondent Validation, and Democratic Participation in Mixed Methods Research. *Journal of Mixed Methods Research*, 20(5), 1–13.

Towler, C., Hall E., & Wall, K. (2009). Developing an Understanding of How Network Diagrams Can Represent and Support Communication across Schools and Colleges Investigating Learning to Learn. Presented at 1st International Visual Methods Conference, September 15–17, Leeds University, UK.

Wall, K., & Hall, E. (2008). *Visually-Based Reflections on a Learning Dispositions Framework*. Paper presented as part of the symposium Using Visual Methods in Educational Research: Issues in Developing Visual Methodologies at the American Educational Research Association Conference, March, New York.

Wall, K., Hall, E., & Woolner, P. (2012). Visual Methodology: Previously, Now and in the Future. *International Journal of Research & Method in Education (Special Issue: Problematising Visual Methods: Philosophy, Ethics and Methodologies)*, 35(3), 223–226.

Wall, K., Higgins, S., Hall, E., & Woolner, P. (2013). 'That's Not Quite the Way We See It': The Epistemological Challenge of Visual Data. *International Journal of Research and Methods in Education*, 36(1), 3–22.

Wall, K., Higgins, S., Remedios, R., Rafferty, V., & Tiplady, L. (2013). Comparing Analysis Frames for Visual Data Sets: Using Pupil Views Templates to Explore Perspectives of Learning. *Journal of Mixed Methods Research*, 7(1), 22–42.

Wittek, L., & Kvernbekk, T. (2011). On the Problems of Asking for a Definition of Quality in Education. *Scandinavian Journal of Educational Research*, 55(6), 671–684.

Woolner, P., Clark, J., Hall, E., Tiplady, L., Thomas, U., & Wall, K. (2010). Pictures Are Necessary but Not Sufficient: Using a Range of Visual Methods to Engage Users about School Design. *Learning Environments Research*, 13(1), 1–22.

Woolner P., Thomas U., Todd, L., & Cummings C. (2009). How Do Visually Mediated Encounters Differ from Traditional Interviews? Presented at 1st International Visual Methods Conference, Leeds, UK. www.ncl.ac.uk/cflat/news/documents/Leeds2009WoolnerThomas.pdf

Part IV
Ethical Issues in Visual Educational Research

13
Ethical Challenges in Visual Educational Research

Kitty te Riele and Alison Baker

Introduction

In educational research, and social research more generally, visual methods pose specific ethical dilemmas that require both researchers and institutional ethical committees to creatively and reflexively consider research ethics guidelines and principles. The purpose of this chapter is to highlight how traditional approaches to applying research ethics principles are challenged by visual research approaches. Ethical challenges are inherently 'grey' rather than 'black and white', so this chapter will not supply solutions. Rather, we hope to make visible ethical challenges that are particularly relevant for visual research. We will use two devices for this:

1. We organise the chapter around three widely recognised principles for research ethics: benefit and harm, respect for persons and justice. This draws on the expertise of the first author (Kitty).
2. We discuss specific challenges for visual research in relation to each principle, drawing on two research projects by the second author (Alison).

Principally our research focuses on young people who hold marginalised positions in society, with a particular interest for Kitty in relation to the ethics of such research and human research in general. She has experience as an active member of university human research ethics committees and has published two books on research ethics: one in relation to youth research (Te Riele & Brooks 2013) and the other on education research (Brooks, Te Riele & Maguire 2014). Alison has extensive expertise in using visual methodologies and has a particular interest in applying those in ways that facilitate young people's sense of social justice and capacity for action (e.g. Baker 2013; Baker & Plows 2015). Her projects have included working with poor-class as well as middle-class young people in El Salvador, and in Australia with urban, indigenous young people, multicultural youth in relation to sport, South African migrants, young street artists, and young people enrolled in inclusive education settings.

The examples presented in this chapter are based on two of our recent research projects. For Project 1, Alison examined an informal education context, namely a legal street art program provided by a metropolitan council for young graffiti writers (Baker 2013). Project 2 (led by Kitty and with a visual component that Alison ran) involved research conducted in a flexible education program across three urban sites, providing access to upper secondary education for students mostly aged fourteen to nineteen. In addition, we draw on relevant examples, from research by others, that are available in the public domain. In our discussions, at times, we will indicate which practices strike us as more or less ethical. However, we realise that such judgements are influenced by each researcher's own sense of research integrity (Macfarlane 2009; NHMRC, ARC & AVCC 2007).

The following three sections address, in turn, the ethical principles of benefit and harm, respect for persons, and justice. These principles stem from the 'Belmont Report' (DHEW 1979) in the USA, and have influenced research ethics guidelines internationally, such as the National Statement on Ethical Conduct in Human Research (NHMRC, ARC & AVCC 2007) in Australia, the Ethical Guidelines for Educational Research (BERA 2011) in the UK, and the Tri-Council Policy Statement: Ethical Conduct for Research Involving Humans (CIHR, NSERC & SSHRC 2010) in Canada. In other words, these principles have worldwide resonance. In each section, we first explain the principle and how it is commonly operationalised in educational research. We then provide actual examples of challenges for and by visual research in relation to that principle of research ethics. In our discussion, we recognise that in some ways traditional approaches by research ethics committees can form an inappropriate imposition on visual research projects, while in other ways these approaches need to be supplemented with additional considerations specific to visual research (Pitt 2014).

Benefit and harm

In ethical approaches based on normative rules (duty-based ethics, or formally referred to as 'deontological ethics'), the term beneficence is used to refer to the duty to act in ways that are good for others (Garrett 2004). As Ross (1930/2002, pp. 21–22) puts it: 'there are other beings in the world whose condition we can make better in respect of virtue, or of intelligence, or of pleasure'. In Australia, the country where we are both working, the Australian Association for Research in Education (AARE), in its *Code of Ethics*, points out, 'educational research is an ethical matter, and...its purpose should be the development of human good' (AARE 1993, section 2). Benefits may be directly to the people participating in the research or to the wider community (i.e. other students, teachers and schools, as well as society at large).

In duty-based ethical theory, both creating benefits ('beneficence', or actively doing good) and preventing harm ('non-maleficence') are duties that are required if one is to be ethical (see Ross 1930/2002). In research ethics guidelines, however, a different approach tends to be taken.

- Rather than aiming for *both* creating benefit and avoiding harm, university research ethics guidelines usually refer to *balancing* potential benefits and risks of a research project. This draws on a very different ethical theory, called Utilitarianism, which is based on looking at consequences rather than on using rules (see Brooks, Te Riele & Maguire 2014, chapter 2).
- Moreover, in practice, research ethics committees tend to prioritise the minimisation of potential harm. The principle, therefore, is not so much about achieving or balancing benefit *and* harm but mainly about *harm prevention*.

As an example of the latter, the Australian National Statement (NHMRC, ARC and AVCC 2007, p. 13) declares that researchers are responsible for:

a. designing the research to minimise the risks of harm or discomfort to participants;
b. clarifying for participants the potential benefits and risks of the research; and
c. the welfare of the participants in the research context.

In medical research, where research ethics guidelines first appeared, avoiding physical harm is important – for example, it is essential to minimise the risk of serious illness or death for participants in a clinical trial for a new medicine. Such dramatic harm is unlikely in most educational research. Instead, the focus is mainly on the risk of psychological or social harm. As examples of potential harm, the AARE (1993) refers to the following:

- For individual participants – 'loss of privacy, whether through exposure to scorn, contumely or victimisation or through the release of data that taken out of context could be misinterpreted' and 'harmful social or psychological consequences, such as loss of self esteem' (section 3).
- For groups – 'the creation or reinforcement of prejudice' and 'damage to the integrity of institutions' (section 4).

To reduce many of these kinds of harm, a common strategy used by researchers and recommended by research ethics committees is to ensure confidentiality (see AARE 1993; BERA 2011; NHMRC, ARC & AVCC 2007, p. 13). This usually involves using pseudonyms rather than participants' or institutions' real names as well as avoiding the use of information in publications that would easily identify a specific participant or institution.

So what does this mean for visual research? In our view, the key concern in relation to the principle of 'benefit and harm' is that implementing confidentiality when conducting visual research poses challenges. Below we discuss two specific issues. The first is the de-identification of people in photos, and the second relates to excluding images that may identify people or institutions.

De-identifying images

To enhance confidentiality, commonly used practices to reduce the potential identification of people in photographs include pixilation of faces and the placement of black bars across the eyes of people. We argue, as have others, that such techniques may themselves be unethical, because they can evoke the impression of the person being a perpetrator or victim of crime (see Blum-Ross 2013). An example of the 'black bar' technique is found in the project *Hope: the everyday and imaginary life of young people on the margins* (Robb et al. 2010). Overall, this book is a warm and moving tribute to the young people who took part in the research, juxtaposing narratives from young people, teachers and the researchers with drawings and photos of the young people, their families and the environments in which they live and learn. Its empowering intent is undermined, unfortunately, by the use of black bars over the eyes of each face in the photos. The book asks, 'How does hope manifest itself for young people on the margins of society?' (Robb et al. 2010, back cover). The barred faces instead imply hopelessness and criminality.

A different project, by Bronwyn Wood in New Zealand, involved asking high school students to take photographs – but with the requirement (due to ethics committee procedures) that photos could not

Ethical Challenges in Visual Educational Research   235

include identifiable people. In response, these teenage students 'devised a range of strategies to ensure they were in the photos, yet unidentifiable' (Wood & Kidman 2013, p. 153), such as the use of shadows and overexposure, or using hands or hair to obscure their faces. Wood admiringly describes,

> One particularly creative group of 14 year-old girls (who referred to themselves as the 'Paperbag Princesses') found three paper bags and drew faces on them, and then appeared clad with these paper bags in most of their photos. ... Cleverly, they also managed to comply with the requirements of the research, remaining non-identifiable, yet subverting the requirements by their unrecognisable presence (rather than absence). (Wood & Kidman 2013, p. 154)

Placing the decision (albeit unintentionally) on how to disguise their identity in the hands of her participants meant that Wood ended up (in our eyes) with a more ethical approach to implementing confidentiality, compared to imposing a de-identification technique such as pixilation or black bars on photographs afterwards.

A further consideration is that the social and political context in which particular groups of young people exist may raise concerns about confidentiality, particularly when an image is used in publicly accessible materials such as promotion by the institution or funder. In Project 1 (see Baker 2013), based on a legal street art program offered by an urban council for young graffiti writers, Alison discussed with young people from the outset the potential uses for the photos and where they would appear. The discussion focused in particular on 'image ethics' as outlined by Wang and Redwood (2001). Risks of participation may include the following:

1. intrusion into one's private space and being filmed/photographed,
2. disclosure of true but embarrassing facts about individuals,
3. placing people in a false light which distorts truth/character, and
4. using someone's image but depriving people of the commercial benefit.

The above points form a useful foundation for developing ethical guidelines to be used with young people when they act as participant-photographers in research projects. In working with young graffiti writers, Alison drew on Wang and Burris' (1994) photovoice method, which forms an ethical frame through its theoretical underpinnings in feminist studies, Freire's understanding of critical consciousness and documentary studies. Wang and Redwood (2001) have highlighted particular ethical concerns in photovoice, based on their work with young people in community settings. First, there is a responsibility for the privacy of people who are not research participants but could appear in photos taken by the research participants (Wang & Redwood-Jones 2001). Given the participants in Alison's project were living in a time of 'selfies' and photographing others with mobile phones, she knew it was important to help the young people consider alternatives to simply taking images that involve people, especially in public spaces. In Project 1, the discussion therefore addressed symbolism, representation, and power to build up young people's visual literacy skills and understandings about the politics of representation. Moreover, the young people were sensitive to being recognised themselves, and to the potential for getting in trouble with police. When they documented their experiences of the legal street art program and their lives more generally, each person decided how they wanted to appear in pictures (if at all) and devised creative ways to communicate their messages. The two photos in Figure 13.1 show some ways in which these young people preferred to capture themselves.

Excluding images

Changing photos to de-identify them, as discussed above, is akin to using pseudonyms in relation to interview data. As another strategy, researchers may exclude some visual data from use for publications altogether, which is similar to not publicly using potentially identifying textual descriptions (e.g. that a participant is the leader of the only school in a certain town). In both visual and textual research, this strategy requires researchers to make a professional and thereby ethical judgement about which data warrants removal and which does

Figure 13.1 Self-representation in the young graffiti writers project (Project 1)

not. Such decision-making is cogently illustrated by Pope, De Luca and Tolich (2010) in relation to photos taken as part of a project investigating student experiences of sport, focusing on a major public regatta (rowing) event in New Zealand. The authors include the researcher, the chair of the researcher's university research ethics committee (REC), and a colleague from another university with extensive expertise in relation to research ethics. Examining six photos taken by the researcher during the regatta, they consider the potential risk of harm that may result from publication of each image and therefore whether it should be excluded. The paper provides insights from each author separately. It is interesting to note that even three expert scholars can sometimes disagree, which highlights the 'grey' areas in the public use of photographs for research. As an example, one photo (referred to as 'figure 5' by Pope et al., 2010) captured one female teenage student comforting another, presumed by the researcher-photographer to be in relation to having lost a race. The photo was used publicly and also reproduced in the paper. Below the competing views of the three authors are explained.

- Author 1 (Researcher): Suggests that such disappointment and support are a natural part of sporting events. He did not ask the young women for their consent as he 'felt that intruding during this delicate time was more harmful than using the image for future publication without their consent' (Pope et al. 2010, p. 310).
- Author 2 (REC Chair): Questions 'the intimacy of the moment being caught on camera and then subsequently made public, and also the intrusion on the part of the researcher who must have stood very close to the pair although they were almost certainly unaware' (p. 310) and would have chosen not to publish this photo in order to protect the students' privacy.
- Author 3 (Colleague): Compares the image with another photo (listed as 'figure 6' by Pope et al., 2010) of tired competitors after a race and suggests that: 'This photo captures exhaustion whereas the other photograph captured emotion. Given this ambiguity, maybe consent is required for Figure 5 but not for Figure 6' (p. 312).

These three reflections from the researchers engaged in this project indicate that decisions about exclusion or inclusion of images need to be based on the context and implications of each photograph, 'mediated by the researcher's ethical considerations at the point of reproduction' (Pope et al. 2010, p. 310). In sum, the example points to the impossibility to impose a general rule upfront and therefore ethical visual research requires trust in the researcher by their research ethics committee (see

NHMRC, ARC & AVCC 2007, p. 12, regarding the personal integrity of researchers).

Excluding certain images, and promising confidentiality, may also strike researchers as unethical because it constrains agency and recognition by/for participants. This is of particular concern for participatory visual research approaches, such as photovoice, and runs counter to their democratic intentions (Berman & Allen 2012; Griebling, Vaughn, Howell, Ramstetter & Dole 2013). As Bronwyn Wood points out in relation to her project (see above), participants may want 'to be included in the project – their images, their faces, their friends and family' (Wood & Kidman 2013, p. 153).

Moreover, participants may expect to be given artistic recognition as the creators of photos, videos and other images. The British Educational Research Association (BERA 2011, p. 7) suggests that participants have 'rights to be identified with any publication of their original works or other inputs, if they so wish'. Alicia Blum-Ross (2013, p. 64) argues that 'often young people want to claim – visually and textually – credit for their own work'. In relation to her research involving young people in participatory film-making, she notes that while her institutional ethics regulations enabled her (in some instances) to give credit to adults and organisations, the same did not apply to the young people. She concludes, 'Ironically, then, the young people's "ownership" of the project ultimately was erased in the public distribution of the research' (p. 64). Including the creator-participant's name in an image caption may be ethical as it gives due credit, while at the same time contravening the usual expectation of confidentiality. Resolving this requires negotiation with both the participants and the relevant research ethics committee to decide which of these concerns is most important in a given project or context. In other words, confidentiality does not always need to be the overriding ethical consideration when applying the principle of benefit and harm.

Respect for persons

The second core ethical principle is 'respect for persons'. It means that every person has intrinsic value and therefore deserves to be treated as an autonomous agent and not be used simply as a means to an end. This conceptualisation comes from deontological (normative, rule-based) ethics (see Brooks, Te Riele & Maguire 2014, chapter 2). In relation to research, the implication is that no matter how beneficial the outcomes of a research project may be too many people, we should not sacrifice even a single participant as a means to achieve that end. The Australian National Statement (NHMRC, ARC & AVCC 2007, p. 13; also see the Belmont Report, DHEW 1979) distinguishes between two elements of autonomy:

> Respect for human beings involves giving due scope, throughout the research process, to the capacity of human beings to make their own decisions.
>
> Where participants are unable to make their own decisions or have diminished capacity to do so, respect for them involves empowering them where possible and providing for their protection as necessary. (p. 13)

The first element means researchers should enable people to make up their own mind about whether and how to take part in the research, not merely in advance (e.g. with a consent form) but throughout the project. The second element means that researchers should attempt to enable everyone (including, for example, children) to similarly make their own decisions – in addition, it is the researchers' responsibility to protect potential participants who may be vulnerable and/or not fully capable of making their own decisions. This applies not only to individual potential participants but also to social groups.

- 'Projects should be discussed with the representatives of the group concerned where such exist (and with other appropriate authorities where they do not)'.
- 'Research on socially disadvantaged groups should be designed for their direct benefit' and 'if the effect of repeating research is likely to be the reinforcing of prejudice against disadvantaged groups, it should not be undertaken'. (AARE 1993, section 4)

The key operationalisation of the principle of respect for persons is through the practice of obtaining consent that is both informed and voluntary. In Australia and similar (mostly Anglophone) countries with formal research ethics regulations for social research, this usually involves at least

- the provision of written information about the project which a potential participant can keep, and
- a formal process of recording consent, often through a written consent form.

For children (or others considered to have reduced autonomy), it is common in educational research to rely on the decision of someone else who is considered to have full autonomy, such as a parent or guardian, in order to adhere to this principle (see Brooks, Te Riele & Maguire 2014, for discussion of this practice).

In relation to visual research, of special interest in relation to consent and respect for persons are challenges relating to the potentially wide dissemination and digital afterlife of visual research artefacts. We discuss this issue below, using examples from recent research and media projects that are accessible in the public domain.

Dissemination and the digital afterlife

The visual products from educational research may be disseminated very widely (e.g. through online distribution) and continue to be available far beyond the lifetime of the project. Even when this is explained in advance to potential research participants, the implications of such widespread dissemination may be difficult to grasp for participants. Moreover, the nature of information distributed through the Internet means is it almost impossible to delete visual products and research findings at a later time if a participant changes their mind during or after the study. Blum-Ross (2013, p. 65) argues this places additional responsibilities on researchers to support young participants to make prudent decisions on what to include in materials that will become publicly available:

> This question of 'afterlife' is one that emerges frequently if there is something particularly questionable in the film product. Perhaps, however, it should be one which, given the 'afterlife' of these products, all youth researchers working with images should be careful to consider. (p. 65)

An example is the Longitudinal Study of Australian Children and its partnership with the Australian Broadcasting Corporation for the production of a related television series that has recently been out to air. The research study has been tracking 10,000 children and their families to examine child development holistically, including 'mental and physical health and development, cognitive ability and learning, social and emotional wellbeing as well as the characteristics of their home and family, childcare and school, and neighbourhood environment' (ABC 2014). In addition, eleven children and families were chosen to feature in eight documentaries (so far) that have been screened on free-to-air television in Australia (ABC 2014). The website about the television series features

- videos and photos for each child,
- detailed and personal information about each child and their family, and
- a link to a related Facebook site.

As a result, the visual artefacts produced through the research are available well beyond the broadcast date of each documentary. The website provides some information about the research project, but there is no explanation about the process for selecting the eleven children and families, nor about the process of gaining consent for how they are being portrayed. Interestingly, one of the children did not take part in *Life at 7* (the most recent documentary), but all her previous information (including photos and videos) continue to be included on the website and there is no comment on why she was not part of *Life at 7*. Her page on the website simply states that she 'and her family were not featured in *Life at 7*. Here's her profile information from *Life at 5*' (ABC 2014).

Based on the principle of respect for persons, we would expect that the research team involved with the *Life* series must have considered – and discussed with the families – the potential positive and negative impacts on the children (and families) created by the digital afterlife of all the visual materials from the research (available through the documentaries and website). The need for such consideration is reinforced by the experience of one of the participants in the famous British *7 Up* television series. Peter Davies withdrew from taking part after the screening of *28 Up*. In a newspaper interview, he explained:

> I pulled out because of the reaction to my participation in the weeks after *28 Up*, particularly from the tabloid press.... They decided they were going to portray me as the angry young Red in Thatcher's England. I was absolutely taken aback, genuinely shocked, at the level of ill-will directed towards me. (Preece 2012, n.p.)

While Peter Davies was able to stop participating (and then re-commence for *56 Up*), he could not remove the record of his participation in the previous four documentaries. The quandary is, as Blum-Ross (2013, p. 65) explains, that 'none of us can know how and when peers or even future employers may see these products'.

It is useful to think of consent as a process rather than as a one-off, written form to sign (Brooks, Te Riele & Maguire 2014; Wood & Kidman 2013). For example, in the photovoice method, there is an emphasis on a multi-stage consent process in regards to images and their uses (Wiles, Prosser, Bagnoli, Clark, Davies, Holland & Renold 2008). Prosser &

Burke (2011, p. 270) note that 'provisional consent' is often appropriate when doing visual research with children and young people because the 'ongoing relationship between researcher and children is seen as evolving and dependent on reciprocal trust and collaboration'. Taking care that young participants understand the potentially far-reaching dissemination, as well as taking steps where possible to remove data from the public domain if requested (e.g. from websites controlled by the research team), enhances trust not only for a specific project but in educational research generally.

Justice

The third principle we discuss is justice. This refers to fairness, in particular the duty to distribute benefits and burdens fairly (Garrett 2004). In relation to research, the Belmont Report reflects this focus on distributive justice by asking, 'Who ought to receive the benefits of research and bear its burdens?' The report recognises that the answer varies depending on the perspective one takes:
There are several widely accepted formulations of just ways to distribute burdens and benefits. Each formulation mentions some relevant property on the basis of which burdens and benefits should be distributed. These formulations are

1. to each person an equal share,
2. to each person according to individual need,
3. to each person according to individual effort,
4. to each person according to societal contribution, and
5. to each person according to merit. (DHEW 1979, part B.3)

The Belmont Report goes on to apply this especially to the selection of potential research participants, warning against choosing some groups 'simply because of their easy availability, their compromised position, or their manipulability, rather than for reasons directly related to the problem being studied' (DHEW 1979, part B.3). Concerns in relation to participant recruitment are not limited to who gets unfairly *included* (or burdened) but also who may be unfairly *excluded* (not given the opportunity to take part). Finally, the principle of justice also involves consideration of fair access to and distribution of the benefits from research processes and outcomes (DHEW 1979; NHMRC, ARC & AVCC 2007).

For visual educational research, two ethical issues are of particular relevance:

- the extent to which different people have a fair opportunity to participate, and
- questions about the purposes for which images are used, and the shared versus individual ownership of images.

These issues are explored below, drawing on examples from Project 2: a commissioned research project to evaluate a high school–level 'flexible learning program' (the Melbourne Academy) with six classroom sites in different suburbs across Melbourne, the capital of the state of Victoria in Australia. For our purposes here, we only discuss the stage of the research that was conducted as a photo project at three of the sites, implemented by Alison, with Kitty as the project team leader.

Fair opportunity to participate

The aim of the arts-based component of Project 2 was to work with students to document their experiences in the school. The research was carried out as a 'creative project' option in the art class over a period of three months, using a photo-elicitation method. The students' work also contributed towards the creation of a photographic display at the school's mid-year exhibition. Embedding the research in the curriculum enabled young people to participate in the activities while having a choice whether to participate in the research. The research project aimed to mirror the flexibility that is central to the operation of flexible learning programs such as the Melbourne Academy (Te Riele 2014) in two ways:

- flexibility in working with young people, and
- flexibility in relation to equipment to ensure fair access.

First, flexibility in working with the students included implementing the project differently across the three sites, to suit the different student cohorts. At one site, Alison worked with two young people over a period of three weeks. At another site, she worked intensively and exclusively with one participant for thirty minutes: a young man who attended school very rarely. At the third site, the project was run as a morning workshop for the group, who created storyboards, took photos and wrote captions, and finally discussed their images as a group. This flexibility allowed for participants to decide how they wanted to participate in the creative project, for example, in relation to working with peers (or not) and time commitment. Gillies and Robinson (2012), who reflect upon the use of creative methods with 'challenging pupils', note that because students' consent is often 'conditional and given on a minute-to-minute basis' (p. 164), it is advantageous to spend a considerable amount of time in each site. They argue for a balance between being flexible and maintaining some structure to avoid the project becoming confusing or overwhelming for students. Such considerations are particularly important when working with socially excluded young people (Matthews 2001). An additional challenge (not just for visual research) is for researchers to make judgements about when to encourage students and when to back off, particularly when working with young people who have had negative experiences in mainstream schools.

Second, flexibility proved to be useful in relation to providing fair access to equipment. The project offered several options for creating photographs, thereby offering choice to the participants:

- five mini Polaroid cameras provided by the researcher,
- 'point and shoot' digital cameras owned by the school, and
- students' own smartphones.

For the latter, the researcher used an application on her iPad to 'convert' digital images participants had taken with their smartphones into Polaroids. The immediacy of the mini Polaroid cameras and the iPad app were especially beneficial as the students could print hard copies and devise captions straightaway. In the lives of most young people – not just at these sites – having digital images on their phones and uploading images onto Instagram or Facebook is a daily activity. However, the introduction of the mini Polaroid cameras to the sites brought about a flurry of excitement, with every student wanting to try out the cameras. Many students did not want to commit to taking pictures for the 'research project' but instead wanted the researcher to take pictures of them that they could keep. While this created an additional cost to the project, it would have been unjust to deny students who were not participating in the project access to these cameras and prints.

Ownership of images

Embedding the research for Project 2 in the curriculum had benefits in terms of fair access but created challenges in relation to the ownership of images. The project was explained as research, but also as an alternative arts activity to those activities being completed in the class at the time, such as painting and print-making. All students were working on some type of arts creation for the school's mid-year exhibition and for them the photo project was no different. When going through the informed consent process initially, students were asked to give permission to use the images they produced. However, in practice, the images often became 'ownerless'. For example, students were passing Polaroids to each other, staff took pictures when students requested. and students jointly documented activities including with students not formally 'in the project'. This made it difficult to discern who some of the pictures belonged to and whom to approach for consent. When moving towards the end of the project, the request to use images for the exhibition was met with confused comments and playful jokes from students. In the context of the art class, they had always assumed that the images were destined for the exhibition.

A month later – using the protocols suggested by Wang and Redwood-Jones (2001, p. 570) to 'provide and review with participants a consent form indicating permission to publish any photographs, or only specified photographs, to promote project goals' – the researcher returned to conduct short interviews with students and attempted to use the form we had created for students to give consent for use of each image. The form consisted of a table with identifiers at the top prompting students to describe each image and to indicate whether it could be used in publications. In practice, many of the students lamented at having to list each image and instead looked through all the images (sometimes only theirs, other times all the images at the site) and then asked, 'how can I say yes to all of them?'. They ended up writing 'yes to all' on the form and signing it. A few participants, as they were looking through, expressed dislike for one or two of the images they were in. In one instance, a participant disliked the way he appeared in a close-up image but later said, 'actually you can use this photo too'. This situation supports the argument by Pope, De Luca and Tolich (2010) that researchers must use their professional judgement in deciding whether to use specific images. In this case, given the student's ambivalence, we decided not to use the close-up image in publications.

Finally, there were challenges related to the individual versus collective ownership of images. Because the images were created as part of an art class, and often it was unclear who took a particular photo, there was a sense of collective ownership. As a result, the decision was made for the photo exhibition from the project to combine images from the three different sites, producing a large collage that fused the visual narrative into a single artwork (see Figure 13.2).

Participants jointly chose the images they wanted to appear in the exhibition and these images (if they were mini Polaroids) were

Figure 13.2 Collective photographic narrative (Project 2)

scanned, enlarged and printed. The display was based upon the theme of 'moments', representing a conglomeration of student experiences that told a broader story about the flexible learning program. It demonstrated the complexities of experience and perspectives – and the fluidity of identities of the young people attending these classrooms. Young people attending these sites often note that 'everyone is here for a reason' (Te Riele 2012, p. 39), giving them a feeling of shared experience. The combined display offered an inclusive representation that was appropriate in this setting, celebrating the students' joint contribution for an audience of their peers, staff and loved ones. Pitt (2014) points to the complexity of establishing the ownership of individual photographs within a family photo collection. Depending on the context, a shared and collaborative approach to ownership may be a useful implementation of the principle of justice. Such shared ownership and representation is well recognised in more communitarian (non-Western) orientations (Hammersley & Traianou 2012; Suaalii & Mavoa 2001).

Concluding thoughts: engaging ethically

Ethical challenges can arise in any educational research project – visual research is no exception – and ethical considerations are inherently complex. Therefore our focus in this chapter has been more on raising awareness for both researchers themselves and their university ethics committees than on supplying straightforward resolutions. Our own projects are not perfect and reinforce the view of ethics as a process, rather than a one-off product through the completion of an 'ethical approval' form. That does not mean, however, that such forms may not be useful. Formal guidelines serve a valuable function to assist research integrity, for example, by alerting researchers to issues they otherwise may not have been aware of.

The principles of benefit and harm, respect for persons and justice – common in research ethics guidelines worldwide – similarly help researchers to identify relevant ethical concerns. For visual research in education, we have pointed especially to questions around

- confidentiality and the risks associated both with de-identification strategies;
- consent and the digital afterlife of visual research products; and
- fairness in taking part in research, accessing equipment, and ownership of images.

For visual researchers, reflecting on how these questions play out in their own project can make the project not only more ethically robust, but also improve its trustworthiness. We agree with Small (2001, p. 405) that

> there is no substitute for the individual's development of the capacity to make ethical decisions about the design and conduct of his or her project. In the end, it is everyone's responsibility to ensure that educational research is ethical research, and the better prepared we are to address this task, the better our research will be.

For RECs in universities and other research institutions, reflecting on these questions may assist in challenging taken-for-granted ways of thinking about the implementation of the principles of benefit and harm, respect for persons and justice. As Brooks, Te Riele & Maguire (2014, p. 37) explain,

> In relation to methods, RECs are commonly charged with not understanding – and therefore preventing or unreasonably modifying – the use of qualitative research methods, especially ethnography, action research, participatory research, and visual research (Schrag 2011; Scott & Fonseca 2010; Sikes & Piper 2010). Such methodological gatekeeping is likely to depend on the specific practices of a particular REC, shaped by the distinctive research strengths of the institution.

Importantly, all research benefits when the application of ethical principles is better tailored to the context and paradigm of each project, and when researchers are enabled 'to develop a research ethic appropriate to the epistemological approach, design and context of their research' (Pitt 2014, p. 323).

As our closing argument, we encourage visual education researchers to engage in ethical conversations with each other as well as with their own research ethics committee. Frankly sharing our challenges, considerations and negotiations supports everyone (researchers, members of ethics committees and research participants) to become clearer about what ethical research means in practice for visual research in education.

Acknowledgements

Project 1 was enabled by a grant from the City of Brimbank, a local council in the west of Melbourne, the capital of the state of Victoria in Australia. Project 2 was enabled by a grant from Melbourne City Mission for research on their high school program (the Melbourne Academy), which operates in six sites in the inner north, centre and west of Melbourne. The preparation of this chapter was supported through the Australian Government's Collaborative Research Networks (CRN) program.

References

AARE [Australian Association for Research in Education] (1993). *Code of Ethics.* Retrieved September 5, 2014. www.aare.edu.au/pages/ethics.html

ABC [Australian Broadcasting Corporation] (2014). *The Life Series.* Retrieved September 5, 2014. http://www.abc.net.au/tv/life

Baker, A. (2013). *More Than Free Paint: Exploring Young People's Experiences of the B-Creative Street Art Program. Final report.* Melbourne: The Victoria Institute for Education, Diversity and Lifelong Learning.

Baker, A., & Plows, V. (2015). Re-presenting or Representing Young Lives? Negotiating Knowledge Construction of and with 'Vulnerable' Young People. In K. te Riele & R. Gorur (Eds), *Interrogating Conceptions of 'Vulnerable Youth' in Theory, Policy and Practice*. Rotterdam: Sense.

BERA [British Educational Research Association] (2011). *Ethical Guidelines for Educational Research*. Retrieved 10 September 2015. www.bera.ac.uk/publications/ethical-guidelines.

Berman, K., & Allen, L. (2012). Deepening Students' Understanding of Democratic Citizenship through Arts-Based Approaches to Experiential Service Learning. *South African Review of Sociology, 43*(2), 76–88.

Blum-Ross, A. (2013). Authentic Representations? Ethical Quandaries in Participatory Filmmaking with Young People. In K. te Riele & R. Brooks (Eds), *Negotiating Ethical Challenges in Youth Research* (pp. 55–68). New York: Routledge.

Brooks, R., Te Riele, K., & Maguire, M. (2014). *Ethics and Education Research*. BERA/SAGE Research Methods Series. London: SAGE.

CIHR, NSERC and SSHRC [Canadian Institutes of Health Research, Natural Sciences and Engineering Research Council of Canada, and Social Sciences and Humanities Research Council of Canada] (2010). *Tri-Council Policy Statement: Ethical Conduct for Research Involving Humans (TCPS 2)*. Retrieved 10 September 2015. http://ethics.gc.ca/eng/policy-politique/initiatives/tcps2-eptc2/Default/.

DHEW [Department of Health, Education and Welfare] (1979). *The Belmont Report: Ethical Principles and Guidelines for the Protection of Human Subjects of Research*. Washington: DWEH. Retrieved September 5, 2014. www.hhs.gov/ohrp/humansubjects/guidance/belmont.html

Garrett, J. (2004). *A Simple and Usable (Although Incomplete) Ethical Theory Based on the Ethics of W. D. Ross*. Retrieved September 5, 2014. http://people.wku.edu/jan.garrett/ethics/rossethc.htm

Gillies, V., & Robinson, Y. (2012). Developing Creative Research Methods with Challenging Pupils. *International Journal of Social Research Methodology, 15*(2), 161–173.

Griebling, S., Vaughn, L., Howell, B., Ramstetter, C., & Dole, D. (2013). From Passive to Active Voice: Using Photography as a Catalyst for Social Action. *International Journal of Humanities and Social Science, 3*(2), 16–28.

Hammersley, M., & Traianou, A. (2012) *Ethics and educational research. British Educational Research Association on-line resource*. Retrieved September 5, 2014. http://www.bera.ac.uk/resources/ethics-and-educational-research

Macfarlane, B. (2009) *Researching with Integrity: The Ethics of Academic Enquiry*. New York: Routledge.

Matthews, H. (2001). Participatory Structures and the Youth of Today: Engaging Those Who Are Hardest to Reach. *Ethics, Place & Environment, 4*(2), 153–159.

NHMRC, ARC & AVCC (2007). *National statement on ethical conduct in human research*. Canberra: National Health and Medical Research Council together with the Australian Research Council and the Australian Vice Chancellors' Committee.

Pitt, P. (2014). 'The Project Cannot Be Approved in Its Current Form': Feminist Visual Research Meets the Human Research Ethics Committee. *Australian Educational Researcher, 41*(3), 311–325.

Pope, C., De Luca, R. and Tolich, M. (2010). 'How an Exchange of Perspectives Led to Tentative Ethical Guidelines for Visual Ethnography', *International Journal of Research and Method in Education, 33*(3), 301–315.

Preece, R. (2012). 'Disillusioned' 7 Up Boy Who Criticised Thatcher Returns to the Documentary Series after a 28-Year Gap. *Daily Mail*, May 14. Retrieved September 5, 2014. http://www.dailymail.co.uk/news/article-2144082/56-Up-7-Up-boy-Peter-Davies-returns-documentary-28-years.html

Prosser, J., & Burke, C. (2011). Image-Based Educational Research: Childlike Perspectives. *Inquiry: Perspectives, Processes and Possibilities*, 4(2), 257–273.

Robb, S., O'Leary, P., Mackinnon, A., & Bishop, P. (2010). *Hope: The Everyday and Imaginary Life of Young People on the Margins*. Kent Town, South Australia: Wakefield Press.

Ross, W. D. (1930/2002). The Right and the Good. In P. Stratton-Lake (Ed.), *Introduction*. New York: Oxford University Press.

Small, R. (2001). Codes are not Enough: 'What Philosophy Can Contribute to the Ethics of Educational Research'. *Journal of Philosophy of Education*, 35(3), 387–406.

Schrag, Z. M. (2011). The Case Against Ethics Review in the Social Sciences. *Research Ethics*, 7(4), 120–131.

Scott, C. L., & Fonseca, L. (2010). Overstepping the Mark: Ethics Procedure, Risky Research and Education Research. *International Journal of Research & Method in Education*, 33(3), 287–300.

Sikes, P., & Piper, H. (2010) Editorial: Ethical Research, Academic Freedom and the Role of Ethics Committees and Review Procedures in Educational Research. *International Journal of Research and Method in Education*, 33(3), 205–213.

Suaalii, T., & Mavoa, H. (2001). Who Says Yes? Collective and Individual Framing of Pacific Children's Consent to, and Participation in, Research in New Zealand. *Childrenz Issues*, 5(1), 39–42.

Te Riele, K. (2012). Negotiating Risk and Hope: A Case Study of Alternative Education for Marginalized Youth in Australia. In W. Pink (Ed), *Schools and Marginalized Youth: An International Perspective* (pp. 31–79). Cresskill, NJ: Hampton Press.

Te Riele, K. (2014). *Putting the Jigsaw Together: Flexible Learning Programs in Australia. Final report*. Melbourne: The Victoria Institute for Education, Diversity and Lifelong Learning. Retrieved September 5, 2014. http://dusseldorp.org.au/priorities/alternative-learning/jigsaw/

Te Riele, K., & Brooks, R. (Eds) (2013). *Negotiating Ethical Challenges in Youth Research*. Critical Youth Studies series. New York: Routledge.

Wang, C., & Burris, M. A. (1994). Empowerment through Photo Novella: Portraits of Participation. *Health Education & Behavior*, 21(2), 171–186.

Wang, C., & Redwood-Jones, Y. A. (2001). Photovoice Ethics: Perspectives from Flint Photovoice. *Health Education & Behavior*, 28(5), 560–572.

Wiles, R., Prosser, J., Bagnoli, A., Clark, A., Davies, K., Holland, S., & Renold, E. (2008). *Visual ethics: Ethical Issues in Visual Research*. ESRC National Centre for Research Methods Review Paper NCRM/011. Retrieved September 5, 2014. http://eprints.ncrm.ac.uk/421/1/MethodsReviewPaperNCRM-011.pdf

Wood, B., & Kidman, J. (2013). Negotiating the Ethical Borders of Visual Research with Young People. In K. Te Riele & R. Brooks (Eds), *Negotiating Ethical Challenges in Youth Research* (pp. 149–162). New York: Routledge.

14
The Gaze and the Gift: Ethical Issues When Young Children Are Photographers

Patricia Tarr and Sylvia Kind

This chapter has emerged from conversations that Sylvia and I have had around her experiences with three- and four-year-olds using cameras and my examination of ethical issues in using photos as part of the documentation processes that teachers use to understand children's thinking (Tarr 2011). We are interested in the intersections of pedagogical documentation (Dahlberg 2012; Dahlberg, Moss & Pence 2007; Rinaldi 2006) research with children, children using cameras to document their own interests (Bitou & Waller 2011; Clark 2005), and a shared space in which educators, children, and cameras blur and blend insider and outsider perspectives into a between-space (Kind 2013; Wilson 2007). In this chapter we will explore the questions and issues that have emerged for us around the use of photography with young children that have implications for both educators and researchers incorporating visual methods with children, especially young children.

Pedagogical documentation as research

Sylvia has been working as an atelierista in a campus daycare, a role similar to an artist in residence, or artist consultant. She works with children and teachers on arts-based projects and uses photography to document the emerging projects and children's processes. In addition much of her recent work has focused on children's own engagements with the camera and photography and how children have used cameras to record, explore and exchange ideas. This chapter will draw on examples from these projects. Pat teaches in a faculty of education where she has been researching pedagogical documentation in elementary and secondary school contexts. We have been inspired by the educators in the infant-toddler and pre-primary schools in Reggio Emilia, Italy, who engage in documenting children's thinking and learning processes through the use of digital and video photography, audio recordings and written notes as the core of their pedagogical work with the children (Dahlberg 2012; Giudici, Rinaldi & Krechevsky 2001). We understand pedagogical documentation as a process of listening to children. It involves processes of photographing and recording children's processes and engagements, revisiting and discussing them together, and collectively proposing new directions for inquiry. It takes seriously children's participation in their own learning and situates children and educators as researchers together. It is a collective search for understanding. For instance, Turner and Wilson (2010) emphasised,

> One of the most common misinterpretations is to understand documentation as a strategy to teach better what we as teachers already know. Instead, documentation needs to be a way to get to know better what the children, in their own way, already know. (p. 8)

Thus pedagogical documentation is an ethical practice. Our definition of ethics comes from Dahlberg, Moss and Pence's (1999/2007) discussion of ethics 'which emanates from respect for each child and cognition of difference and multiplicity, and which struggles to avoid making the Other into the same as oneself' (p. 156). This engages educators and researchers in an inquiry where we look for disruptions to our own understandings while exploring children's processes and perspectives. As Olsson (2009) wrote, 'there is a risk that we document that which we already know about children and learning and by doing that we immobilize and close down the event' (p. 113). Bucknall (2014) has cautioned researchers in a similar vein:

> The concepts and categories which adult researchers identify in the data often correspond to the knowledge they bring to the study.... even when the aim of the research is to privilege the voices of children and young people, these voices can still be misrepresented or silenced during the process of data selection and representation. (pp. 78–79)

Additionally, researchers have increasingly used photography to understand children's perspectives of their lives within early childhood educational settings (e.g. Bitou & Waller 2011; Clark 2005, 2010). Thus, we

The Gaze and the Gift: Ethical Issues   253

understand photography as both a visual research method and pedagogical practice.

As educators and researchers, we take children seriously as co-participants and researchers of our lives together. Carlina Rinaldi (2006), in describing this as a search for meaning, asked, 'How can we help children find the meaning of what they do, what they encounter, what they experience? And how can we do this for ourselves?' (p. 63).

Understanding pedagogy as research into meaning within a system of relationships (Rinaldi 2006) brings complexity into the research process. We have discovered that the children's use of cameras to document their interests has made this search for meaning multi-layered and more complex than we anticipated. We liken this complexity to the shifting images in a kaleidoscope where pieces combine and recombine to create complex designs as the kaleidoscope is turned. We will focus this kaleidoscopic array around two themes: the gaze and the gift. Like educational/sociological researchers, Pat lives outside of the kaleidoscope of the classroom and brings an outsider's perspective to this work having only had the opportunity to see the work that Sylvia does with children through photographs she has shared. Sylvia, who works directly with children, brings an insider perspective. Both of us take seriously the implications of the *UN Convention on Rights of the* Child (1989) that states that children have a right to be listened to and to have a voice in matters that concern them. This document has led to researchers from the fields of both education and sociology of childhood to engage in dialogues and debates about what it means ethically to involve children as participants in research (e.g. Einarsdottir 2007; Harcourt, Perry & Waller 2011; Soto & Swadener 2005), to gain informed consent/assent from young children (Flewitt 2005; Harcourt & Conroy 2011), and to use photographs in research with children in an ethical manner (Nutbrown 2010; Olsson 2009; Quinn & Manning 2013).

As one living outside of the early childhood classroom, one of Pat's questions has been whether children consent to being photographed and having their images and words made visible in the classroom that is part of the pedagogical documentation process. Negotiating consent with children may remain unexamined or taken for granted by teachers. For example, Cheeseman (2006) wrote,

> We are tempted to make assumptions that children don't mind this, that it is part of being in an early childhood center. We have always listened into children's conversations and used this material to inform our future planning. The public display of these conversations within

documentation may represent an assumption on behalf of the teacher that children consent to this practice. (p. 194)

Have we asked directly, or have we asked, about the use of photography in ways that children understand so that they can refuse to participate? When we negotiate consent with children, are we truly involving them in informed assent/consent on an ongoing basis (see Harcourt & Conroy 2011; Quinn & Manning 2013; Sargeant & Harcourt 2012)? While this has been an issue for Pat as an academic, it has not been such an issue for Sylvia in her more intimate relationship with the children and co-inquirer and collaborator with the children in their interests and projects. While we will not pursue this issue at length within the scope of this chapter, we feel it should be part of the ongoing dialogue around ethical practices for educators and researchers using photography in their work with children. This is something that Quinn and Manning (2013) discussed using the lens of power relationships between stakeholders that include educators, parents and children to raise critical issues about taking and using photographs in educational settings. Quinn and Manning (2013) cautioned, 'It is also important to recognize that the systems of knowledge under which the photographs are interpreted also have considerable power over both the interpreted and the interpreter of a photograph' (p. 273).

Children and photography

Embedded in this chapter are questions about what it means for young children to engage in the act of 'making' pictures (Navab 2001) and what it means to be in a co-researcher relationship with children as they engage in picture making. We use Navab's (2001) idea of making rather than taking pictures because this concept fits more closely into the role that photography played in the studio space of the school and its connection to children's engagement with other materials (Kind 2013). In our exploration of this, we crossed the boundaries between pedagogy and research as the children challenged us to rethink our notions of children using cameras to document their interests as a way to understand their thinking and as a way for support their learning.

To engage in dialogue with children around pedagogical documentation and their engagement with cameras and making photographs is a complex process because it involves a search for understanding on both the part of the teacher and the children (Rinaldi 2006). When children are using the camera, the complexity increases and becomes even more multi-layered. We begin with two questions: 'what is a photograph?' and 'what might making photographs mean to young children?' Sontag (1977) has written, 'photographs alter and enlarge our notions of what is worth looking at and what we have a right to observe. They are a grammar and, even more importantly, an ethics of seeing' (p. 3). She stated, 'picture taking is an event in itself, and one with ever more peremptory rights – to interfere with, to invade, or to ignore whatever is going on' (p. 11). In what way then do the children's photographs challenge and deepen our understanding of what is worth looking at?

Tinkler (2008) has argued that research into children's use of photography is fragmented and falls into one of three categories: 'uncovering and understanding young people's lives using photographic methods; documenting and explaining how young people produce photographs; exploring young people's cultural responses to photographic technologies' (p. 256). She has found that individual studies are usually dominated by a single approach, although some may contain elements of more than one. All three approaches contribute valuable insights into young people's photographic practices, but these insights are partial and fragmented. She has stated, 'It is necessary to keep in mind the distinction between, on the one hand, photographs and photography as research tools, and on the other hand, photographs and photography as the subjects of research' (p. 256). We argue that this is not as simple as Tinkler has suggested. In the following, we find this distinction to be blurred and complex.

Episode 1: Photos as Provocations

For several months Sylvia was engaged in a photography project with three- and four-year-old children. In this project, children, often accompanied by another teacher, were invited in to the studio where cameras were available for them to use. The children took photos of each other, themselves, the adults in the room (who were also taking photos), and things that interested them, following directions that the children proposed as well as those that Sylvia invited. Teachers and children together explored photography's processes. Sylvia describes her experience of engaging with children and the resulting photographs as follows:

> As we took photos, they were printed and posted on the studio walls and gradually took over the space. Silently the photos filled the walls, and as different groups of children came to work in the studio, chairs were drawn up in front and children momentarily

sat together and talked about the images. I attended to the ways the photos prompted stories, evoked memories and provided other photographic compositions. The children's own discussion rarely engaged with questions of who took the photo, what it meant, how it reflected a particular view, experience or perception, or how it gave insight into a particular individual's process. Instead they engaged with the photos by acting in response to the images, posing as the figures in the photos, enacting and re-enacting moments and playing in their company.

In this example, the focus was on both adults and children looking at the photographs and the possibilities and the meaning that the children brought to their photography. In this episode, the photographs served as provocations or invitations for children to engage with the photos as prompts for stories, memories and the creation of new photographs. This is a way that photographs, taken by children or adults, have been used as part of pedagogical documentation. We want to reveal a much more complex process than using photographs as a memory but also provide an invitation for 'becoming' (Olsson 2009) to the children. We want to make this past/present and future relationship of the photos even more complex through the following discussion on 'the gaze'.

The gaze

The field of early childhood education has long been dominated by a developmental psychology perspective which has positioned children as deficit models of adults (Canella 1997; Dahlberg, Moss & Pence 2007; Pacini-Ketchabaw, Nxumalo, Kocher, Elliot & Sanchez 2015) studied through the gaze of the psychologist or educator as objectively as possible to fit a 'scientific model' in order to uncover the 'truth' about children. These observations, which may have included photo documentation served to 'Other' and 'objectify the child', result in issues of power and surveillance (Quinn & Manning 2013). This is the 'colonial' (Navab 2001) gaze, and it is fraught with issues of power. It tends to award more power to the one doing the looking and objectify the one being looked at. But there are ' ways of looking at this, and the gaze can be much more complicated than simply a polarity of power. A polarity of power, for instance, tends to underestimate the self-awareness and self-knowledge of the person being photographed and overestimates the power and abilities of the photographer (Navab 2001; Sturken &

Cartwright 2009). Nevertheless, it is important that we reconstruct this notion of the gaze in order to disrupt the use of photographs as sites of power.

Claudia Mitchell (2011) asked, 'What does the gaze look like when those who are typically the subjects and not the agents are behind the camera?' (p. 143). Young children are most frequently the objects of the photograph and not the creators of the photograph. How does using cameras empower young children to be constructors of their lives with teachers? To have real agency in their lives in a educational setting? In this kaleidoscopic context, at various times, we have the gaze of the children using the camera on the subject of their photo; the other children's gaze on the subject because this may be a collaborative or community effort; and on the act of picture taking, our (adult) gaze on the children using the camera, and the children gazing back at us as we gaze at them. Additionally, we have the camera's gaze, which is not the same as the children's gaze, nor the adult's gaze. Then we have the images the children created, in which we gaze at the children gazing out from the photographs.

To illustrate this, we can look at a moment from Sylvia's photography project.

Episode 2: Looking

We are in the studio and a game begins. The children have been creating creatures through sculptural work and drawings, tangents of crafting appendages where they become the creatures, decorating themselves and others. A curled wire is placed behind a friend's ear, and other fragments tucked into tufts of hair and into the waistband of pants.

'Don't look!' a voice calls out and her hands cover an emerging structure. Other voices join in, 'Yeah, don't look!' 'It's not finished yet. Don't look!'

'Only kids can look, not adults.'

'Only girls can look, not boys.' There are no boys in the studio today so this is not contested.

I pose a question, 'Can the camera look?'

There is a pause, a momentary silence as the idea seems to settle in the room. Then a chorus of voices: 'Yes, the camera can look. But no adults!'

I am puzzled and intrigued by this as today as I am the only one with the camera. What does it mean that I, as an adult, cannot look, but the camera can? It is evident to the children that I need to look through the viewfinder and my eye is behind the camera's lens. Yet it seems that other ways of seeing are proposed and the camera is invited to play in this game as its own entity with its own agency and particular way of looking. Later while using a video camera I am provoked to turn the display screen around to face the children so they can more evidently see what the camera sees as it records our movements and conversations. The video camera stands on its own legs, the tripod, and watches. (Kind 2013, pp. 432–433)

Bloustien (1996) found a similar situation where the camera seemed to have its own identity in research with teen girls:

Frequently in situations like this, the camera was invited in as an additional member of the group. It 'joined in' their activities and was often beckoned to as though it were a new friend who needed encouragement to feel at home. It was far from an objective voyeur but instead treated like an additional participant in the group's activities. (Bloustien 1996, Fantasy vs Play, para.1)

Sylvia describes the episode as an event of learning (see Atkinson 2011) that didn't just consider the child's view and participation, or even just the adult's point of view, but was a complicated way of seeing that considered multiple perspectives. It raised the question of who 'owned' the photos, whose view did they represent, and what did it mean to take and make photographs?

We think it is the very awareness of the complexity and multi-layered nature of this looking that can help move educators away from documenting or responding to what they expect, or already think they know to understand more fully the nature of reciprocity of this situation and how to engage in ethical responses. As Dahlberg, Moss and Pence (1999/2007) emphasised, 'The art of listening and hearing what the Other is saying, and taking it seriously, is related to the ethics of the encounter' (p. 156). Pacini-Ketchabaw et al. (2015) brought a poststructural perspective to their discussion of ethics and spoke to a contextual and situational nature of ethical relationships:

A code of ethics can guide us, but codes don't speak to the small acts and words we exchange every day. We believe that at times we need to interrogate preset codes of ethics for their colonial legacies – as they are usually founded on colonial practices. (p. 175)

Our interest here is in how we might create and improvise with the camera and consider complicated ways of seeing. We are interested in ways of seeing that recognise the power and complexity of the gaze, resist straightforward understandings, and allow for a continuum of complicity and resistance (Kind 2013).

Gazing back – the photo as gift

As we think about this between space, a space of exchange can be opened up if we consider the photograph as an encounter, or as a gift, something that is both given and received rather than something that is simply taken or 'captured' (see Navab 2001). For example, Les Back (2007), a sociologist at Goldsmith's College, London, described a photographic project in Brick Lane where a large-format camera was set up and people chose to pose for the camera. The result was a large number of photos of people visiting Brick Lane over a period of time. Back said, 'It is a mistake, I think, to see the lens only looking one way. The figures in these portraits look back. They stare back at us' (p. 104). We often talk about taking photos. We take something away. Back reframed this to think about the photo as a gift. The people who chose to pose for the students and camera gave their presence, and this momentary presence has been preserved as a photograph. Back (2007) wrote, 'Part of what is compelling about them is they contain voices that are present yet inaudible. We have to listen for them with our eyes' (p. 100).

How will we, as educators, receive these photographic gifts from children? And how will we facilitate engagement with children's photos as gifts given to each other as well as to ourselves? In the first episode, the children's photographs on the studio wall acted as gifts returned to the children. Individual children's photos did not belong to them but were extended to other children to reinterpret, engage with, and respond to. It is this ethical encounter with the gift, to fully listen to the gift in a spirit of reciprocity and dialogue, that concerns and engages us. The gift places a responsibility upon us: a responsibility of response, an ethical response in which we truly listen to the meaning of the gift from the giver's perspective and also allow the gift to take on its own life and meaning as others engage with it. Olsson (2009) suggested,

They [children] sometimes engage in a production of sense that leads to truths that we as adults can have a very hard time understanding. Therefore it is necessary to approach the pedagogical documentation by focusing on how the children's construction of a problem relates to the sense under production. (p. 116)

This attentive listening is not an easy process, and as educators we must be continually reflexive about what the selves or lenses are that we bring to our listening.

Bitou and Waller (2011), who provided video and digital cameras to children under the age of three years to understand children's view of the curriculum in an early childhood setting, found that it would have been easy to misunderstand children's actual engagement in activities had they not had children's thoughts and comments connected to the photographs. While it appeared that one boy was enjoying playing with toy tools because he had taken a photo of the tools, in fact, he told them he did not like the plastic tools available but preferred to use real tools like at his grandfather's house.

In ethical relationships, we must continually return a new gift to children. This gift has at its core their gift, valued and reformed with our propositions and proposals of meaning, through questioning, confirming or disconfirming what we think we understand about children's intentions. In this process we recognise that there are multiple meanings possible (Quinn & Manning 2013). It is as Rinaldi (2006) wrote, 'listening with all of our senses' (p. 65), and is about, as Olsson (2009) suggested, 'tak[ing] into account thoughts, speech, actions, but also material and environments' (p. 119). Sylvia says, 'I am interested, as Rose (2004) described, in embracing "noisy and unruly processes capable of finding dialogue with each other and with the world...a dialogue that requires a "we" who share a time and space of attentiveness"' (p. 21).

What does it mean to listen and ethically respond, when children push the boundaries of acceptability when they take photos? Grace and Tobin (1997), in a study of children's video productions with children grades 1–6, 'found that as the students incorporated their own interests and pleasures into the videos, they pushed at the borders of propriety, reminding us of the fragility of classroom equilibrium' (p. 167). Children were sensitive to their audience and created different videos depending on whether the audience comprised their peers or their parents. It was in the videos created for peers where they pushed the boundaries that included the 'fantastic, horrific, the grotesque and the forbidden' (p. 169). The students also used parody and humor in their productions.

'The teachers eventually came to perceive children's use of parody in a generally prosocial light' (p. 170). The researchers found that they needed to look beneath the surface to see how the videos might help the children address and deal with particular issues and topics.

It is easy to dismiss or shut down photos or videos that push boundaries of acceptability in an educational setting; however, ethically, teachers, and researchers, must then respond in a way that goes beneath the surface to see how such images can serve positive purposes. This is consistent with Olsson's direction, 'Do not look for knowledge, look at learning processes, that is, look for and construct how the involved bodies join in a problematic field' (p. 119).

There were other moments in Sylvia's project where children took photos of the 'blood in their body', pulling down eyelids to see the red veins in their own eyes, taking photos of the insides of each others' mouths; and peered into closed classrooms where adult students were studying, taking photos through small windows on the classroom doors. Walking outside while holding a camera allowed them a certain boldness to approach strangers, asking, 'Can I take a photo of your bag? What do you have in there?' The camera, it seemed, gave them permission to look at things not normally visible, accessible or permissible.

Between-spaces

In this third episode, we refocus on the complex, reciprocal interactions around taking pictures that blur the separate roles of children and educator to create a dynamic space of listening and creating.

Episode 3: Between-spaces

This morning I am in the classroom with the four-year-old children and we are drawing together with coloured pencils, watercolour crayons, and charcoal. The light is low, so I have my camera mounted nearby on a tripod. It is my regular morning to draw and paint with the children. Over the months, they have become accustomed to the presence of my camera, and we have developed a rhythm of taking photos together. During the art explorations, the children often interject with their own vision of what they want recorded, direct me in how they want to be photographed, or most usually, use the camera as a way of seeing for themselves. Like a dance, they interrupt me as I photograph, asking, 'Can I take a picture?' and I interject with my own requests when something appears before me that I would like to have photographed in a particular way. There is space for both our interests. The camera moves between us, the tripod allowing for a slower, more deliberate, cautious movement as the photographer, whether child or adult, stands behind the camera, looks through the lens, and makes adjustments to the position of the tripod and angle of the view. My photos are more deliberate, slower, carefully composed, and most often move with the rhythm of the events – slow when things are placid, and quicker and somewhat more intrusive when the energy intensifies. Their photos have a rhythm as well. There is a click-click-click of the shutter, always it seems a rhythm of three, and as the child stands back to look at the image in the viewfinder, small groups collect to look at and consider the resulting images. Collectively there are rhythms of looking, focusing, composing, capturing, considering, representing and inventing.

And so as it often happens as we draw together, the events begin to intensify as charcoal begins to creep on to hands and then faces. There is a momentary pause as one child looks around at the charcoal on the other children's faces and announces, 'We're the Monster High girls!' The children are drawn to attention at this exclamation, and then there is a sudden eruption of activity.

Watercolour crayons are dipped in water and faces are coloured with green, black, blue, pink, yellow and white. Children check themselves in mirrors to evaluate how accurately they are beginning to resemble the characters from Monster High: Howleen Wolf and Lagoona Blue, in particular. Other children join in with characters they are familiar with and others that they invent in order to join in the game. Two boys begin to compose themselves as Ninja Boy and Queen Monster High, bodies becoming black and blacker, intense pink on lips, forehead, arms and eyelids. Bodies are marked, symbols drawn on arms and torsos, faces transformed. Mirrors and camera reflect back and provoke the emergence of the characters. The children become hybrid composites. They become characters they are familiar with, and also those that are partially known, out of reach and known only through their friends. The children borrow, transform, and extend each others' ideas and speculations. The adults in the room have to check the Internet to find out about Monster High as we seem to be ignorant of the source that compels the children at this moment. Children gather around to judge their emerging bodied representations with the images on the screen.

I am unsure what to make of this, but the energy of the event is compelling. 'Look at me!' 'Take my picture!' 'Did you get a picture of my face?' 'Take a picture of me like this!' 'Let me use the camera!' It is difficult to enter into this now highly energetic and intense experimentation in my usual ways as no one seems interested in slowing enough to talk about their processes. But the camera and photographic exchanges connect us. The children perform for the camera and each other, and together we record the events as they unfold.

Brent Wilson (2007) described collaboration as a process of mutual transformation, a hybrid co-production or hypertext. In this situation, authority is shared as each participant contributes to the emergence and documentation of the event through posing, composing, interjecting, inventing and recording. The photos reflect children's desire to look, and to be looked at and noticed. The photos also record their desire to interrupt, interject and cut into a single viewpoint. Documentation becomes a collective event.

Wilson describes moments such as this as 'other-than' – other-than children's productions and other-than adult's interests – 'each has an opportunity to contribute, to propose changes in direction, to innovate, and to exercise power and control' (Wilson 2007, p. 11).

We have been challenged to look beneath the surface of what at first appears to be a relatively simple process, giving children cameras to document their lives and using these photos as a means to understand their points of view in order to support their learning. Through conscious awareness of the complexity of the 'gaze' and 'gifts' that children offer us through their photography, we can now more ethically see photography serving as a process of collaborating and moving with the world (Kind 2013) in a between-space, rather than a view from either the outside or inside. We think that to be immersed in this between-space offers both educators and researchers opportunities to engage ethically with children.

We have chosen the three vignettes to speak to the complexities of teaching and research with young children and photography. In the first episode, the photos served as provocations for the children to re-engage with the images by acting out the moments or posing like the figures. While the photos served as memories for the children, the children were focused on their present interactions with the photos or on a process of becoming (Olsson 2009) rather than on the past, as to what the photos meant at the time they were taken. When researchers use photographs with children, including photos that children have taken, the focus tends to be oriented to the child's choice of subject matter photograph: why did you take this picture? How does this picture represent your desire, interest or life? In other words, using photos to elicit/understand children's experiences. Stepping back from this process and seeing the photo as a memory for the group but also as a provocation for becoming, opens new possibilities for understanding and entering into a dialogue with children and understanding their perspectives.

The second episode challenged us to consider the acts of looking and the complexity of the gaze: who can look, what lens do they bring to the looking and what are the ethical implications when the gaze pushes our boundaries or requires us to respond? 'Ethical action involves being present in every relationship without following obvious or comfortable answers. Being present involves much more than being physically present; it requires us to acknowledge and respond to power injustices, both historical and ongoing' (Pacini-Ketchabaw et al. 2015, p. 184).

In the third episode, we have a 'between-space' in which educators and children interact as co-partners where adult-child boundaries disappear. This was possible in part because Sylvia, in her role as atelierista, was very much part of the learning community. However, we wonder how might educational researchers design their studies in ways that might blur the boundaries between researcher and researched through using photography with children?

We have drawn from the literature and image of the child coming from the preschools in Reggio Emilia, Italy (Dahlberg 2012; Rinaldi 2006), and pedagogical documentation that places teachers as researchers with children. We have done so in the belief that when teachers and children are researching their lives together through photography, the issues that emerged for us may also inform researchers using photography as part of their research with children.

Note

Previous versions of this chapter have been presented at the International Visual Arts Society Conference, London, UK, July 2013; and at the 66th OMEP World Assembly and Conference, Cork, Ireland, July 2014 under the title, 'The Gaze and the Gift: Ethics, Young Children and Photography'.

References

Atkinson, D. (2011). *Art, Equality and Learning: Pedagogies Against the State*. Rotterdam: Sense.
Back. L. (2007). *The Art of Listening*. New York: Berg.

Bitou, A., & Waller, T. (2011). Researching the Rights of Children under Three Years Old to Participate in the Curriculum in Early Years Education and Care. In D. Harcourt, B. Perry & T. Waller (Eds), *Researching Young Children's Perspectives: Debating the Ethics and Dilemmas of Educational Research with Children* (pp. 52–67). New York: Routledge.

Bloustien, G. (1996, September). Striking a Pose! *Youth Studies Australia*, 10382569 15(3). Retrieved from www.web.b.ebscohost.com.

Bucknall, S. (2014). Doing Qualitative Research with Children and Young People. In A. Clark, R. Flewitt, M. Hammersley, & M. Robb (Eds), *Understanding Research with Children and Young People*. Thousand Oaks, CA: Sage.

Burke, C. (2008). 'Play in Focus': Children's Visual Voice in Participative Research. In P. Thomson (Ed.), *Doing Visual Research with Children and Young People* (pp. 23–36). New York: Routledge.

Canella, G. (1997). *Deconstructing Early Childhood Education: Social Justice and Revolution*. New York: Peter Lang.

Cheeseman, S., & Robertson, J. (2006). Unsure – Private Conversations Publicly Recorded. In A. Fleet, C. Patterson, & J. Robertson (Eds), *Insights: Behind Early Childhood Pedagogical Documentation* (pp. 191–204). Castle Hill, NSW, Australia: Pademelon Press.

Clark A. (2005). Ways of Seeing: Using the Mosaic Approach to Listen to Young Children's Perspectives. In A. Clark, A. Kjorhot, & P. Moss (Eds), *Beyond Listening: Children's Perspectives on Early Childhood Services* (pp. 29–49). Bristol, UK: The Policy Press.

Clark, A. (2010). *Transforming Children's Spaces: Children's and Adults' Participation in Designing Learning Environments*. New York: Routledge.

Dahlberg, G. (2012). Pedagogical Documentation: A Practice for Negotiation and Democracy. In C. Edwards, L. Gandini, & G. Forman (Eds), *The Hundred Languages of Children: The Reggio Emilia Experience in Transformation*, 3rd ed. (pp. 225–231). Denver, CO: Praeger.

Dahlberg, G., Moss, P., & Pence, A. (1999/2007). *Beyond Quality in Early Childhood Education and Care*. Philadelphia, PA: Falmer Press; New York: Routledge.

Einarsdottir, J. (2007). Research with Children: Methodological and Ethical Challenges. *European Early Childhood Education Research Journal*, 15(2), 197–211, DOI: 10.1080/13502930701321477.

Flewitt, R. (2005). Conducting Research with Young Children: Some Ethical Considerations. *Early Child Development and Care*, 175(6), 553–565. DOI: 10.1080/03004430500131338.

Giudici, C., Rinaldi, C., & Krechevsky, M. (Eds) (2001). *Making Learning Visible: Children as Individual and Group Learners*. Reggio Emilia, Italy: Project Zero and Reggio Children.

Grace, D., & Tobin, J. (1997). Carnival in the Classroom: Elementary Students Making Videos. In J. Tobin (Ed.), *Making a Place for Pleasure in Early Childhood Education* (pp. 159–187). New Haven, CT: Yale University.

Harcourt, D., & Conroy, H. (2011). Informed Consent: Processes and Procedures in Seeking Research Partnerships with Young Children. In D. Harcourt, B. Perry, & T. Waller (Eds), *Researching Young Children's Perspectives: Debating the Ethics and Dilemmas of Educational Research with Children* (pp. 38–51). New York, NY: Routledge.

Kind, S. (2013). Lively Entanglements: The Doings, Movements, and Enactments of Photography. *Global Childhoods, 3*(4), 427–441.
Mitchell, C. (2011). *Doing Visual Research*. Thousand Oaks, CA: Sage.
Navab, A. (2001). Re-picturing Photography: A Language in the Making. *Journal of Aesthetic Education, 35*(1), 69–84. http://www.jstor.org/stable/3333772
Nutbrown, C. (2010). Naked by the Pool? Blurring the Image? Ethical Issues in the Portrayal of Young Children in Art-Based Educational Research. *Qualitative Inquiry, 17*(1), 3–14. DOI: 10.1177/1077800410389437.
Olsson, L. (2009). *Movement and Experimentation in Young Children's Learning*. New York: Routledge.
Pacini-Ketchabaw, V., Nxumalo, F., Kocher, L., Elliot, E., & Sanchez, A. (2015) *Journeys: Reconceptualizing Early Childhood Practices through Pedagogical Narration*. Toronto, ON: University of Toronto Press.
Quinn, S., & Manning, J. (2013) Recognizing the Ethical Implications of the Use of Photography in Early Childhood Educational Settings. *Contemporary Issues in Early Childhood, 14*(3), 270–278.
Rinaldi, C. (2006). *In Dialogue with Reggio Emilia*. New York: Routledge.
Rose, D. B. (2004). *Reports from a Wild Country: Ethics for Decolonisation*. Sydney, Australia: University of New South Wales.
Sargeant, J., & Harcourt, D. (2012). *Doing Ethical Research with Children*. New York: Open University Press.
Sontag, S. (1977). *On Photography*. New York: Picador.
Soto, L. D., & Swadener, B. B. (Eds) (2005). *Power and Voice in Research with Children*. New York: Peter Lang.
Sturken, M., & Cartwright, L. (2009). *Practices of Looking*. New York: Oxford University Press.
Tarr, P. (2011). Reflections and Shadows: Ethical Issues in Pedagogical Documentation. *Canadian Children, 36*(2), 11–16.
Tinkler, P. (2008). A Fragmented Picture: Reflections on the Photographic Practices of Young People. *Visual Studies, 23*(3), 255–266. DOI: 10.1080/14725860802489916.
Turner, T., & Wilson, D. (2010 winter). Reflections on Documentation: A Discussion with Thought Leaders from Reggio Emilia. *Theory into Practice, 49*(1), 5–13.
United Nations. (1989). *The United Nations Convention on the Rights of the Child*. New York: UNICEF. http://www.ohchr.org/en/professionalinterest/pages/crc.aspx www.ohchr.org/english/law/crc.htm
Wilson, B. (2007). Art, Visual Culture, and Adult/Child Collaborative Images: Recognizing the Other-than. *Visual Arts Research, 33*(2), 6–20.

15
Conclusion

Barbara Pini and Julianne Moss

In this concluding chapter our purpose is two-fold. The first is to draw out some of the common themes which underpin the chapters. In part, we commenced this task in arranging the book into the four sections of Images of Schooling, Performing Pedagogy Visually, Power and Representation and Ethical Issues. However, in recognition that, like all categorisations, this was arbitrary and potentially reductive, we now revisit the contributions making connections across and between the chapters. A related and second task of this conclusion is to highlight gaps and limitations of what we have gathered together in this collection. Inevitably, this book does not speak to all of the issues embedded in a visual approach to educational research. In recognising this partiality, our aim is to gesture towards the types of questions and concerns that VRMs raise and still require educational researchers to think about – and in differing ways.

Commonalities, gaps and the future

A scan of the chapters in this book demonstrates the versatility of visual methods. Visual research methods renders obsolete divisions of educational research according to whether the focus is on a particular site, a precise temporal period, and a certain group of actors or a specific area of inquiry. In a disciplinary field such as education that has often been preoccupied by categorisations this is remarkable. Daycare centres (Tarr and Kind), alternative education (McLeod, Goad, Willis and Darian-Smith), university settings (Metcalfe and Thomson and Hall), elite schools (Pini, McDonald and Bartlett), secondary schools (Dixon and Senior and Moss), the tutoring industry (Koh), kindergartens (Luttrell) and informal education (Te Riele and Baker) are all explored through visual approaches. Further, as Rowe and Margolis reveal in Chapter 3, and as others detail later in the collection, visual sources in educational research are as vital for understanding the past as they are the present. What is suggested by the diversity of educational sites explored by authors is that visual methods have potential to provide insights across the complex, overlapping and multiple spatialities of the educational landscape. In this regard, there is still much to be done, particularly given that new educational spaces are emerging all the time. Koh shows in his examination of the private tutoring industry and Pini, McDonald and Barlett delineate the way in which marketers at elite schools engage with global consultancy companies in media, advertising and social media as part of their remit. While engaging the visual to elicit meanings associated with new educational spaces, we should not forget some of the more traditional and overlooked sites in which education has and continues to occur. For example, as recent work drawing on the visual to investigate the Boys' Brigade Camps and The Scouts (Mills 2014; Kyle 2014; Bannister 2014) has revealed, a study of iconography in these well-known organisations can tell us a great deal about the pedagogic lives of youth beyond the classroom.

The richness of visual data as a source that can be engaged to address research questions across the educational field is further evidenced in this book by the incredible variety of images utilised by authors. Pauwel's (2012, p. 254) claim that camera-based representations 'have lost [their] almost exclusive position' in visual research' is exemplifed in the text as contributors utilise architectural designs (McLeod, Goad, Willis and Darian-Smith), student drawings (Senior and Moss), data maps (Dixon), children's books (Hassett) and billboards and flyers (Koh). Again, however, while celebrating this incredible diversity we are aware that it simultaneously unlocks that there is so much more to the visual in education than has been covered within these pages. In the recent literature, educational researchers are showing us that there continue to be gaps in the field; moreover, educational researchers are continuing to innovate, critique and foreground the fissures and cracks of education as a global, complex and highly scrutinised policy space. Recent examples of research that demonstrate and engage visual research methods in education include:

- the use of visual methods as a pedagogic tool in teacher education, demonstrated by Bjartveit and Panayotidis (2014) and Bailey and Van Harken (2014);

- the proliferation of the visual in policy-driven/evidence-driven/practice-driven discourse that in its very visibility can equally be educative and/or seductive (see Nguyen & Mitchell 2012, who argue that visual methods are important for critiquing policy itself);
- the challenging of an anthropocentric analysis of visual data as outlined by Hultman and Taguchi (2010);
- the close attention to ethical issues where new issues are emerging as the materiality of research practices evolve and change as illustrated by Korkiakangas (2014), who identifies the challenges in archiving and sharing video data; and
- the use of wearable cameras and 'too much information' as highlighted by Mok, Cornish and Tarr (2014).

The extraordinary significance of the visual in contemporary 21st century life is also evident in the phenomena of 'big data' (Mayer-Schönberger & Cukier 2013). In the next section of our concluding chapter, we raise 'bigness' of 'big data' and 'datafication' as introducing a further range of contested spaces for visual methodologists.

Big data and visual methodologies

On Facebook and YouTube alone it has been estimated that 2,083,000 photos and 300 hours of video are uploaded respectively each minute (Horaczek 2013). This unprecedented access to visual data sources offers exciting potential for research providing a platform to use images as a means to understand and explore the lives of diverse groups of geographically distant people and/or the experiences of people from the past. Margolis' (1999) readings of school photographs from visual archives richly illustrate this potential. In part, these issues are encapsulated in the commonly engaged definition of 'big data', as encompassing volume, velocity and variety (Gandomi & Haider 2015). It is claimed that these are data of extraordinary and growing magnitude, not only generated at a rapid speed often in real time but able to be analysed and acted upon quickly. These data can be inclusive of the numerical, such as transactional data; the textual, such as blogs and tweets; YouTube videos; surveillance footage; medical images and Flickr accounts.

In the growing body of academic literature on the subject of big data, the tripartite of volume, velocity and variety trigger 'both utopian and dystopian rhetoric' (Boyd & Crawford 2012, p. 663). Indeed, some taking up the latter view have added to the alliterative definition of big data around the letter 'v' with terms such as valueless, vampire-like, venomous, vulgar, violating and very violent (Uprichard 2013). As we reflect on what the proliferation of big data might mean for visual methods, we find ourselves shifting between and across these dual perspectives. In the era of big data, we see both possibilities and problems for the future of visual methodologies. As Margolis (1999, p. 8) opines, big data images are 'ripped free from context' so that 'photographs become free-floating signifiers'.

In addition, critics of big data have highlighted how a technological elite in the private sector is positioned most strongly to access the knowledge inherent in big data (e.g. Manovich 2011). This group has the resources necessary to access and work with big data, and furthermore, they often has ownership of the sites/programs through which significant big data are generated (e.g. Google). They may sell data to researchers who can afford it, creating 'a rift between data-rich and data-poor researchers' (Halavais 2015, p. 590). As big data is inextricably tied up with neoliberal capitalism, its democratic potential for researchers in public institutions is highly circumscribed.

A second and related issue mediating celebratory discourses around the volume of visual data now available on the Internet is that of ethics and privacy, and they were raised in the fourth part of this collection. As Boyd and Crawford (2012, pp. 671–673) so cogently argue, 'just because it is accessible does not make it ethical' particularly as 'researchers are rarely in a user's imagined audience'. They remind us that the public posting of a visual by a user does not necessarily indicate they agree to it being used for different purposes in the future, potentially de-contextualised for analysis and critique by an unknown third party. As the furor over the 2008 study by Lewis et al., which utilised Facebook data of students from a U.S. university demonstrated, issues of consent and privacy, and strategies for anonymising data nominally 'public' are not straightforward (see Zimmer 2010). Adding to the debate on ethics and big data, Tene and Polonestsky (2012, p. 63) address some of the more sinister ways in which big data, including visual data, may be used, such as for the purposes of 'profiling, tracking, discrimination, exclusion, government surveillance and loss of control'.

As well as increased concerns around ethics, the rise of big data is also problematic for visual scholars as it is associated with the increased privileging of the numerical as a way of knowing and understanding the social world to the exclusion of qualitative methods. In the world of big data, the emphasis is primarily on volume, velocity, and variety, not quality. Big data are often afforded status over qualitative data as they are positioned as benign and uncontaminated by subjectivity (Callebaut

2012). For example, in preparing big data for analysis (i.e. in deciding what to retain, ignore or collate), scholars use the verb 'clean', suggesting objectivity and neutrality. What we would suggest is that there is an important role here for visual researchers whose expertise can be used to uncover the 'emergent political economies of data including the politics of measurement attached to it' (Adkins & Lury 2012, p. 15). We can utilise our critical capacities to document how big data are generated, by whom and for what purposes, to uncover how big data are analysed and why, and to detail the subjects of big data and the power relations in the constituting of these subjects. As Beer (2015) demonstrates in an instructive case study of how big data are produced and circulate in the game of football, we need detailed ethnographic work which reveals how data practices are embedded in everyday life. Such work brings to the fore the political dimensions of big data and opens up the space for challenge and resistance.

A further way in which our capacities as visual researchers can be enrolled in relation to big data is in terms of visualisation practices. According to Ruppert et al. (2013), one of the most striking aspects of big data is that it has afforded visualisation a new status in social analysis which has otherwise relied upon numerical and textual devices. As a means to translate and communicate big data, visualisation involves techniques such as graphs, models, diagrams, maps and flow charts. While visualisation (like the big data from which it emanates) is often heralded as accurate, clear and objective, it is as inflected by subjectivity as any human process. Decisions about which of the many visualisation designs to use are made by scholars using big data alongside judgements about positioning, size, shape and colour (Heer, Bostock & Ogievetsky 2010). What this suggests is that the visualisations that have become ubiquitous with the emergence of big data require a critical lens so that the interpretive and representational politics that inform their selection, production and circulation are uncovered. This is labour to which those trained in visual methods could contribute substantially. Emerging studies in this vein which approach the images as socially constructed and framed by point of view and authorial power are suggestive of the type of analytical critiques visual scholars could make of big data visualisations (e.g. Galloway 2011; Mackenzie & McNally 2013).

While the rise of big data does appear to implicitly marginalise visual approaches (given it is typically pitted against qualitative approaches), it has also had some contradictory impacts, which suggest positive developments for image-based approaches. Most promisingly, the ascendancy of big data has enlivened debates about methodological orthodoxies in the social sciences and led to calls for greater methodological innovation and plurality in order to 'reinvigorate a sociological imagination' (Burrows & Savage 2014, p. 3). In an early polemical piece on big data, Savage and Burrows (2007) criticised sociologists for their insularity and conservatism and lamented the discipline's lack of willingness to engage inventive methods. Also arguing for methodological plurality is Halavais (2015, p. 585) who contends that big data is not new but rather part of the 'ongoing evolution of social methods and theories'. He posits the concerns with connecting the micro with the macro in society, and problems with large data sets have a long history in the social sciences. Like others contributing to the discussion, he invokes C. W. Mills and suggests that the data deluge of today requires a 'new, bigger sociological imagination' that is underpinned by variety of methods and theories (Halavais 2015, p. 1). In another contribution, Uprichard (2012, p. 136) welcomes the 'refocus on method in sociology' that has been wrought by big data but cautions that we must not simply focus on what we can and cannot do in relation to method but instead ask 'why we are doing it'. The collective sociological contestations around big data usefully bring to the fore debates that have been of central concern to visual scholars; that is, questions about the politics of knowledge production and methodological diversity. Reflections on big data have also been used to argue that qualitative methods, including visual approaches, are more important than ever, as a means to probe and mediate big data (Montgomery 2015). That is, to generate 'wide data' rather than simply 'big data' (Tinati 2014, p. 16).

The ontological and epistemological grounds which underpin image-based research and big data research are potentially diametrically opposed. Importantly, those who utilise visual methods have typically done so as a means to redress disparities in power relations between the researcher and participant and as part of a larger commitment to emancipatory research goals (Prosser 1998; Pink 2006). This is not to further any simplistic conflation between visual methods and participation but to acknowledge that collaboration and equality have often guided visual scholars. Such concerns have not featled heavily in research using big data even as more critical approaches to quantitative methods have become popularised (Kitchen 2014). In fact, questions of ethics, power relations, exclusions and inequalities surrounding big data have often been ignored or discounted by big data advocates. For visual scholars these same issues are often paramount. As such, we need to continue to participate in the debates about the implications of big data for socially just research, actively voice the need for micro-level, image-focused understandings of the social world, and add to the work ably undertaken by McCosker and Wilken (2014, p. 163) in challenging the 'often uncritical fascination with data visualisation' of big data enthusiasts.

Generative futures

It is a salutary exercise to revisit the literature on visual methods as we have done for this book. That is, to note that just a few decades ago it was customary for scholars to begin work on the subject by acknowledging the invisibility and marginality of the image in social science research (Chaplin 1994; Fyfe & Law 1998). More recently, writers proclaim the method is now being widely taken up across the social sciences (e.g. Knoblauch et al. 2008; Pauwels 2011). At the same time, Rose's (2013, p. 18) claim that there is an 'uninterest in visuality' in the academy cannot be dismissed. It remains the case that despite exciting and radical epistemic shifts, traditional orthodoxies which undermine visual approaches continue to hold considerable currency. These purported truths about what research is and how research is done remain as dominant in education as they do in other fields. However, this book demonstrates that visual methods materialise the heterogeneity of visual data and are shaping the emergence and resurgence of old and new issues for educational researchers. The contributors provide a strong rationale for critically and reflexively engaging visual methods in educational research more comprehensively and into the future.

References

Adkins, L., & Lury, C. (2012). Introduction: Special Measures. In L. Adkins & C. Lury (Eds), *Measure and Value* (pp. 5–23). Oxford: Wiley-Blackwell.
Bailey, N. M., & Van Harken, E. M. (2014). Visual Images as Tools of Teacher Inquiry. *Journal of Teacher Education*, 65(3), 241–260.
Bannister, C. (2014). 'Like a Scout Does...Like a Guide Does...': The Scout or Guide Camp's Lessons of Identity. In S. Mills & P. Kraftl (Eds), *Informal Education Childhood and Youth: Geographies, Histories, Practices* (pp. 36–47). London: Palgrave Macmillan.
Beer, D. (2015). Productive Measures: Culture and Measurement in the Context of Everyday neoliberalism. *Big Data & Society*, 2(1). DOI: 10.1177/2053951715578951.
Bjartveit, C. J., & Panayotidis, E. L. (2014). Pointing to Shaun Tan's the Arrival and Re-imagining Visual Poetics in Research. *Contemporary Issues in Early Childhood*, 15(3), 245–261.
Boyd, D., & Crawford, K. (2012). Critical Questions for Big Data: Provocations for a Cultural, Technological, and Scholarly Phenomenon. *Information, Communication & Society*, 15(5), 662–679.

Burrows, R., & Savage, M. (2007). The Coming Crisis of Empirical Sociology. *Sociology, 41*(5), 885–899.

Burrows, R., & Savage, M. (2014). After the Crisis? Big Data and the Methodological Challenges of Empirical Sociology. *Big Data & Society*, April–June, 1–6.

Callebaut, W. (2012). Scientific Perspectivism: A Philosopher of Science's Response to the Challenge of Big Data Biology. *Studies in History and Philosophy of Biological and Biomedical Science, 43*(1), 69–80.

Chaplin, E. (1994). *Sociology and Visual Representation*. London: Routledge.

Fyfe, G., & Law, J. (Eds) (1998). *Picturing Power: Visual Depiction and Social Relations*. London: Routledge.

Galloway, A. (2011). Are Some Things Unrepresentable? *Theory, Culture and Society, 28*(7), 85–102.

Gharabaghi, K., & Anderson-Nathe, B. (2014). Big Data for Child and Youth Services? *Child and Youth Services, 35*(3), 193–195.

Halavais, A. (2015). Bigger Sociological Imaginations: Framing Big Social Data Theory and Methods. *Information, Communication & Society*. In Press.

Herr, J., Bostock, M., & Ogievetsky, V. (2010). A Tour through the Visualization Zoo. *Communications of the ACM, 53*(6), 59–67.

Horaczek, S. (2013). How Many Photos Are Uploaded to the Internet Every Minute? *Popular Photography*. http://www.popphoto.com/news/2013/05/how-many-photos-are-uploaded-to-internet-every-minute

Hultman, K., & Taguchi, H. L. (2010). Challenging Anthropocentric Analysis of Visual Data. *International Journal of Qualitative Studies in Education, 23*(5), 525–542.

Kitchen, R. (2014). Big Data, New Epistemologies and Paradigm Shifts. *Big Data & Society*, April–June, 1–12.

Knoblauch, H., Baer, A., Laurier, E., Petschke S., & Schnettler, B. (2008). Visual Analysis. New Developments in the Interpretive Analysis of Video and Photography. *Forum: Qualitative Social Research, 9*(3). http://www.qualitativeresearch.net/index.php/fqs/article/view/1170/2587

Korkiakangas, T. (2014). Challenges in Archiving and Sharing Video Data: Considering Moral, Pragmatic, and Substantial Arguments. *Journal of Research Practice, 10*(1), 1–18.

Kyle, R. G. (2014). Inside-Out: Connecting Indoor and Outdoor Spaces of Informal Education through the Extraordinary Geographies of the Boys' Brigade Camp. In S. Mills and P. Kraftl (Eds), *Informal Education Childhood and Youth: Geographies, Histories, Practices* (pp. 21–35). London: Palgrave Macmillan.

Mackenzie, A., & McNally, R. (2013). Living Multiples: How Large-Scale Scientific Data-Mining Pursues Identity and Difference. *Theory, Culture and Society, 30*(4), 72–91.

Manovich, L. (2011). Trending: The Promises and the Challenges of Big Social Data. In M. K. Gold (Ed.), *Debates in the Digital Humanities*. Minneapolis, MN: University of Minnesota Press. Online.

Margolis, E. (1999). Class Pictures: Representations of Race, Gender and Ability in a Century of School photography. *Visual Sociology, 14*(1), 7–38.

Mayer-Schönberger, V., & Cukier, K. (2013). *Big Data: A Revolution That Will Transform How We Live, Work and Learn*. London: John Murray.

McCosker, A., & Wilken, R. (2014). Rethinking 'Big Data' as Visual Knowledge: The Sublime and the Diagrammatic in Data Visualisation. *Visual Studies, 29*(2), 155–164.

Mills, S. (2014). 'A Powerful Educational Instrument': The Woodcraft Folk and Indoor/Outdoor 'Nature', 1925–75. In S. Mills & P. Kraftl (Eds), *Informal Education Childhood and Youth: Geographies, Histories, Practices* (pp. 65–80). London: Palgrave Macmillan.

Montgomery, K. (2015). Children's Media Culture in a Big Data World. *Journal of Children and Media, 9*(2), 266–271.

Mok, T. M., Cornish, F., & Tarr, J. (2015). Too Much Information: Visual Research Ethics in the Age of Wearable Cameras. *Integrative Psychological and Behavioural Science, 49*(2), 309–322. DOI: 10.1007/s12124-014-9289-8.

Nguyen, X. T., & Mitchell, C. (2012). On the Use of Visual Methodologies in Educational Policy Research. *South African Journal of Education, 32*(4), 479–493.

Parkin, S., & Coomber, R. (2009). Value in the Visual: On Public Injexting, Visual Methods and Their Potential for Informing Policy (and Change). *Methodological Innovations Online, 4*(2), 21–36.

Pauwels, L. (2011). An Integrated Conceptual Framework for Conceptual Visual Research. In E. Margolis & L. Pauwels (Eds), *The SAGE Handbook of Visual Research Methods* (pp. 3–23). London: Sage.

Pauwels, L. (2012). Contempolating the State of Visual Research: An Assessment of Obstacles and Opportunities. In S. Pink (Ed.), *Advances in Visual Methodology* (pp. 248–264). London: Sage.

Pink, S. (2006). *Doing Visual Ethnography*. London: Sage.

Prosser, J. (Ed.) (1998). *Image-Based Research: A Sourcebook for Qualitative Researchers*. London: Falmer Press.

Raghupathi, W., & Raghupathi, V. (2014). Big Data Analytics in Healthcare: Promise and Potential. *Health Information Science and Systems, 2*(3), 1–10.

Rose, G. (2014). On the Relation between 'Visual Research Methods' and Contemporary Visual Culture. *Sociological Review, 62*(1), 24–46.

Ruppert, E., Law, J., & Savage, M. (2013). *Theory, Culture & Society, 30*(4), 22–46.

Tene, O., & Polonestsky, J. (2012). Privacy in the Age of Big Data: A Time for Big Decisions. *Standford Law Review Online, 64*, 63–69.

Tinati, R., Halford, S., Carr, L., & Pope, C. (2014). Big Data: Methodological Challenges and Approaches for Sociological Analysis. *Sociology*, 1–19.

Uprichard, E. (2013). Image in Public Domain. *Discover Society*. http://www.discoversociety.org/2013/10/01/focus-big-data-little-questions/

Zimmer, M. (2010). But the Data Is Already Public: On the Ethics of Research in Facebook. *Ethics and Information Technology, 12*, 313–325. DOI: 10.1007/s10676-010-9227-5.

Index

AARE (Australian Association for Research in Education), 83, 233
ABER (Arts Based Educational Research), 77
ACARA (Australian Curriculum Assessment and Reporting Authority), 105, 106, 107
advertisements
  visual ecology, 8–9
  see also tutorial advertisements
AERA (American Educational Research Association), 80, 81
Ahmed, Sarah, 193–4, 198, 199
Albuquerque Indian School, class photograph, 46, 52
American Memory project, 46, 54
ARC (Australian Research Council), 5
Arnie the Doughnut (Keller), 144–5
art creations, ownership of images, 244–7
audit trails, educational research, 56

Baker, Alison, 9, 231–50
Bartlett, Jennifer, 5–6, 59–71
basketball court, photographs, 86–89
Becker, Howard, 173
Belmont Report, 232, 239, 242
benefit and harm
  de-identifying images, 234–6
  ethical challenge, 232–8
  excluding images, 236–8
big data, visual methodologies, 269–73
Blum-Ross, Alicia, 238, 240–1
Boys-Only, Catholic School, 63, 64
Boys-Only, Independent School, 67
branding, 64–5, 191–3
Bray, Mark, 189, 195
Britzman, Deborah, 79
Burton, Linda, 182

cartography
  classroom images, 103–5
  learning spaces, 100–1
  merging data of learning spaces, 108–14
  numerical pedagogical images, 105–8
  pedascapes, 109–14
Catholic School, marketing, 63–4, 68
childhood, photography describing, 173–4
children
  Children Framing Childhoods project, 8, 172, 175–83
  ethics of, and photography, 254–6
  photo as gift, 259–61
  photography, 175–7, 179, 181–3
  pictures of homeplaces, 177, 182–3, 185
  roles of educators and, 261–3
Cixous, Hélène, 91
CMI (Chinese Medium-of-Instruction) schools, 195
Cochran-Smith, Marilyn, 79–81, 85
collaborative seeing approach, 181
collaborative work, 76–8, 105, 119, 162, 213, 246, 257
communication, marketing and, in elite schools, 59–61, 68–70
copyright, photographs, 54–5
corporatisation, visual in elite schools, 63–5
CP (Creative Partnerships) program, 119–20, 122
Cuban, Larry, 81–2

Daguerreian Society, 49
Danesi, Marcel, 193
Darder, Antonia, 85
Darian-Smith, Kate, 5, 12–35
Darling-Hammond, Linda, 79
Davies, Peter, 241
Debord, Guy, 190–1
digital files, photographs, 45–9
Dilthey, Wilhelm, 49
Disney, 54

Dixon, Mary, 6, 77, 100–15
DMCA (Digital Millennium Copyright Act), 40, 54, 56n4
'Dr Koopa Koo' advertisements, 199–201, 203
DSS (Direct Subsidy School), 195
Du Bois, W. E. B., 173, 174

education
 early childhood, 9–10, 256–9
 Hong Kong, 194–6
 photography relationship with, 39–40
 politics in Hong Kong, 8–9
 visual research methods, 10–11, 267–9
 see also elite schools; schools; teacher education research
Educational Magazine, The (magazine), 20, 28, 29, 33
educational research
 audience for film, 127
 benefit and harm, 232–8
 Creative Partnerships (CP) program, 119–20, 122
 ethics of visual methods, 231–2, 247–8
 film-maker, 28, 127
 film-making, 128–9
 Get Wet project, 123–6
 justice, 242–7
 pedagogical film, 126–9
 respect for persons, 238–42
 Signature Pedagogies project, 119–23, 125
 teacher learning, 127–8
 teachers' work and learning, 116–17
 using film in, 118–19
Eisner, Elliot, 76
elite schools
 branding, 64–5
 corporatisation of visual in, 63–5
 document production in, 68–70
 managing the visual in, 65–8
 marketing and communication, 59–61, 68–70
 methodology, 61
 producers of visual in, 62–3
 visual research and, 59–61

Ellsworth, Elizabeth, 84, 85
EMI (English Medium-of-Instruction) schools, 195, 201
emotional geography, 181, 183, 185, 196
Enlightened Eye, The (Eisner), 76
Ephemera Society of America, 49
ethics
 benefit and harm, 232–8
 big data, 270–2
 children and photography, 254–6
 collaboration, 263–4
 educational research, 231–2, 247–8
 gaze of child photographer, 256–8
 justice, 242–7
 pedagogical documentation as research, 251–4
 photo as gift, 259–61
 respect for persons, 238–42
 roles of children and educators, 261–3
ethnography, 40–1, 51, 56n2
 film in educational research, 118–19

Facebook, 5, 20
 Huntingdale Technical School, 22, 24, 30
 school pages, 63, 183
 social media, 38, 47, 241, 244, 269–70
family, photography, 173–4
family album, photography, 176, 184
film
 audience for, 127
 authors of, 127
 designers of, 127
 educational researchers making, 128–9
 film-maker, 127
 teachers' work and learning, 116–17, 127–8
 see also educational research
fixed meanings, 91, 128
found object photographs
 audit trails, 56
 copyright and limitations of use, 54–5
 educational research, 55–6
 ethnography, 40–1, 51

found object photographs – *continued*
evolution of education over time, 36–9
interpretivist tools, 41, 49–53
photoforensics, 40, 42–9
photography and education, 39–40
photovoice, 36
FSA (Farm Security Administration), 50, 51

Gay, Geneva, 79, 85
Geertz, Clifford, 50
Gershwin, George, 54
Get Wet project, 123–6
action research cycles, 123–4
film for communication, 125–6
Girls-Only, Catholic School, 68
Girls-Only, Independent School, 62–7
Goad, Philip, 5, 12–35
Goffman, Erving, 176

Hall, Christine, 7, 116–32
Hall, Elaine, 9, 209–27
harm prevention, 233
Hassett, Dawnene D., 7, 133–49
heuristics, learning aid, 121–2, 125, 126, 127, 141
Hine, Lewis, 173, 174
HKDSE (Hong Kong Diploma in Secondary Education) exam, 195, 201
homeplaces, children's pictures of, 177, 182–3, 185
Hong Kong, 8–9
media spectacle of tutorial advertisements, 191–2
social context and culture of education in, 194–6
tutoring industry, 189–90
see also tutoring industry
Huntingdale Technical School, 20, 21
curriculum hints, 27–8
diagram of school, 22
external photograph of, 23–4
interior view of classroom, 28, 29
interrogating images of, 32–3
school grounds, 30–1

iconography, 41, 52, 60, 268
ICSEA (Index of Community Socio-Educational Advantage), 105, 106, 107, 108, 110
Innovative Learning Environments Study, 100–1
interpretivist tools, photoforensics, 49–53
Irvine, Jacqueline, 79

Jackson, William Henry, 157
Jewitt, Carey, 199
Joyce, William, 144
J. Paul Getty Museum, 46, 55
justice
ethics, 242–7
fair opportunity to participate, 243–4
ownership of images, 244–7

Kellner, Douglas, 8, 190–2
Kind, Sylvia, 9–10, 251–66
Klett, Mark, 157, 158, 160, 161
Knowledge, co-production in visual research, 92–4
Kodak EasyShare™ method, 6, 75, 86
Koh, Aaron, 8, 189–208
Kuhn, Annette, 38
Kwo, Ora, 195

Lau, Jeffrey, 202, 203–5
learning environments, 15, 79, 100–1, 103, 108, 112–13
Lenski, Susan David, 80
literacy, 7
LOC (Library of Congress), 46, 54–5
Lucas, Tamara, 80
Luttrell, Wendy, 9, 172–88

McDonald, Paula, 5–6, 59–71
McLeod, Julie, 5, 12–35
manga format, photographs, 92–4
Margolis, Eric, 5, 36–58
marketing
corporatisation of visual in elite schools, 63–5
elite schools, 59–61, 69–70
managing visual in elite schools, 65–8

280 Index

mathematical reasoning, visual process, 214–22
'Math God' tutorial advertisements, 200–201, 203
MCDA (Multimodal Critical Discourse Analysis), 197
media spectacle, 190
   multimodal discourse analytical framework, 197–9
   theoretical framing, 190–1
   tutorial advertisements in Hong Kong, 191–2, 197–9, 205–6
   see also tutoring industry
Meerkat Mail (Gravett), 143
Meow Ruff (Sidman), 140, 142, 143
Metcalfe, Amy Scott, 7–8, 153–71
Metropolitan Museum of Art, 46, 55
Mitchell, Claudia, 257
Morris, Errol, 38–9
Moss, Julianne, 1–11, 75–99, 267–75
My Map Book (Fanelli), 144
My School website, 100, 105–8, 110, 112–13
myths, teacher education, 81, 83, 84

NAPLAN (National Assessment Program – Literary and Numeracy), 105, 108, 110, 113
Nieto, Sonia, 79, 85

OASC (Open Access for Scholarly Content), 55
OECD Innovative Learning Environments Study, 100–1
OECD (Organisation for Economic Co-operation and Development), 6
Orellana, Marjorie Falstich, 182
O'Sullivan, Timothy H., 157

panopticon, 23, 111
partnerships, collaborative and arts-based, 7
Pauwels, Luc, 154–6, 158, 197, 268
pedagogy, 41
   classroom images, 103–5
   disrupting visual method and representation, 90–2
   encounters, 102–3

knowledge, 82–6
language in, 102
learning space, 101, 109–14
living, 77, 78
merging data and new cartographies, 108–14
numerical representations and images, 105–8
pedagogical documentation as research, 251–4
quality of, 78–81
responsibility of teachers, 80
teacher education, 76
visual data, 102–3
pedascapes, data mapping, 109–14
Phillips, Michelle, 174
photoforensics
   digital, 45–9
   early history, 42–4
   snapshot, 44
   stereographs, 43–4
photographs
   basketball court, 86–9, 86–89
   class at Albuquerque Indian School, 52
   co-production of knowledge, 92–4
   copyright, 54–5
   de-identifying images, 234–6
   ethics of, as gifts, 259–61
   evoking school memories, 30–1
   excluding images, 236–8
   Huntington Technical School, 24, 29, 30
   mathematics lesson in English classroom, 37
   men's gymnastics class, 39
   ownership of images, 244–7
   as provocations, 255–6
   schools, 18–19
   shifting role in research project, 86–90
   see also found object photographs
photography
   agricultural facilities at UBC, 165, 166
   ethics of children and, 254–6
   family and childhood, 173–4
   relationship with education, 39–40
   see also repeat photography

photovoice, 36
picturebooks
  classroom use, 143–6
  illustrations, 139–40
  models of comprehension, 138–43
  multimodal, 133–4, 138–43, 143–6
  reading comprehension, 141, 142
  transaction instructional dynamics, 143–6
  words and visuals, 137–8
Pini, Barbara, 1–11, 59–71, 267–75
Pinterest, social media, 5, 38, 47
postmarks, 49
Potter, Beatrix, 139
progressivism, 19, 23, 117
provocations, photos as, 255–6

quality, teacher education research, 94–5

REC (research ethics committee), 237, 247–8
repeat photography, 7–8, 168–9
  methodological framework for, 159–60
  practice of, 162–8
  as sociological method, 156–62
  technological aspects, 163–4
  theory and analysis of, 162–3
  UBC (University of British Columbia), 162–7
  visualising sociology, 153–6
rephotography, 153, 157, 160–2, 165
respect for persons, ethical challenges, 238–42
Riis, Jacob, 173
Rose, Gillian, 2, 126, 172, 181, 195
Rosenblatt, Louise, 134, 142, 143, 145
Rowe, Jeremy, 5, 36–58

Saussure, Ferdinand de, 136
scape, 109
schools
  architectural eye, 21–5
  classroom images, 103–5
  contextual lens, 31–3
  curriculum hints, 27–8
  design innovations, 16, 33–4
  environment, 28, 29
  methodological questions and contexts, 17–20
  photographs evoking memories, 30–1
  photographs of, 18–19
  Resource Centre, 27
  Self-discovery, 19–20
  space, 15–17
  view from education, 26–31
  see also elite schools; Huntingdale Technical School
Sekula, Alan, 50
semiotics, 136, 146
  media spectacles, 198
  tutorial advertisements, 193–4
Senior, Kim, 6, 75–99
shadow education, 189, 190, 205
Sidman, Joyce, 140
signature method, 3–4
Signature of All Things on Method, The (Agamben), 4
Signature Pedagogies project, 119–23, 125
  film communicating results, 122–3
  generating and analysing film data, 120–2
  idea of, 120
signs
  meaning of, 134
  semiotics, 136
snapshot, photographs, 30, 40, 44, 48, 107, 116, 176
social semiotics, 136
sociology
  photography, family and childhood, 173–4
  repeat photography, 156–62
  visual, 10, 153–6, 158
Solomon-Godeau, Abigail, 41
Sontag, Susan, 32
space
  cartography of learning, 100–1
  pedagogy and, 101
stereographs, photoforensics, 43–4

Tale of Peter Rabbit, The (Potter), 139
Tan, Shaun, 89
Tarr, Patricia, 9–10, 251–66

teacher education research
  co-production of knowledge in visual research, 92–4
  disrupting visual method and representation, 90–2
  framing the story, 78–82
  learning and learning to teach, 76–8
  native/observer as framer, 82–6
  practitioner inquiry, 82–6
  school culture and pedagogy, 75–6
  seeing quality in, 94–5
  shifting role of photographs in project, 86–90
  vision for students, 81–2, 84
  see also educational research
TEMAG (Teacher Education Ministerial Advisory Group), 78, 94
Te Riele, Kitty, 9, 231–50
Thomson, Pat, 7, 116–32
ThumbsPlus, 51, 56*n*3
Tinkler, Penny, 31, 173, 255
Top of the Class (2007 report), 83
tutorial advertisements
  analysis of, 199–205
  'Dr Koopa Koo', 199–201, 203
  Jeffrey Lau, 202–5
  'Math God', 200–201, 203
  media spectacle, 191–2, 197–9, 205–6
tutoring industry, 189–90
  market size, 189
  situated visual methodology, 196–7
  visual production in, 192–4

UBC (University of British Columbia)
  agricultural facilities, 165, 166
  repeat photography, 162–7

value, visual sources, 18
Villegas, Ana Maria, 79
vision for students, 81–2, 84
visual data
  pedagogy encounters, 102–3
  visual methodologies, 269–73
visual ecology, advertisements, 8–9

visual language, definition, 137
visual literacy
  definitions, 137
  picturebooks, 133–4
  poststructural caveat, 134–6
  social semiotics, 136
  transaction instructional dynamics, 143–6
visual management, elite schools, 65–8
visual production
  elite schools, 62–3
  tutorial industry, 196–7
  tutorial industry in Hong Kong, 192–4
visual research, 1–3
  co-production of knowledge in, 92–4
  disrupting method and representation, 90–2
  elite schools, 59–61
  film in educational research, 118–19
visual sociology, 10, 153–6, 158
VRMs (visual research methods), 1–3
  analytic matrix, 223
  appeal of, 210–14
  big data and, 269–73
  commonalities, gaps and future, 267–9
  education, 10–11
  models of mixed methods use, 212
  participation and intent, 209–10
  participation and quality, 222–5
  repeat photography, 156–62
  use of abductive reasoning, 214–22

Wall, Kate, 9, 209–27
Weber, Max, 49, 50
Wexler, Laura, 176
Whitlam, Gough, 33
Williams, Raymond, 205
Willis, Julie, 5, 12–35
Wilson, Brent, 263
Wood, Bronwyn, 234–5, 238

YouTube, 8, 144, 147, 184, 189, 269

The manufacturer's authorised representative in the EU is Springer Nature Customer Service Centre GmbH, Europaplatz 3, 69115 Heidelberg, Germany. If you have any concerns regarding our products, please contact ProductSafety@springernature.com

Printed and bound by CPI Group (UK) Ltd, Croydon, CR0 4YY

23/03/2026

02076460-0012